Collins

AQA GCSE

Spanish

with Audio

Spanish

with Audio

AQA
GCSE

Revision
Guide

Allison Macaulay

Contents

Contents

Review Questions

Key Concepts from Key Stage 3

1 Write out these numbers as figures (e.g. cincuenta y dos = 52).

a) treinta y siete ....

b) sesenta y cinco ....

c) cuarenta y uno ....

d) setenta y ocho ....

e) noventa y nueve ....

f) ciento veinticinco ....

g) setecientos cuarenta ....

h) quinientos ochenta y dos ....

i) mil trescientos ....

j) cuatrocientos setenta y tres .... [10]

2 Draw lines between the boxes to match the times on the left with the digital times on the right.

Son las ocho y diez	01:20
Son las nueve y cuarto	03:25
Son las once menos cuarto	06:35
Son las tres y veinticinco	02:05
Son las cuatro menos cinco	08:10
Es la una y veinte	10:45
Son las siete menos veinticinco	03:55
Son las dos y cinco	09:15

[8]

3 Are the following statements **true** or **false**?

a) 15/03 = **cinco de marzo** ....

b) 22/06 = **veintidós de julio** ....

c) 30/11 = **treinta de noviembre** ....

d) 18/08 = **dieciocho de agosto** ....

e) 25/02 = **veinticinco de marzo** ....

f) 14/12 = **quince de diciembre** ....

g   27/05 = **veintiséis de mayo** ....

h) 31/01 = **treinta y uno de enero** ....

i) 11/10 = **diez de octubre** ....

j) 21/04 = **veintiuno de abril** .... [10]

4 Match the weather descriptions **A**, **B**, **C**, **D**, **E**, **F**, **G** and **H** with the symbols **1–8**.

A   Hace mucho frío hoy. ☐

B   ¡Qué viento hace! ☐

C   Creo que está nevando. ☐

D   Hoy hace mucho sol. ☐

E   ¡Qué pena! Está lloviendo. ☐

F   Ayer, hizo mucho calor. ☐

G   Está nublado. ☐

H   ¡Cuidado! Hay tormenta. ☐ [8]

Relationships with Family and Friends 1

You must be able to:

- Give and ask for personal information such as name, age, birthday and personality
- Describe your family and give personal details about your family
- Use possessive adjectives and different parts of the verbs **ser** and **tener**.

My Name

- **¿Cómo te llamas?** — What are you called?
  Me llamo… — I am called…
- **Mi nombre es…** — My first name is…
- **Mi apellido es…** — My surname is…
- **¿Cómo se escribe tu nombre?** — How do you spell your (first) name?
  Se escribe… — It is spelt…

My Age

- **¿Cuántos años tienes?** — How old are you?
  Tengo quince años. — I am fifteen years old.
  Pronto, voy a cumplir dieciséis. — Soon, I will be sixteen.
- **¿Cuándo es tu cumpleaños?** — When is your birthday?
  Mi cumpleaños es el tres de mayo. — My birthday is the 3rd of May.
- **¿Cuándo naciste?** — When were you born?
  Nací en el año dos mil uno. — I was born in the year 2001.

Describing Personality

- **¿Cómo eres de carácter?** — What sort of person are you?
  Soy… — I am…

	Masculine	Feminine
pleasant	agradable	agradable
kind/nice	simpático	simpática
funny	gracioso	graciosa
shy	tímido	tímida
lazy	perezoso	perezosa
sporty	deportivo	deportiva
naughty	travieso	traviesa
talkative	hablador	habladora

- **En mi opinión soy muy tímido.** — In my opinion I am very shy.
- **A veces soy graciosa, pero normalmente soy tímida.** — Sometimes I am funny, but usually I am shy.

Key Point

Don't forget that when forming questions, you need to put **¿** at the beginning of the question as well as **?** at the end. The same rule applies when using exclamation marks (**¡** and **!**):
¿Cuántos años tienes?
¡Qué calor!

Family Members

- **En mi familia hay… personas.** — In my family there are… people.
- **En mi familia somos cinco.** — There are five of us in my family.

la familia	the family	**la hermanastra**	stepsister
la madre	mother	**el tío**	uncle
el padre	father	**la tía**	aunt
los padres	parents	**el primo**	cousin (male)
el padrastro	stepfather	**la prima**	cousin (female)
la madrastra	stepmother	**el abuelo**	grandfather
el hermano	brother	**la abuela**	grandmother
la hermana	sister	**los abuelos**	grandparents
los hermanos	siblings	**el hijo**	son
el hermanastro	stepbrother	**la hija**	daughter

- **Soy hijo único.** — I am an only child. (male)
- **Soy hija única.** — I am an only child. (female)
- **No tengo hermanos.** — I don't any have brothers or sisters.
- **En mi familia hay mi madre y yo.** — In my family there is my mum and me.
- **En mi familia somos mi padre y yo.** — It's me and my dad in my family.

Possessive Adjectives

- Possessive adjectives are used a lot when talking about family and friends.
- Possessive adjectives include my, your, his and her.

mi hermano	my brother	**tu madre**	your mother
mis padres	my parents	**sus primos**	his/her cousins

Information about Others

- **Se llama… / Se llaman…** — He / She is called… / They are called…
- **Tiene… años.** — He / She is… years old.
- **Tienen… años.** — They are… years old.

- **Mi hermana menor se llama María y tiene once años.**
  My younger sister is called María and she is eleven years old.
- **Tengo dos hermanos mayores que se llaman David y Leo.**
  I have two older brothers called David and Leo.
- **David es hablador y Leo es tímido.**
  David is talkative and Leo is shy.

> ### Key Point
>
> Possessive adjectives must agree with the object that is owned (possessed), not the person who owns (possesses) them.

> ### Quick Test
>
> 1. Say in Spanish your name and how old you are.
> 2. Ask someone in Spanish what their name is and how old they are.
> 3. What is the Spanish for 'stepsister'?
> 4. Translate into English: **Hola. Me llamo Carmen y tengo trece años. Mi cumpleaños es el doce de agosto y pronto voy a cumplir catorce años. Tengo dos hermanas que se llaman Laura y Elena y tienen ocho y cinco años.**

Relationships with Family and Friends 2

You must be able to:

- Give a physical description of yourself and others
- Describe your relationships with friends and family
- Use conjunctions and quantifiers/intensifiers to lengthen sentences.

Describing Hair and Eyes

- **Tengo/Tiene…**   I have/He/She has…

el pelo	hair	**los ojos**	eyes
rubio	blonde	**azules**	blue
pelirrojo	red	**verdes**	green
castaño	chestnut brown	**marrones**	brown
moreno/a	dark brown	**grises**	grey
largo/a	long		
corto/a	short (hair)		
liso/a	straight		
rizado/a	curly		

- **Mi hermana tiene los ojos azules y el pelo moreno y largo.**
  My sister has blue eyes and long, dark brown hair.
- **Mis padres tienen los ojos verdes pero yo tengo los ojos azules.**
  My parents have green eyes but I have blue eyes.

Describing Size and Appearance

- **Soy/Es…**   I am/He/She is…

	Masculine	Feminine
tall	**alto**	**alta**
short	**bajo**	**baja**
of medium height	**de estatura mediana**	**de estatura mediana**
fat	**gordo**	**gorda**
thin/slim	**delgado**	**delgada**
nice-looking/pretty	**bonito**	**bonita**
handsome/good-looking	**guapo**	**guapa**
ugly	**feo**	**fea**

- **Soy bastante baja y delgada pero mi hermano es muy alto y gordo.**
  I am quite short and slim but my brother is very tall and fat.
- **Mi madre dice que soy guapo pero yo creo que soy bastante feo.**
  My mother says that I am handsome but I think that I am quite ugly.
- **Llevo gafas y tengo barba y bigote.**
  I wear glasses and I have a beard and moustache.
- **Mi hermana tiene muchas pecas y creo que es muy bonita.**
  My sister has lots of freckles and I think that she is very pretty.

Talking About Relationships

- Here are some useful verbs for describing relationships:

aguantar	to put up with/bear
charlar	to chat
conocer a	to know (person)
detestar	to hate
discutir	to argue/discuss
enfadarse con	to get annoyed with
jubilarse	to retire
llevarse bien/mal con	to get on well/badly with
molestar	to bother/annoy
odiar	to hate
parecerse	to look like/resemble
reír	to laugh
sonreírse	to smile

> **Key Point**
>
> Use quantifiers and intensifiers to make your writing and speaking more interesting:
>
> | | |
> |---|---|
> | **bastante** | quite |
> | **demasiado** | too |
> | **mucho** | a lot/lots |
> | **muy** | very |
> | **(un) poco** | (a) little |

- **¿Te llevas bien con tu familia?**
  Do you get on well with your family?

- **Pues, a veces sí, pero también discuto bastante con mis padres sobre los deberes.**
  Well, yes sometimes, but I also argue quite a lot with my parents about my homework.

- **¿Y qué tal con tus hermanos? ¿Te llevas bien con ellos?**
  And what about with your brothers and sisters? Do you get on well with them?

- **Bueno, me llevo muy bien con mi hermana porque es muy madura y comprensiva pero mis hermanos son tontos y me enfado mucho con ellos.**
  Well, I get on well with my sister because she is very mature and understanding, but my brothers are stupid and I get really annoyed with them.

- **¿Cómo son tus amigos?**
  What are your friends like?

- **Mi mejor amiga es justa y divertida y siempre habla conmigo de todo.**
  My best friend is fair and good fun and she always talks to me about everything.

> **Key Point**
>
> Using a variety of conjunctions will make your writing and speaking flow much better:
>
> | | |
> |---|---|
> | **y** | and |
> | **pero** | but |
> | **porque** | because |
> | **por eso** | therefore |
> | **también** | also |

> **Quick Test**
>
> 1. Translate into Spanish:
>   I am very tall and I have blonde, short hair.
> 2. Choose the correct forms:
>   **Mi hermana es bastante <u>alto</u>/<u>alta</u> y es <u>bonito</u>/<u>bonita</u>.**
> 3. Say in Spanish that you don't get on well with your mother.
> 4. Translate into Spanish:
>   In my opinion, I get on quite well with my siblings because they are good fun and we always chat a lot.

Marriage and Partnership

You must be able to:

- Describe marital status and describe relationships
- Give more detail about those around you
- Use higher-level adjectives to add complexity.

Talking about Marital Status

- Here are some useful words for talking about marital status (**el estado civil**):

Está…	He/She is…
casado/a	married
separado/a	separated
divorciado/a	divorced
viudo/a	widowed
soltero/a	single

- **Mi hermana está casada pero mis tíos están divorciados.**
  My sister is married but my aunt and uncle are divorced.
- **Mi primo estaba casado pero ahora está separado de su mujer.**
  My cousin was married but now he is separated from his wife.

Marriage and Relationships

- Here are some useful verbs and nouns for talking about marriage and relationships:

casarse	to get married	**preocuparse de**	to worry about
compartir	to share	**relacionarse con**	to get on with (people)
comprometerse	to get engaged	**querer**	to love
confiar en	to trust	**separarse**	to separate
divorciarse	to get divorced	**el/la adolescente**	teenager
enamorarse de	to fall in love with	**el esposo/el marido**	husband
estar harto/a de	to be fed up with	**la esposa/la mujer**	wife
		el hombre	man
fastidiar	to annoy	**el matrimonio**	married couple
llorar	to cry	**la mujer**	woman
molestar	to bother/ annoy	**el novio**	boyfriend/ groom
pelearse	to fight/argue	**la novia**	girlfriend/bride
perdonar	to forgive	**la pareja**	couple/ partner

- **Espero casarme en el futuro.**
  I hope to get married in the future.
- **Mis padres se enamoraron con veinte años.**
  My parents fell in love at the age of twenty.
- **Mi novia y yo compartimos todo y confío en ella totalmente.**
  My girlfriend and I share everything and I trust her completely.

Using the Verbs 'Estar' and 'Ser'

- The verb **estar** (to be) is used to talk about temporary states and marital status:

Estoy	I am
Estás	You are
Está	He/She is
Estamos	We are
Estáis	You are (pl)
Están	They are

- The verb **ser** (to be) is used to talk about personal characteristics:

Soy	I am
Eres	You are
Es	He/She is
Somos	We are
Sois	You are (pl)
Son	They are

> **Key Point**
>
> Use the verb **estar** to talk about temporary states and marital status. Use the verb **ser** to talk about personal characteristics.

- **Estamos casados.**
  We are married.

- **Eres muy atrevido.**
  You are very daring.

Higher-level Adjectives to Describe People

atrevido/a	daring	**encantador/a**	charming
avaro/a	mean/miserly	**glotón/a**	greedy
callado/a	quiet/reserved	**orgulloso/a**	proud
celoso/a	jealous	**seguro de sí mismo/a**	self-assured
cortés	polite		
cuidadoso/a	careful	**sensible**	sensitive
cariñoso/a	caring	**torpe**	clumsy
bien/mal educado/a	well/badly behaved, well/bad mannered	**vago**	lazy/unreliable

- **Mi novio es bastante avaro en cuanto al dinero.**
  My boyfriend is quite miserly when it comes to money.
- **El marido de mi amiga es siempre muy callado.**
  My friend's husband is always very quiet.
- **Mi pareja es muy sensible.**
  My partner is very sensitive.
- **Mi novia es muy segura de sí misma.**
  My girlfriend is very self-assured.

Wedding Bells

- Here are some useful words for talking about weddings and engagements:

el amor	love	**el compromiso**	engagement
el anillo	ring	**la felicidad**	happiness
la boda/el casamiento	wedding	**la fiesta**	party
		los parientes	relatives
el cariño	affection	**el sentimiento**	feeling

- **Mi novio me ha dado un anillo precioso.**
  My boyfriend has given me a lovely ring.
- **En el verano, voy a ir a la boda de mi prima.**
  In summer, I'm going to go to my cousin's wedding.

> ## Quick Test
>
> 1. Translate into Spanish: My parents are separated.
> 2. Translate into Spanish: The couple is charming.
> 3. What is the Spanish for 'married couple'?
> 4. Choose the correct forms: **Mi madre es <u>animado</u>/<u>animada</u>. Mis padres son <u>cariñosos</u>/<u>cariñosas</u>.**

Social Media

You must be able to:

- Talk about the Internet and mobile phones
- Talk about social networking
- Talk about the positive and negative effects of technology.

Useful Technology Verbs

- Here are some useful verbs for talking about technology:

acceder	to access
adjuntar	to attach
borrar	to erase
cargar	to load
chatear	to chat (electronically)
colgar	to put (photos on social media, etc.)
crear	to create
desactivar	to block (screen)
descargar	to download
enviar	to send
funcionar	to work
grabar	to record, to burn (a disk)
guardar	to save
mandar	to send
navegar	to surf
publicar	to publish
recibir	to receive

Learn

- **Me gusta usar el portátil por la noche para hacer mis deberes.**
  I like to use my laptop on an evening to do my homework.
- **A mí me encanta descargar música del Internet.**
  I love to download music from the Internet.
- **Suelo mandar correos electrónicos en vez de escribir cartas tradicionales.**
  I usually send emails instead of writing traditional letters.
- **Generalmente paso cuatro horas al día jugando a los videojuegos.**
  I generally spend four hours a day playing video games.
- **Prefiero usar mi iPad porque lo llevo conmigo a todos lados.**
  I prefer to use my iPad because I take it with me everywhere.

Key Point

When talking about a brand name, for example Xbox or PlayStation, the name of the brand stays the same. The same goes for social network sites such as Facebook and Twitter.

Mobile Phones

- **Mando mensajes a mis amigos.** I send messages to my friends.
- **Navego por Internet con mi móvil.** I surf the Internet with my mobile.
- **En mi móvil tengo muchos juegos.** I have lots of games on my mobile.
- **Uso mi móvil para escuchar música en el autobús.**
  I use my mobile to listen to music on the bus.
- **Para mí, mi móvil es una herramienta importantísima; lo uso para todo.**
  For me, my mobile is a really important tool; I use it for everything.

Social Media

- **Me encanta usar las redes sociales como Facebook y Twitter.**
  I love using social network sites such as Facebook and Twitter.
- **Suelo acceder a las salas de chat para conectarme con mis amigos en otros países.**
  I usually access chatrooms to get in contact with friends in other countries.
- **Anoche colgué unas fotos de mi cumpleaños.**
  Last night I posted some photos of my birthday.
- **Las redes sociales son útiles para buscar trabajo e informarte de lo que está pasando en tu región local.**
  Social network sites are useful for searching for jobs and finding out what is happening in your local area.

Positive and Negative Effects of Technology

- **En mi opinión hacer compras por Internet es más barato que ir de compras en la ciudad.**
  In my opinion shopping on the Internet is cheaper than going shopping in the city.
- **La tecnología me ayuda a quedarme en contacto con mis amigos todos los días.**
  Technology helps me to keep in contact with my friends every day.
- **He descargado muchas aplicaciones diferentes porque son muy útiles.**
  I have downloaded lots of different apps because they are very useful.
- **Navegar la red es la mejor manera de estar al día.**
  Surfing the Internet is the best way to be up to date.
- **Publicar tu número de teléfono en algunas de las redes sociales puede ser peligroso.**
  Posting your phone number on some of the social network sites can be dangerous.
- **La tecnología me distrae mucho.** *Learn*
  I get very distracted by technology.
- **La tecnología puede ser muy adictiva y puede causar trastornos de sueño y concentración.**
  Technology can be very addictive and can cause sleep and concentration disorders.
- **El cíberacoso es un problema serio hoy en día.**
  Cyberbullying is a serious problem these days.

Opinion Phrases

- Here are some useful phrases for giving your opinion:

En mi opinión…	In my opinion…
Para mí…	For me…
Creo que…	I think that…
Prefiero…	I prefer…
Diría que…	I would say that…

Quick Test

1. Translate into Spanish: I surf the net every day.
2. What is the Spanish for 'email'?
3. Say in Spanish that you use your mobile to do your homework.
4. Translate into English: **Me gusta chatear con mis amigos**.

Music and Free Time

You must be able to:

- Talk about your musical interests
- Say how you prefer to listen to music
- Talk about other free-time activities.

Playing an Instrument

- **Sé tocar...**   I can play...
  la batería   drums
  las castañuelas   castanets
  el clarinete   clarinet
  la flauta   flute
  la guitarra   guitar
  el piano   piano
  la trompeta   trumpet
  el violín   violin

- **¿Sabes tocar un instrumento?**
  Can you play an instrument?
- **Sé tocar la trompeta y la guitarra.**
  I can play the trumpet and the guitar.
- **Me encanta tocar el piano porque me relaja mucho.**
  I love playing the piano because it really relaxes me.
- **En el futuro me gustaría aprender tocar la flauta.**
  In the future I would like to learn to play the flute.
- **Me gusta mucho escuchar música sobre todo cuando hago mis deberes.**
  I really like listening to music, especially when I'm doing my homework.
- **Lo que más me gusta es la música pop pero no soporto la música hip-hop.**
  What I like the most is pop music but I can't stand hip-hop.
- **Siempre llevo mi iPod conmigo a todos sitios y así puedo escuchar música cuando quiera.**
  I always take my iPod everywhere with me and then I can listen to music whenever I want.
- **Mi cantante preferido es... porque tiene una voz preciosa.**
  My favourite singer is... because he has a lovely voice.
- **No aguanto la música rock. La música clásica es mi música preferida.**
  I can't stand rock music. Classical music is my favourite.
- **Esta noche quiero ensayar la nueva canción en el clarinete.**
  Tonight I want to practise the new song on my clarinet.

> **Key Point**
>
> To play a sport you use the verb **jugar** to play, but to play a musical instrument the verb is **tocar**.

> **Key Point**
>
> The article is used when talking about different types of music:
> - **Prefiero escuchar la música rap.**

> **Key Point**
>
> After verbs of liking and disliking, you need a verb in the infinitive form:
> - **Me gusta <u>tocar</u> la flauta.**
> - **Detesto <u>escuchar</u> la música rap.**

Free-time Activities

- **En mi tiempo libre me gusta…** — In my free time I like…
  bailar — to dance
  cantar — to sing
  charlar con amigos — to chat to friends
  dar una vuelta — to go for a walk
  divertirme (divertirse) — to enjoy myself (to enjoy oneself)
  escuchar música — to listen to music
  ir a la bolera — to go bowling
  ir al cine/al teatro — to go to the cinema/theatre
  ir a una corrida de toros — to go to a bullfight
  ir de compras — to go shopping
  jugar al ajedrez/a las cartas — to play chess/cards
  jugar con los videojuegos — to play video games
  leer — to read
  navegar por Internet — to surf the Internet
  pasarlo bien/bomba — to have a good/great time
  pintar — to paint
  quedar con amigos — to meet up with friends
  salir con amigos — to go out with friends
  ver la televisión — to watch television
  ver un partido — to watch a match/game

- **En mi tiempo libre prefiero salir con mis amigos.**
  I prefer to go out with my friends in my free time.
- **A veces voy a la bolera con mis primos y me divierto mucho.**
  Sometimes I go bowling with my cousins and I really enjoy myself.
- **Me apasiona jugar al ajedrez y suelo jugar todos los días.**
  I am passionate about playing chess and I usually play every day.
- **Intento ver todos los partidos de mi equipo favorito en mi tiempo libre.**
  I try to watch all of my favourite team's matches in my free time.
- **Cuando sea mayor quiero aprender a bailar salsa.**
  When I am older, I want to learn how to dance salsa.

Key Point

Show off your knowledge of tenses; don't just stick to the present tense:

- **El sábado pasado fui de compras con mis amigos.** Last Saturday I went shopping with my friends.
- **En el pasado solía leer mucho más.** In the past I used to read much more. *Learn*
- **La semana que viene, voy a ir al cine con mi prima.** Next week I'm going to go to the cinema with my cousin.

Quick Test

1. Translate into Spanish:
   I prefer to listen to pop music.
2. Say in Spanish that you know how to play the drums.
3. Translate into Spanish:
   I love to chat to my friends.
4. Translate into Spanish:
   Going out with my friends is really good fun.

Cinema and Television

You must be able to:

- Talk about your cinema preferences
- Talk about television
- Make comparisons with other free-time activities.

At the Cinema

- Here are some useful words for talking about the cinema:

la actuación	performance, role
la banda sonora	soundtrack
el cine	cinema
la comedia	comedy
los dibujos animados	cartoons
la película	film
la película romántica / de amor	romantic film
la película de acción / aventura	action / adventure film
la película de ciencia-ficción	science-fiction film
la película de guerra	war film
la película de terror	horror film
la película del oeste	western
la película policíaca	detective film
la taquilla	ticket office

- **A mí me gustan las películas de aventura y también las comedias.**
  I like adventure films and comedies as well.
- **No me gustan las películas de ciencia-ficción porque me parecen aburridas y tontas.**
  I don't like science-fiction films because they seem boring and stupid to me.
- **Ayer fui al cine con mis amigos y vi una película de James Bond que me encantó.**
  Yesterday, I went to the cinema with my friends and I saw a James Bond film, which I loved.
- **Se trata de un espía que trabaja por el gobierno británico. ¡Fue muy emocionante!**
  It's about a spy who works for the British Government. It was really exciting!
- **Me encanta la banda sonora de las películas de Harry Potter.**
  I love the soundtrack from the Harry Potter films.
- **Yo prefiero descargar películas de la Red y verlas en casa.**
  I prefer to download films from the Internet and watch them at home.
- **Para mí, ir al cine es algo especial, sobre todo cuando voy con mis amigos.**
  For me, going to the cinema is special, specially when I go with my friends.

> ### Key Point
>
> When using impersonal verbs such as **gustar**, the definite article must also be used:
> - **Me gustan las películas de terror.**
> - **No me gustan las comedias.**

Watching Television

- Here are some useful words for talking about television:

los anuncios	adverts
el canal	channel

los concursos	game shows
los documentales	documentaries
las emisiones	programmes/broadcasts
las emisiones deportivas	sports programmes
el espectáculo	show
las noticias/el telediario	(TV) news
la pantalla	screen
los programas musicales	music programmes
las series	series
las telenovelas	soaps

- **¿Qué ponen en la tele esta noche?**
  What's on TV tonight?
- **Hay un concurso muy gracioso a las ocho. ¿Te apetece verlo?**
  There's a very funny game show on at eight o'clock. Do you fancy watching it?
- **Vale, sí. ¿Viste el documental anoche en la 2? Fue muy informativo e interesante.**
  Ok, yes. Did you see the documentary last night on Channel 2? It was really informative and interesting.
- **Esta noche voy a ver mi serie preferida y la veré en el portátil.**
  Tonight, I am going to watch my favourite series and I will watch it on my laptop.

Making Comparisons

- Comparisons can make your speaking and writing more interesting.
- Some common comparative phrases include:
  - **más... que** — more... than
  - **menos... que** — less... than
  - **mejor que** — better than
  - **peor que** — worse than
  - **tan... como** — as ... as
- Don't forget that where necessary the adjectives must agree:
  - **Me gustan los dibujos animados porque son *más* divertidos *que* los documentales.**
    I like cartoons because they are more fun than documentaries.
  - **Los programas musicales son *mejores que* las emisiones deportivas.**
    Music programmes are better than sports programmes.
  - **Para mí, ir al cine es *mejor que* ver una película en la tele.**
    For me, going to the cinema is better than watching a film on the TV.
  - **Creo que navegar por Internet es *menos* interesante *que* leer una novela.**
    I think that surfing the Internet is less interesting than reading a novel.

Key Point

To make comparisons between activities, you can use the infinitive:
- **En mi opinión, <u>ver</u> la tele es más aburrido que <u>salir</u> con mis amigos.**

Quick Test

1. Complete the sentences with **el/la/los/las**:
   Me encantan .... películas románticas.
   No me gustan nada .... programas musicales.
2. Say in Spanish that you like watching cartoons.
3. Translate into English:
   Creo que las telenovelas son más divertidas que las noticias.
4. Translate into Spanish: I love documentaries.

Food

You must be able to:

- Talk about food and drink
- Ask for food at the market
- Say what you eat at different mealtimes.

At the Market

- **¿Qué desea?** What would you like?
- **Póngame…** I'll have…

la fruta	fruit	**el melón**	melon
la cereza	cherry	**la naranja**	orange
la ciruela	plum	**la pera**	pear
la frambuesa	raspberry	**la piña**	pineapple
la fresa	strawberry	**el plátano**	banana
el limón	lemon	**el tomate**	tomato
la manzana	apple	**la uva**	grape
el melocotón	peach		

la verdura	vegetable	**los guisantes**	peas
el ajo	garlic	**las judías verdes**	green beans
la cebolla	onion	**la lechuga**	lettuce
el champiñón	mushroom	**las legumbres**	vegetables, pulses
la col	cabbage		
las coles de bruselas	sprouts	**la patata**	potato
		el pepino	cucumber
el espárrago	asparagus	**la pimienta**	pepper
las espinacas	spinach	**la zanahoria**	carrot

- **¡Qué rico! Me encantan las fresas.** How delicious! I love strawberries.
- **Lo que no me gusta mucho es el ajo.** What I don't like much is garlic.

- **¿Cuánto cuestan las manzanas?**
  How much are the apples?
- **Un euro cincuenta el kilo.**
  One euro fifty a kilo.
- **Pues, deme dos kilos por favor y medio kilo de uvas.**
  Well, give me two kilos, please, and half a kilo of grapes.
- **¿Algo más?**
  Anything else?
- **No, nada más, gracias. ¿Cuánto es?**
  No, nothing else thanks. How much is it?

At the Supermarket

- Here are some useful words for items at the supermarket:

una lata de atún	tin of tuna
un cartón de leche	carton of milk
una botella de vino tinto	bottle of red wine

> ### Key Point
>
> To say that someone is hungry/thirsty, etc., Spanish uses the verb 'to have' and not the verb 'to be':
> - **Tengo hambre.** I am hungry.
> - **Tengo sed.** I am thirsty.

un kilo de tomates	1 kilo of tomatoes
doscientos gramos de queso	200 grams of cheese
5 lonjas de jamón de york	5 slices of cooked ham
un bote de café	jar of coffee
dos barras de pan	two loaves of bread
un paquete de azúcar	packet of sugar
una docena de huevos	a dozen eggs
un litro de agua	1 litre of water
una caja de galletas	box of biscuits
una pastilla de mantequilla	block of butter

- **¿En qué puedo servirle?**
  How can I help you?
- **Póngame quinientos gramos de queso y dos kilos de jamón serrano, por favor.**
  I'll have five hundred grams of cheese and two kilos of cured (serrano) ham, please.
- **Aquí tiene. ¿Algo más?**
  Here you are. Anything else?
- **Sí, deme seis chuletas de cerdo también.**
  Yes, give me six pork chops as well.
- **Lo siento, sólo quedan cuatro. ¿Las quiere?**
  I'm sorry, there are only four left. Do you want them?
- **Sí, me las llevo, gracias.**
  Yes, I'll take them, thank you.

Mealtimes

- **¿Qué sueles desayunar?**
  What do you usually have for breakfast?
- **Pues, normalmente tomo un vaso de leche con tostadas.**
  Well, I usually have a glass of milk and toast.
- **Yo desayuno cereales durante la semana pero el sábado me gusta tomar churros con chocolate caliente.**
  I have cereal for breakfast during the week, but on a Saturday I like to have fritters and hot chocolate.
- **Para el almuerzo me gusta comer algo ligero como un bocadillo o una ensalada de atún.**
  For lunch, I like to have something light such as a sandwich or a tuna salad.
- **Suelo merendar algo como fruta por la tarde.**
  I usually have something like fruit for a snack in the afternoon.
- **Para la cena anoche comí pollo asado con patatas y verduras.**
  For dinner last night I had roast chicken with potatoes and vegetables.

> ### Key Point
>
> Mealtimes have their own verbs:
> - Breakfast (**El desayuno**) → **desayunar**
> - Lunch (**El almuerzo**) → **almorzar**
> - Snack (**La merienda**) → **merendar**
> - Dinner (**La cena**) → **cenar**
>
> **La comida** is another noun for 'lunch', and is also the noun for 'food'. **Comer** is the verb for 'to eat', but can also be used to say 'to eat lunch'.

> ### Quick Test
>
> 1. What is the correct Spanish verb to use when talking about eating lunch?
> 2. Say in Spanish that you love sprouts.
> 3. Translate into English: **Póngame ciento cincuenta gramos de jamón**
> 4. Which is the odd one out?
>   a) **el plátano**   b) **la pera**   c) **las uvas**   d) **los guisantes**

Eating Out

You must be able to:

- Understand a menu
- Order something to eat and drink
- Recognise when to use the formal 'you'.

The Menu

La carta/El menú Menu

Primer plato	*First course (starter)*	el pollo (frito)	(fried) chicken
		la ternera	veal
el chorizo	cured pork sausage		
la ensalada	salad	el pescado	fish
los espaguetis	spaghetti	el bacalao (asado)	(roast) cod
el fiambre	sliced meat (e.g. salami)	la merluza	hake
el gazpacho	cold vegetable soup	las sardinas (a la plancha)	(grilled) sardines
la salchicha	sausage	la trucha	trout
la sopa de verduras	vegetable soup	los mariscos	seafood
		los calamares	squid
la tortilla española	Spanish omelette	las gambas	prawns
		la paella de mariscos	seafood paella
Segundo plato	*Second course (main course)*	*Postres*	*Desserts*
		el arroz con leche	rice pudding
la carne	meat		
las albóndigas	meatballs	el flan	crème caramel
el bistec	steak	el helado de vainilla	vanilla ice-cream
la carne de cerdo/de vaca	pork/beef		
el cordero	lamb	la tarta de chocolate	chocolate cake

At a Restaurant

- **¿Tiene una mesa para dos, por favor?**
  Do you have a table for two, please?
- **¿Qué van a tomar?**
  What are you going to have?
- **De primero, quisiera el gazpacho y de segundo, la paella de mariscos.**
  For the first course, I'd like the gazpacho and for the second course, the seafood paella.
- **Y ¿para beber?**
  And to drink?

- **Quiero vino blanco, por favor.**
  I'd like white wine, please.
- **¿Quiere algo de postre?**
  Would you like anything for dessert?
- **¿Recomienda usted algo?**
  Do you recommend anything?
- **La tarta de chocolate es muy rica.**
  The chocolate cake is really delicious.
- **Bien, yo quiero probarla.**
  Good, I would like to try it.
- **Pues, yo estoy de régimen, voy a tomar fruta.**
  Well, I am on a diet, I am going to have fruit.
- **La cuenta, por favor.**
  The bill, please.

Problems at a Restaurant

- **No hay…**   There isn't/aren't…
  cuchara   a spoon
  cuchillo   a knife
  tenedor   a fork
  servieta   a serviette/napkin
  vaso   a glass

- **La comida está…**   The food is…
  demasiado picante too spicy
  fría   cold
  salada   salty
  grasienta   greasy, oily

Drinks

las bebidas	drinks	**la leche**	milk
el agua	water	**la limonada**	lemonade
el agua mineral (con/sin gas)	mineral water (fizzy/ still)	**la naranjada**	orangeade
		el refresco	soft drink
el café (con leche/solo)	coffee (with milk/ black)	**el té**	tea
		el tinto	red wine
la cerveza	beer	**el vino (blanco)**	(white) wine
la Coca-Cola	Coca-cola	**el zumo de fruta/manzana**	fruit/apple juice
la gaseosa	lemonade/pop		

- **Tengo sed. ¿Quieres tomar algo?**
  I'm thirsty. Do you want something to drink?
- **Sí, para mí, un café con leche y agua mineral sin gas, por favor.**
  Yes, I'll have (for me) a white coffee and still mineral water, please.

> **Key Point**

In a restaurant, you speak to the waiter or waitress using the **usted** form of the verb:
- **¿Tiene una mesa para cuatro personas?**
- **¿Qué recomienda usted?**

> **Quick Test**
>
> 1. Order something in Spanish for your first and second course.
> 2. Say in Spanish that you don't like meatballs.
> 3. Which is the odd one out?
>   a) **el café**   b) **la gaseosa**
>   c) **la leche**   d) **el zumo de fruta**

Sport

You must be able to:

- Talk about different sports
- Say how long you have been practising a sport
- Recognise when to use **hacer**, **practicar** or **jugar** with sports.

Types of Sports

- Here are some words for sports and activities:

el alpinismo	climbing	**la gimnasia**	gymnastics
el atletismo	athletics	**el monopatín**	skateboard
el baloncesto	basketball	**la natación**	swimming
el balonmano	handball	**el patinaje**	skating (ice)
el béisbol	baseball	**(sobre hielo)**	
el billar	billiards	**la pelota**	Basque pelota
el boxeo	boxing	**la pesca**	fishing
el ciclismo	cycling	**el ping-pong**	table-tennis
los deportes	sports	**el rugby**	rugby
los deportes	extreme sports	**el tenis**	tennis
de riesgo		**el tenis de mesa**	table-tennis
la equitación	horse-riding	**la vela**	sailing
el esquí	skiing	**el voleibol**	volleyball
el footing	jogging	**el windsurf**	windsurfing
el fútbol	football		

Verbs for Talking about Sports

- For sports and activities use the following verbs:
  - **jugar a**   to play
  - **practicar**   to practise
  - **hacer**   to do.
- In general, if it is a game (such as football) use **jugar a** (to play) and for the other activities use **practicar** or **hacer**. (In English we often translate these verbs as 'go' + activity) For example:
  - **Practico/Hago la vela los fines de semana.**
    I practise/do/go sailing at weekends.
- **Jugar** is always followed by **a**. If the sport is masculine, which the majority are, you will need to contract the **a + el = al**:
  - **Juego al fútbol todos los días**. I play football every day.

Talking about Sports

- **Practico el monopatín los fines de semana en el parque.**
  I go skateboarding at weekends in the park.
- **Me encantan los deportes. Juego al hockey dos veces a la semana y también practico la natación y el footing.**
  I love sports. I play hockey twice a week and I also go swimming and jogging.
- **Soy miembro del club de tenis de mesa en mi colegio.**
  I am a member of the table-tennis club at my school.

- **Cuando era más joven no me gustaban mucho los deportes, pero ahora me encanta practicar el esquí.**
  When I was younger I didn't really like sports, but now I love to go skiing.
- **En el futuro me gustaría practicar un deporte de riesgo porque ¡es más emocionante!**
  In the future, I would like to do an extreme sport because it's more exciting!

Sports Verbs

- Here are some useful verbs for talking about sports:

correr	to run
dar un paseo	to go for a walk
entrenarse	to train
esquiar	to ski
ganar la copa	to win the cup
marcar un gol	to score a goal
montar	to ride
nadar	to swim
patinar	to skate
pescar/ir de pesca	to fish/go fishing
perder	to lose
saltar	to jump
ser hincha de	to be a fan of
ser aficionado a	to be keen on/fond of (activity)

- **Soy hincha del atletismo y lo practico con mi equipo escolar cada semana.**
  I am an athletics fan and I practise it every week with my school team.
- **Mi deporte preferido es la natación y entreno en la piscina todos los días.**
  My favourite sport is swimming and I train at the pool every day.
- **Practico el boxeo desde hace un año.**
  I've been doing boxing for one year.
- **Ayer, marqué un gol en el torneo. ¡Fue estupendo!**
  Yesterday, I scored a goal in the tournament. It was brilliant!

Quick Test

1. Which one is the odd one out?
   a) **el esquí**
   b) **el balonmano**
   c) **el baloncesto**
   d) **el tenis**
2. Say in Spanish that you are going fishing with your brother on Sunday.
3. Translate into Spanish:
   I play rugby every Saturday.
4. What is wrong with this sentence?
   Juego al footing todos los días.

Key Point

There is often more than one way of saying the same thing in Spanish, particularly when talking about sports and activities. For example, to talk about swimming you could use:
- **nadar**
  to swim
- **practicar/hacer la natación**
  to go swimming
- **bañarse**
  to bathe/swim
- **ir a la piscina**
  to go to the pool

Key Point

Use **desde hace** with the present tense to say how long you have been doing something:
- **Practico la gimnasia desde hace cinco años.**
  I have been doing gymnastics for five years.

Use **desde hacía** with the imperfect tense to say how long you *had* been doing something:
- **Jugaba al béisbol desde hacía un año cuando ganamos la copa.**
  I had been playing baseball for a year when we won the cup.

Customs and Celebrations

You must be able to:

- Talk about traditional customs and festivals in Spanish countries and communities
- Describe what happens during particular festivals
- Use the gerund to describe events.

Special Events

- **Celebramos…**   We celebrate…
  El Año Nuevo   New Year
  El Día de los Inocentes   28th December
  El Día de los Muertos   All Souls' Day
  El Día de Navidad   Christmas Day
  El Día de Reyes   Epiphany (6th January)
  El Día del santo   Saint's Day
  La Noche Buena   Christmas Eve
  La Noche Vieja   New Year's Eve
  La Navidad   Christmas
  La Pascua   Easter
  La Semana Santa   Easter, Holy Week
  Los San Fermines   Bull-running festival
  La Tomatina   Tomato-throwing festival

- **¡A mí me encanta la Semana Santa! El año pasado fui a Sevilla para ver las procesiones y ¡fue muy impresionante!**
  I love Holy Week! Last year I went to Seville to see the processions and it was really impressive!

- **En mi casa, solemos celebrar el Día de Navidad con mis abuelos.**
  At my house, we usually celebrate Christmas Day with my grandparents.

- **En España los niños reciben los regalos el día de Reyes, que es el 6 de enero.**
  In Spain, children receive their presents on the Epiphany, which is the 6th of January.

- **Durante el Día de los Muertos, las familias visitan los cementerios para adornar las tumbas de sus parientes.**
  During All Souls' Day, families visit cemeteries to decorate the graves of their relatives.

Celebration Verbs and Vocabulary

- Here are some useful words for talking about celebrations, customs and festivals:

  adornar/decorar   to decorate
  cantar   to sing
  celebrar   to celebrate
  dar   to give
  disfrazarse de   to dress up as
  esperar con ilusión   to look forward to
  felicitar   to congratulate

festejar	to celebrate
mandar	to send
ofrecer	to offer/give
recibir	to receive
regalar	to give as a present
rezar	to pray
tener lugar	to take place
la corrida (de toros)	bullfight
la costumbre	custom, way
el cumpleaños	birthday
el día festivo	public holiday
el disfraz	fancy dress
el gaucho	cowboy
la feria	fair
la fiesta	festival
el jugete	toy
el mariachi	Mexican musician
la muñeca	doll
Papá Noel	Father Christmas
el paso	statue paraded at Easter
los Reyes Magos	the Three Kings
el villancico	Christmas carol
el Año Nuevo Chino	Chinese New Year
la fiesta de Januka	Hanukkah

> **Key Point**
>
> Although there are lots of different festivals celebrated throughout the Spanish-speaking world, the language used to describe them is fairly standard, so don't be put off if you read or hear about a festival that you are unfamiliar with. (28th December is the equivalent of April Fools' Day.)

- **Todos los años celebramos mi cumpleaños en el mismo restaurante.**
  Every year we celebrate my birthday in the same restaurant.
- **Algún día iré a Sudamérica para celebrar las fiestas de Carnaval.**
  Some day, I will go to South America to celebrate the Carnival festival.
- **Durante la Navidad, mi familia pasa mucho tiempo junta comiendo, jugando, a veces cantando villancicos y generalmente pasándolo bien.**
  During Christmas, my family spends a lot of time together eating, playing, sometimes singing Christmas carols and generally having a good time.
- **Me encanta celebrar el Año Nuevo con mis amigos. La Nochevieja se bebe champán y a las doce se come doce uvas, que es típico en España.**
  I love to celebrate New Year with my friends. On New Year's Eve, people drink champagne and at twelve o'clock, they eat twelve grapes, which is the tradition in Spain.
- **No celebramos la Navidad sino Diwali, el festival de las luces.**
  Instead of celebrating Christmas, we celebrate Diwali, the festival of lights.
- **En el festival de Eid intercambiamos tarjetas, regalos y dulces.**
  During the festival of Eid we exchange cards, gifts and sweets.

> **Key Point**
>
> Use the gerund ('-ing' in English) after a main verb to describe a sequence of events:
> – **Me gusta pasar el Día de Reyes charlando, comiendo y descansando con mi familia.**
> – I like to spend the Epiphany chatting, eating and resting with my family.
> Remember, **-ando (-ar)** **-iendo (-ir** and **-er)**.

> ### Quick Test
>
> 1. Say in Spanish that you love to celebrate Christmas Eve.
> 2. Translate into Spanish: We decorate the house.
> 3. Say in Spanish that you are looking forward to the bull-running festival.
> 4. Translate into English: **Mi madre preparó una cena muy rica.**

Relationships with Family and Friends & Marriage and Partnership

1 Choose the correct verbs from the options given to complete the following sentences.

es ~~tiene~~ se llama somos ~~eres~~ tengo ~~son~~

a) Mi padre _Se llama_ Jorge.

b) Y tú, ¿cómo _eres_ ?

c) _Tengo_ dos hermanos y una hermana.

d) ¿Cómo _es_ tu padre, bajo o alto?

e) Tus primas _Son_ muy guapas.

f) _Somos_ cinco en mi familia.

g) Mi amiga no _tiene_ hermanos. [7]

2 Rearrange the words into the correct order to form the sentences.

a) tiene y pelo el prima rizado mi castaño (My cousin has chestnut brown curly hair.)

Mi Prima tiene el pelo castaño rizado

b) alto los y azules bastante ojos soy tengo (I am quite tall and I have blue eyes.)

Soy bastante alta Y tengo los ojos azules.

c) mediana es padre estatura mi de (My dad is of medium height.)

Mi Padre es de estatura mediana

d) son y hermanos bajos bastante mis delgados (My brothers are quite short and slim.)

Mis hermanos Son bastante bajos e delgados. [4]

3 Are the following opinions positive (P) or negative (N)? Write **P** or **N** for each.

Mi marido es muy comprensivo y sensible y le quiero mucho.	Pilar
Mi novia es bastante impaciente, sin embargo es muy cariñosa.	Ramón
Mis padres discuten mucho y estoy harto de sus peleas.	Victoria

a) Pilar _____ b) Ramón _____ c) Victoria _____ [3]

Social Media

1 Choose the correct verbs from the options given to complete the sentences.

cargar   descargué   enviar   navegar   mando   utilizar

a) Suelo _____ correos electrónicos en vez de escribir cartas tradicionales.

b) Normalmente _____ mensajes de texto a mis amigas.

c) Ayer _____ la nueva canción de mi grupo preferido a mi móvil.

d) Me gusta mucho _____ las redes sociales para estar en contacto con mis amigos.

e) Lo que me gusta hacer por la noche es _____ por Internet.

f) Esta noche tengo que _____ mi iPad porque me he quedado sin batería.   [6]

2 Read the comments from parents about social media and technology and decide whether the opinions are positive (P) or negative (N). Write **P** or **N** for each.

> Mi hijo pasa largas horas en su dormitorio jugando con los videojuegos o navegando por Internet. Aunque está comunicándose con sus amigos mientras juega, creo que rompe la comunicación familiar porque no viene nunca al salón para hablar con nosotros, sus padres, solo quiere encerrarse en su cuarto. DAVID

> A mi hija le encanta usar las redes sociales todos los días. Las usa para quedarse en contacto con sus amigas, pero también para informarse de lo que está pasando en la ciudad. Siempre encuentra algo nuevo o algún lugar nuevo como cafeterías o tiendas nuevas que usan las redes sociales para anunciarse. MARISOL

> Cuando mis hijos tienen deberes del colegio, siempre usan la tecnología para ayudarles. Si necesitan información sobre un tema histórico o geográfico, la pueden buscar con el Internet. Si no entienden algo, siempre pueden encontrar la respuesta con el portátil o el móvil. Me parece imprescindible usarla hoy en día. JESÚS

a) David _____

b) Marisol _____

c) Jesús _____   [3]

Practice Questions

Music and Free Time & Cinema and Television

1 Choose the correct form of the verb to complete the following sentences. Tick the correct option.

a) Anoche _____ con los videojuegos.

A juego ☐ B jugaré ☐ C jugué ☐

b) Por la tarde me gusta _____ una vuelta con mi perro.

A dar ☐ B doy ☐ C daré ☐

c) Cuando era pequeña _____ mucho al ajedrez con mi hermano.

A juego ☐ B jugaré ☐ C jugaba ☐

d) Suelo _____ la tele por la noche.

A veo ☐ B ver ☐ C vi ☐

e) Mañana voy a _____ con mis amigos al centro.

A salí ☐ B salir ☐ C salía ☐

f) Después de _____ un poco, normalmente me duermo en seguida.

A leo ☐ B leía ☐ C leer ☐ [6]

2 Match the descriptions **A**, **B**, **C**, **D** and **E** with the programmes **1–5**.

1 Las noticias 2 Las telenovelas 3 Los documentales

4 Los concursos 5 Las emisiones deportivas

A Esta noche voy a ver el partido entre los dos mejores equipos de la liga. ☐

B El premio esta vez va a pasar un millón de euros. ☐

C No quiero perder el capítulo hoy porque mi personaje favorito va a casarse. ☐

D Esta noche ponen un programa muy interesante sobre los elefantes en África. ☐

E Tenemos que verlo para saber lo que está pasando en el mundo. ☐ [5]

Food, Eating Out, Sport & Customs and Celebrations

1 Translate the items on the shopping list below into English, including the quantities.

a) **Tres botellas de vino blanco**

b) **Una botella de vino tinto**

c) **Dos kilos de plátanos**

d) **Un kilo de naranjas**

e) **Medio kilo de uvas**

f) **Dos kilos de cebollas**

g) **Una lechuga**

h) **Medio kilo de chorizo** [8]

2 Match the descriptions **A**, **B**, **C**, **D**, **E** and **F** with the correct celebrations **1–6**.

1 Christmas   **2** Easter

3 Birthday   **4** New Year's Eve

5 Bull-running festival   **6** 28th December

A **Recibimos regalos de familia y amigos y normalmente tenemos una tarta especial con velas.**

B **Adornamos un árbol y también montamos un belén. Comemos pavo con verduras y hay siempre muchos regalos.**

C **Esta fiesta es muy graciosa. Todo el mundo cuenta chistes y, en la tele, leen noticias en broma que parecen serias.**

D **Durante esta fiesta comemos muchos huevos de chocolate y vamos a misa para cantar y rezar.**

E **Mis amigos y yo asistimos a esta fiesta todos los años. Puede ser peligroso porque los toros son muy grandes y corren rápidamente.**

F **Mucha gente sale a la calle y a las doce cantamos y nos abrazamos. También hay fuegos artificiales y en España la gente come doce uvas.** [6]

House and Home

You must be able to:

- Talk about your house
- Use prepositions to say where things are in your house
- Describe your bedroom.

At Home

- Here are some useful words for talking about your home:

la casa (adosada)	house (semi-detached)	**el cuarto de baño**	bathroom
el chalé/el chalet	detached house/ bungalow	**el dormitorio**	bedroom
		la escalera	stairs
		el garaje	garage
		la habitación	room
el domicilio	address, home	**el jardín**	garden
la granja	farm	**la pared**	wall
el piso	flat, floor	**el pasillo**	corridor
la vivienda	dwelling, housing	**la planta baja**	ground floor
		la primera planta	first floor
el árbol	tree	**el salón**	lounge
el aseo	bathroom, WC	**el sótano**	basement
el césped	lawn	**la terraza**	patio, terrace
la cocina	kitchen	**el vestíbulo**	entrance hall, foyer
el comedor	dining room		
el cuarto	room	**arriba**	upstairs
el cuarto de estar	living room	**abajo**	downstairs

- **Vivo en una casa adosada con tres habitaciones en la planta baja. El cuarto de baño está en la primera planta. No tenemos garaje.**
  I live in a semi-detached house with three rooms on the ground floor. The bathroom is on the first floor. We don't have a garage.

- **Detrás de la casa hay un jardín bastante grande con un césped y muchas flores. También tenemos un garaje.**
  Behind the house there is quite a big garden with a lawn and lots of flowers. We also have a garage.

- **En mi piso, el salón comunica con la cocina y luego hay un baño pequeño y mi dormitorio.**
  In my flat, the lounge connects with the kitchen and then there is a small bathroom and my bedroom.

Key Point

Note that after a negative expression the article is not used:

- **En mi casa no hay comedor.** In my house there is no dining room.
- **No tenemos ni jardín ni garaje.** We don't have a garden or a garage.

Describing Where Things Are

- When describing the location of a person or thing, use **estar** with a preposition:
- **Está/Están...**   It is/They are…

al final de	at the end of	**detrás de**	behind
al lado de	next to	**en**	in/on
a la derecha de	to the right of	**encima de**	above/on
a la izquierda de	to the left of	**en el suelo**	on the floor
cerca de	near to	**enfrente de**	opposite
debajo de	below/under	**en medio de**	in the middle of
delante de	in front of	**entre**	in between

- Remember: **de + el = del** and **de + la = de la**
  - **Mi casa está <u>al final de la</u> calle.** My house is at the end of the street.
  - **La cocina está <u>al lado del</u> salón.** The kitchen is next to the lounge.

Describing Your Bedroom

En mi dormitorio hay…	In my bedroom there is…	**la lámpara**	lamp
		la luz	light
		la manta	blanket
la alfombra	rug	**la moqueta**	carpet
el armario	wardrobe	**los muebles**	furniture
la cama	bed	**la puerta**	door
las cortinas	curtains	**la sábana**	sheet
el despertador	alarm clock	**el secador**	hairdryer
el espejo	mirror	**el techo**	ceiling
el estante	shelf	**la ventana**	window

- **En mi dormitorio hay una cama, un armario y una mesa para mis cosas del instituto.**
  In my bedroom there is a bed, a wardrobe and a table for all of my school things.
- **Los muebles en mi dormitorio son muy anticuados. Me gustaría tener un cuarto moderno con un póster de mi cantante preferido.**
  The furniture in my bedroom is old-fashioned. I would like a modern room with a poster of my favourite singer.
- **Antes, tenía un dormitorio muy feo pero ahora es muy bonito y acogedor.**
  Before, I used to have a very ugly bedroom but now it's really lovely and cosy.

Quick Test

1. Describe your house in Spanish, naming the rooms.
2. Complete these sentences using **de la** or **del**:
   Mi dormitorio está al lado _____ cuarto de baño.
   El garaje está detrás _____ casa.
   El salón está enfrente _____ comedor.
3. Translate into Spanish: My flat is on the first floor.
4. Translate into English: **En mi dormitorio hay una cama grande.**

Key Point

Always try to justify an opinion with a reason. **Me gusta mi casa** on its own conveys some information but you will always gain better marks if you can say *why*:
- **No me gusta mi casa porque es demasiada pequeña y no tenemos jardín.**
  I don't like my house because it is too small and we don't have a garden.

Neighbourhood and Town

You must be able to:

- Say what is in your town
- Describe your town or neighbourhood
- Talk about how you travel around.

Describing your Town

- **Vivo…**   I live…
la aldea	village
el barrio	neighbourhood, district
la ciudad	city, town
el pueblo	small town, village
en las afueras	on the outskirts
en el centro	in the centre
en el campo	in the countryside
en la costa	on the coast
en la sierra	in the mountains

- **Vivo en las afueras de la ciudad**. I live on the outskirts of the city.
- **Vivo en un pueblo pequeño en el campo**. I live in a small town in the countryside.

- **En mi pueblo hay…**   In my town there is…

el ayuntamiento	town hall	**la panadería**	baker's
el banco	bank	**la papelería**	stationery shop
la biblioteca	library	**el parque infantil**	children's playground
la carnicería	butcher's		
el castillo	castle	**la pastelería**	pastry shop
el centro comercial	shopping centre	**la peluquería**	hairdresser's
		la pescadería	fish shop
el cine	cinema	**la piscina**	swimming pool
la comisaría	police station	**la plaza**	town square
Correos	post office	**la plaza de toros**	bullring
el estanco	tobacconist's		
la fábrica	factory	**el polideportivo**	sports centre
la frutería	fruit shop	**el supermercado**	supermarket
la iglesia	church	**la tienda (de comestibles)**	shop (grocer's)
la joyería	jeweller's		
la mezquita	mosque	**la zapatería**	shoe shop
el mercado	market	**la zona peatonal**	pedestrian area

- **Me encanta mi ciudad porque hay muchas tiendas muy buenas y unos museos estupendos.**
  I love my city because there are lots of very good shops and some excellent museums.

- **En el pasado no había mucho para los jóvenes, pero ahora hay la piscina y un polideportivo estupendo.**
  In the past there wasn't much for young people but now there is the swimming pool and an excellent sports centre.

Key Point

When writing or speaking, you must use a range of complex structures. So if you are describing your neighbourhood or town, don't just list the facilities; try to think of other ways of expressing yourself.

Describing a Place

- Here are some useful adjectives for describing a place:

aislado/a	isolated	**limpio/a**	clean
animado/a	lively	**pequeño/a**	small
antiguo/a	old	**pintoresco/a**	picturesque
bonito/a	pretty	**precioso/a**	lovely/beautiful
comercial	commercial	**residencial**	residential
concurrido/a	busy, crowded	**ruidoso/a**	noisy
contaminado/a	polluted	**sucio/a**	dirty
feo/a	ugly/unsightly	**tranquilo/a**	peaceful
histórico/a	historic	**turístico/a**	attractive to
industrial	industrial		tourists

- **Mi pueblo es muy bonito pero a veces puede ser bastante aislado.**
  My town is very pretty but at times it can be quite isolated.
- **Prefiero vivir en el campo porque es siempre muy tranquilo.**
  I prefer to live in the countryside because it's always very peaceful.
- **Vivo en un barrio residencial que es muy limpio y antiguo.**
  I live in a neighbourhood that is very clean and old.

Getting Around

- **el medio de transporte**   means of transport

el autobús	bus	**el metro**	underground train
el autocar	coach	**la moto**	motorbike
el avión	plane	**la tranvía**	tram
el barco	boat	**el tren**	train
la bicicleta, bici	bicycle, bike	**andar**	to walk
el camión	lorry	**coger (cojo)**	to catch (I catch)
el coche	car	**esperar**	to wait (for)

- **El viaje es...**   The journey is...

barato	cheap	**económico**	economical
caro	expensive	**lento**	slow
(in)cómodo	(un)comfortable	**rápido**	fast
ecológico	ecological		

- **Prefiero ir en coche porque es cómodo.**
  I prefer to go by car because it's comfortable.
- **No me gusta ir en coche a causa de los atascos. ¡Siempre hay retrasos!**
  I don't like to go by car because of the traffic jams. There are always delays!
- **Intento ir a pie a menudo porque es más ecológico.**
  I often try to go on foot because it is more ecological.

> ### Key Point
>
> When saying how you travel, use **en** + transport, for example, **en coche** (by car). You do not need the definite article **el/la**. Note that 'on foot' is **a pie**.

Quick Test

1. Which sentence describes a city?
   a) **Hay mucho que hacer como el cine, las tiendas y muchos restaurantes.**
   b) **Es muy tranquilo y verde y hay pocas tiendas.**
   c) **Donde yo vivo solo hay una iglesia y una tienda.**
2. Is this sentence past, present or future tense?
   Van a construir un nuevo centro comercial.
3. Translate into Spanish: I like to go by bus because it's fast.

My Region

You must be able to:

- Say what you can do in your region
- Describe the positives and negatives of your area
- Talk about getting around in your area.

Talking About What You Can Do

- To say what you/one can or can't do in your town or region, use **se puede +** infinitive:
  - **En mi pueblo <u>se puede cenar</u> en un restaurante.**
    In my town you can eat out in a restaurant.
  - **En el campo <u>se puede dar</u> un paseo o montar a caballo.**
    In the countryside you can go for a walk or go horse-riding.
  - **En mi región <u>se puede visitar</u> el castillo e ir a la playa.**
    In my region one can visit the castle and go to the beach.
  - **En la sierra <u>se puede ver</u> el paisaje precioso.**
    In the mountains you can see the beautiful landscape.

Expressing Opinions About Your Region

- A slightly different way of expressing an opinion about something is to talk about the good or bad 'thing'. Use **lo +** adjective to mean 'the .... thing'. For example:

lo bueno	the good thing
lo malo	the bad thing
lo mejor	the best thing
lo peor	the worst thing
lo interesante	the interesting thing
lo raro	the strange thing
lo positivo	the positive thing
lo negativo	the negative thing
lo único	the only thing

- **Lo mejor de mi pueblo es que está en la costa.**
  The best thing about my town is that it is on the coast.
- **Lo malo es el desempleo.**
  The bad thing is the unemployment.
- **En el pasado lo bueno era que no había tanto tráfico.**
  In the past, the good thing was that there wasn't as much traffic.

Getting Around

- Here are some useful question phrases and words to help you talk about how to get around:

¿Dónde está...?	Where is...?
¿Para ir a...?	To get to...?
¿Por dónde se va a...?	How do I get to...?
Baje	Go down
Cruce	Cross

Key Point

At higher level, in particular, meaning is often inferred rather than obvious. Words such as **lo bueno/mejor** and adjectives such as **bonito/interesante/precioso** all express an idea of positivity, even if the words **me gusta/encanta** are not used.

Está a cien metros	It's 100 metres away
Está a la derecha/izquierda	It's on the right/the left
Tome la primera/segunda/tercera calle	Take the first/second/third street
a la derecha	on the right
a la izquierda	on the left
Siga todo recto	Go straight on
Suba…	Go up…
Tuerza…	Turn…

la calle	street
la carretera	main road
el cruce	crossroads
la esquina	corner
la glorieta	roundabout
el paso de peatones	zebra crossing
la plaza (mayor)	(main) square
el puente	bridge
el puerto	port
el río	river
los semáforos	traffic lights
la señal	sign
la zona peatonal	pedestrianised area
cerca	near
lejos	far
hasta	as far as/up to

Directions

- As conversations about directions often occur between strangers, **usted** is usually used as it would be a formal situation:
- **¡Perdone! ¿Por dónde se va al polideportivo, por favor?**
  Excuse me! How do I get to the sports centre, please?
- **A ver, siga todo recto, cruce la plaza y está a la izquierda cerca del puente.**
  Let's see, go straight on, cross the square and it's on the left near the bridge.
- **¿Está lejos la catedral?**
  Is the cathedral far?
- **No, está muy cerca. Suba la calle hasta los semáforos y tuerza a la derecha. Está a cincuenta metros.**
  No, it's very close. Go up the street to the traffic lights and turn right. It's 50 metres away.

Quick Test

1. Translate into Spanish: In my region you can go to the beach.
2. Complete the sentences with **del** or **de la**:
   La catedral está cerca _____ mercado.
   El ayuntamiento está lejos _____ plaza.
3. Translate into English: **Lo bueno de mi región es el paisaje.**
4. Is this sentence positive or negative? **En mi región se puede hacer mucho: ir a los parques, visitar museos o ir de compras.**

Charity and Voluntary Work

You must be able to:

- Talk about the main issues affecting society
- Give your opinions on a number of issues
- Discuss voluntary work and its benefits.

Issues Affecting Society

- **Hay problemas con…**   There are problems with…

la delincuencia	delinquency, crime
el desempleo	unemployment
la desigualdad	inequality
la exclusión social	social exclusion
la falta de respeto	lack of respect
los gamberros	hooligans
la indignidad	indignity
los inmigrantes	immigrants
el maltrato	mistreatment, abuse
el racismo	racism
el robo	theft, burglary
el sida	AIDS
los sin techo	homeless people
la violencia	violence

- **Tenemos que luchar contra la desigualdad.** We have to fight against inequality.
- **El desempleo es algo que afecta a gente por todo el país.** Unemployment is something that affects people all over the country.
- **Me preocupa mucho el maltrato de animales.** I am very worried about the mistreatment of animals.

Tackling the Issue

- Here are some useful verbs for talking about social issues:

apoyar	to support
ayudar	to help
beneficiar	to benefit
compartir	to share
contribuir	to contribute
cuidar	to look after
dedicar(se)	to do, go in for, devote oneself
discutir	to discuss
educar	to educate
formar parte de	to be part of
hacerse voluntario/a	to become a volunteer
lograr	to achieve
mejorar	to improve
provocar	to cause/provoke

Key Point

You will have to understand/ give opinions on a number of issues to achieve a high level. You must also justify your opinions with a reason.

- **Me gustaría trabajar como voluntario/a en/con…**
  I would like to work as a volunteer in/with…
una tienda solidaria	a charity shop
una residencia para ancianos	an old people's home
una escuela (en África)	a school (in Africa)
los minusválidos	disabled people

- **Voy a hacerme voluntario/a con…**   I'm going to become a volunteer with…
una organización benéfica	a charitable organisation
una ONG	an NGO (non-governmental organisation)
una organización ecologista	an environmental organisation
una organización humanitaria	a humanitarian organisation

- **Tenemos que luchar contra el racismo porque creo que los derechos humanos son muy importantes.**
  We have to fight against racism because I believe that human rights are very important.

- **Voy a hacerme voluntario para ayudar a los demás.**
  I'm going to become a volunteer to help others.

- **En el pasado era un poco egoísta pero ahora trato de dar mi tiempo a otros.**
  In the past I was a bit selfish, but now I try to give my time to others.

- **Si nos juntamos y trabajamos juntos, lograremos mejorar nuestra sociedad.**
  If we all come together and work together, we will manage to improve our society.

- **Hay un problema con la delincuencia en muchos sitios y tenemos que crear oportunidades para que esto se acabe.**
  There is a problem of delinquency in many places and we have to create opportunities so that it stops.

- **Cuando sea mayor tengo la interción de hacerme voluntario.**
  When I am older I have the intention of becoming a volunteer.

Key Point

Use **si** + present + future to talk about things that are likely to happen:
- **Si me hago voluntaria contribuiré a la sociedad.**
  If I become a volunteer I will contribute to society.
- **Si educamos a la población cambiaremos la situación.**
  If we educate the population we will change the situation.

Giving Opinions

- You can give an opinion using a number of phrases:
Creo que	I think/believe that
Diría que	I would say that
En mi opinión	In my opinion
Me parece que	It seems to me that
Opino que	I think that
Para mí	For me
Pienso que	I think that
Por un lado	On the one hand
Por otro lado	On the other hand
Reconozco que	I recognise that

- **Reconozco que tenemos que mejorar la sociedad en la que vivimos.**
  I recognise that we have to improve the society in which we live.

Quick Test

1. Give an opinion in Spanish on one of the issues that affect society.
2. When might you use the phrases **por un lado** and **por otro lado?**
3. Translate into English: **Si trabajamos juntos mejoraremos la comunidad.**
4. Give an example in Spanish of a way that we can help society.

Healthy Living

You must be able to:

- Talk about your health
- Say what you will do to be more healthy
- Use the infinitive to give advice.

Health and Fitness

- Here are some useful words for talking about health and fitness:

el alimento	food	**el estrés**	stress
el apetito	appetite	**las golosinas**	sweet things
el ataque cardíaco	heart attack	**gordo/a**	fat (adjective)
el cansancio	tiredness	**la grasa**	fat
la comida basura	junk food	**los granos**	spots
la comida rápida	fast food	**los/las modelos**	size zero
delgado/a	slim	**de talla cero**	models
la dieta	healthy/	**la obesidad**	obesity
sana/malsana	unhealthy diet	**perjudicial**	harmful
la dieta	balanced diet	**poco sano**	not healthy
equilibrada		**la salud**	health
el dolor de oídos	earache	**saludable**	healthy
los dulces	sweet things	**sano/a**	healthy,
el ejercicio físico	physical		wholesome
	exercise	**el sobrepeso**	overweight

- **Creo que estoy en forma. Intento comer una dieta equilibrada, o sea carne, pescado, fruta, verduras, etc., y practico el deporte tres veces a la semana.**

  I think I am fit. I try to eat a balanced diet, that's to say meat, fish, fruit, vegetables, etc., and I do sport three times a week.

- **Cuando era más joven, comía muchas golosinas y comida que contiene grasa. Ahora estoy intentando seguir una dieta más saludable.**

  When I was younger, I used to eat lots of sweet things and food that contains fat. Now I am trying to follow a healthier diet.

- **En el futuro haré más ejercicio físico y cambiaré mi estilo de vida.**

  In the future I will do more physical exercise and I will change my lifestyle.

- **Mi amiga quiere estar flaca como las modelos en la tele y por eso trata de no comer mucho. Yo no estoy de acuerdo con eso.**

  My friend wants to be thin like the models on TV and because of that she tries not to eat much. I don't agree with that.

> ### Key Point
>
> Look for time indicators to help you understand whether someone is talking about the past, present or future. Phrases such as **antes** (before), **cuando era joven** (when I was young), **de pequeño** (as a youngster), **ahora** (now), **cuando sea mayor** (when I am older), etc., will all help with understanding.

Useful Verbs

- Here are some useful verbs for talking about lifestyle:

acostarse	to go to bed	**hacer ejercicio**	to exercise
adelgazar	to lose weight, slim down	**inyectarse**	to inject
		levantarse	to get up
correr el riesgo	to run the risk	**mantenerse en forma**	to keep fit
despertarse	to wake up		
estar bien/mal	to be well/ill	**oler**	to smell
estar en forma	to be fit/healthy	**perder peso**	to lose weight
evitar	to avoid	**relajarse**	to relax
fumar	to smoke	**respirar**	to breathe

Giving Advice

- Use the following expressions plus an infinitive to give advice:

Se debe/Se debería	One/You should
Deberías	You should
Hay que	One must, has to
Tienes que	You have to

- **Para estar en forma hay que hacer ejercicio físico cuatro veces a la semana.**
  To be fit, you should do physical exercise four times a week.

- **Para llevar una vida más sana, no deberías comer demasiada comida rápida.**
  To lead a more healthy life, you should not eat too much fast food.

- **Para perder peso tienes que evitar los dulces.**
  To lose weight, you have to avoid sweet things.

- **En mi opinión, hay que acostarse temprano y dormir ocho horas por noche para evitar el estrés.**
  In my opinion one must go to bed early and sleep eight hours a night, to avoid stress.

Saying Something Hurts

- To say that something hurts, use **tener dolor de** plus the body part:
  - **Tengo dolor de estómago.** I have stomach ache.
  - **Mi hermano tiene dolor de oídos.** My brother has earache.
- You can also use **dolerse** plus body part, which works in the same way as **gustar:**
  - **Me duele la cabeza.** My head hurts.

Quick Test

1. Which is not healthy?
   a) **Evito comer la comida rápida.**
   b) **Siempre como mucha fruta y verduras.**
   c) **Nunca hago ejercicio y como muchas golosinas.**
   d) **Como una dieta equilibrada.**
2. Translate into English:
   Comer mucha grasa es muy perjudicial para la salud.
3. Give some advice in Spanish about how to be more healthy.
4. Do the following phrases refer to past, present or future?
   a) **De momento**   b) **En el pasado**   c) **La semana que viene**

Unhealthy Living

You must be able to:

- Talk about alcohol and drugs
- Say what you think about smoking
- Express strong opinions.

Alcohol

- Here are some useful words for talking about alcohol:

adictivo	addictive
el alcohol	alcohol
el alcoholismo	alcoholism
el alcohólico	alcoholic
el botellón	drinking party in the street
borracho/a	drunk
la enfermedad	illness
con moderación	in moderation
emborracharse	to get drunk

- **En mi opinión, el alcohol puede ser adictivo para alguna gente.**
  In my opinion, alcohol can be addictive for some people.
- **Cuando sea mayor, no voy a beber alcohol porque puede ser perjudicial para la salud.**
  When I am older, I am not going to drink alcohol because it can be harmful to your health.
- **Mis amigos y yo nos emborrachamos los fines de semana y no veo nada mal en eso.**
  My friends and I get drunk at weekends and I don't see anything wrong with that.
- **En España el botellón causa muchos problemas ya que los jóvenes hacen mucho ruido y tiran basura al suelo.**
  In Spain, drinking parties in the street cause lots of problems given that the young people make a lot of noise and throw rubbish on the floor.

> ### Key Point
>
> Even if you don't particularly have a strong opinion on these matters, you need to form one, as they are very topical issues and will come up in all four skills.

Drugs

- Here are some useful words for talking about drugs:

la adicción	addiction
el/la adicto/a	addict
la cocaína	cocaine
la droga blanda/dura	soft/hard drug
el/la drogadicto/a	drug addict
drogarse	to take drugs
el hábito	habit
la muerte	death
peligroso	dangerous
el porro	joint
probar	to try
el síndrome de abstinencia	withdrawal symptoms

- **No quiero probar las drogas porque me dan miedo.**
  I don't want to try drugs because they scare me.
- **Alguna gente toma drogas a causa de la presión por el grupo paritario.**
  Some people take drugs because of peer pressure.

Smoking

- Here are some useful words for talking about smoking:

el cigarrillo	cigarette
el fumador	smoker
el fumar pasivo	passive smoking
el humo	smoke
el olor	smell
asqueroso/a	disgusting
los pulmones	lungs
los problemas respiratorios	respiratory problems
respirar	to breathe
el tabaco	tobacco
el tabaquismo	smoking habit

- **Para mí, el humo de los cigarrillos es asqueroso.**
  For me, cigarette smoke is disgusting.
- **Fumar es muy perjudicial para los pulmones.**
  Smoking is very harmful for the lungs.
- **Mi padre fuma veinte cigarrillos al día y no quiere dejarlo.**
  My dad smokes 20 cigarettes a day and he does not want to stop.

Expressing Strong Opinions

- When talking about topics such as drugs and smoking, you could express your opinions in a slightly stronger way than **pienso que**, with phrases such as:

– **Estoy a favor de**	I am in favour of
– **Estoy en contra de**	I am against
– **No estoy ni a favor ni en contra de**	I'm neither for nor against
– **Desde mi punto de vista**	From my point of view
– **A mi modo de ver**	In my view
– **Está claro que**	It's clear that
– **(No) estoy de acuerdo con**	I (dis)agree with

- **No estoy ni a favor ni en contra de fumar y, desde mi punto de vista, todo el mundo tiene que tomar sus propias decisiones.**
  I'm neither for nor against smoking, and from my point of view, everyone has to make their own decisions.

 Key Point

Using a variety of structures (opinions, change of tense, time frames, etc.,) in your speaking and writing will enrich your language and earn you more marks in the exam.

 Quick Test

1. Translate into English:
   Estoy totalmente en contra de tomar drogas.
2. Translate into Spanish:
   To lead a healthier life, you should not smoke.
3. Rearrange the following words to make a sentence:
   tres a deporte la debes semana practicar veces
4. Use a strong opinion phrase to give your views on alcohol.

Local Environment

You must be able to:

- Describe local environmental issues
- Suggest some solutions to environmental issues
- Make links between word families and recognise noun exceptions.

Local Environment

- Here are some useful words for talking about your local environment:

el aire	air	**la gasolina sin plomo**	unleaded petrol
el atasco	traffic jam		
la atmósfera	atmosphere	**el medio ambiente**	the environment
la basura	rubbish		
la belleza	beauty	**la naturaleza**	nature
la bolsa plástica	plastic bag	**el planeta**	planet
la campaña	campaign	**el problema**	problem
la capa de ozono	ozone layer	**los productos químicos**	chemical products
el combustible	fuel		
la contaminación	pollution	**el reciclaje**	recycling
el daño	damage	**los recursos naturales**	natural resources
los desechos	rubbish, waste		
los desperdicios	waste	**el tráfico**	traffic
la electricidad	electricity	**el transporte**	transport
la energía	energy	**el vehículo**	vehicle
el envase	wrapping		
los gases de escape	exhaust fumes		

> ### Key Point
>
> Use your knowledge of verbs and vocabulary to help work out new words from the same 'family':
> - **mejor** means *better* or *best* and **mejorar** means to *improve*
> - **preocuparse** means *to worry* and **preocupante** means *worrying*.

- **Mi pueblo es bonito con pocos edificios y muchas zonas verdes. Realmente no tenemos problemas con el tráfico ni la contaminación.**
  My town is lovely with few buildings and lots of green spaces. We don't really have traffic or pollution problems.
- **Mi ciudad está sucia y hay muchos atascos a causa de tanto tráfico.**
  My city is dirty and there are lots of traffic jams because of so much traffic.
- **Mi ciudad es muy industrial y me preocupa el problema de los desechos tóxicos de las fábricas.**
  My city is industrial and I am worried by the problem of toxic factory waste.
- **Hay contaminación del aire y de los ríos también y no veo ninguna solución.**
  There is air pollution and also river pollution and I don't see any solution.

Useful Environment Verbs

- Here are some useful verbs for talking about your local environment:

ahorrar	to save	**dañar**	to damage, harm
apagar	to turn off	**desaparecer**	to disappear
consumir	to consume	**desarrollar**	to develop
contaminar	to pollute	**destrozar**	to destroy

ducharse	to have a shower	**producir**	to produce
emitir	to emit	**proteger**	to protect
encender	to light/turn on	**reciclar**	to recycle
ensuciar	to get dirty	**reducir**	to reduce
estropear	to spoil	**reutilizar**	to reuse
gastar	to use (energy)/ spend (money)	**salvar**	to save
		separar la basura	to sort the rubbish
malgastar	to waste		
mejorar	to improve	**tirar**	to throw (away)
preocuparse por	to worry about	**usar**	to use

Looking After the Environment

- **Yo siempre intento andar en vez de ir en coche.**
  I always try to walk instead of going by car.
- **Se debe reciclar todo lo posible como el vidrio, el plástico, el papel y el cartón y meterlo todo en los contenedores de reciclaje.**
  You should recycle as much as possible such as glass, plastic, paper and cardboard and put it all into the recycling containers.
- **Para reducir la contaminación es mejor llevar una bolsa a la compra en vez de pedir una bolsa de plástico.**
  To reduce pollution, it's better to take a bag to do the shopping, instead of asking for a plastic one.
- **Deberíamos usar el transporte público para reducir las emisiones de los coches y para ayudar a prevenir la lluvia ácida.**
  We should use public transport to reduce car emissions and to help prevent acid rain.
- **Hay que construir más zonas peatonales y carriles de bicicleta para disminuir la contaminación de ciudades.**
  They have to build more pedestrianised areas and cycle lanes to reduce the pollution of cities.

Noun Exceptions

- Generally, nouns ending in **–o** are masculine and nouns ending in **–a** are feminine. However, there are a few exceptions that need to be learnt.

Masculine		Feminine	
el clima	climate	**la foto**	photograph
el día	day	**la mano**	hand
el mapa	map	**la moto**	motorbike
el planeta	planet	**la radio**	radio
el problema	problem		
el programa	programme		
el sistema	system		
el tema	topic/theme		

> ### Quick Test
>
> 1. In Spanish, give five examples of local environmental problems.
> 2. Translate into English: **Mi ciudad está muy contaminada.**
> 3. Suggest two solutions starting with **Hay que** and **Se debe**.
> 4. Translate into Spanish: We should consume less energy.

Global Issues

You must be able to:

- Describe global environmental issues
- Talk about poverty and homelessness
- Use verbs with a preposition.

Global Issues

- Here are some useful words for talking about global issues:

agotar	to exhaust	**la energía**	renewable
amenazar	to threaten	**renovable**	energy
aumentar	to increase	**la escasez**	scarcity
el aumento	increase	**inquietante**	worrying,
el calentamiento	global warming		disturbing
global		**inquietar(se)**	to worry
el cambio	climate change	**la inundación**	flood
climático		**la marea negra**	oil slick
el combustible	fossil fuel	**el petrolero**	oil tanker
fósil		**el recurso**	resource
el consumo	consumption	**la selva (tropical)**	jungle/(rain)
el cultivo	crop		forest
echar la culpa	to blame	**la sequía**	drought
el efecto	greenhouse	**la Tierra**	Earth
invernadero	effect	**el vertedero**	tip

- **Lo que más me inquieta es el calentamiento global. Tenemos que usar alternativas a los combustibles fósiles.**
  What worries me the most is global warming. We have to use alternatives to fossil fuels.
- **En mi opinión la deforestación es un problema muy serio. Es esencial que protejamos los bosques y las selvas tropicales.**
  In my opinion, deforestation is a very serious problem. It is essential that we protect the forests and tropical rainforests.
- **Debemos crear un mundo mejor para nuestros hijos.**
  We should create a better world for our children.

Useful Adjectives

- Here are some useful adjectives for talking about global issues:

ecológico/a	ecological
medioambiental	environmental
mundial	worldwide
peligroso/a	dangerous
químico	chemical
recargable	rechargeable
reciclable	recyclable
tóxico	toxic

> ### Key Point
>
> In translation tasks, always use a 'best fit' approach. If something sounds odd when it has been translated, you probably need to re-word it to make it sound better.

Poverty and Homelessness

- **Lo que me preocupa es…** — What worries me is…
  la discriminación — discrimination
  el paro — unemployment
  la pobreza — poverty
  el prejuicio — prejudice
  los sin techo/hogar — homeless people, homelessness

- **A mi modo de ver es totalmente injusto que todavía existan hambre y pobreza en algunas partes del mundo.**
  To my mind it is totally wrong that there is still hunger and poverty in some parts of the world.
- **En todos los países del mundo hay gente que vive en la calle. Es muy preocupante.**
  In every country in the world there are people living on the street. It's very worrying.
- **Para mí, lo peor es la pobreza que existe en el mundo.**
  For me, the worst thing is the poverty that exists in the world.
- **Hay que educar a la gente para cambiar su manera de pensar.**
  We must educate people to change their way of thinking.
- **Perdí mi trabajo hace un año y ahora vivo en la calle porque no tengo nada.**
  I lost my job a year ago and now I live on the street because I have nothing.
- **Tenemos que intentar combatir el prejuicio que daña la sociedad.**
  We have to try to fight the prejudice that harms society.

Verbs with the Infinitive

- Some verbs can be directly followed by an infinitive, for example, **espero mejorar…** 'I hope to improve…'. However, others require a preposition before the infinitive:
  - **tratar de** — to try to
  - **acordarse de** — to remember to
  - **olvidarse de** — to forget to
  - **acabar de** — to have just
  - **terminar de** — to finish… –ing
  - **aprender a** — to learn to
  - **ayudar a** — to help to
  - **empezar a** — to begin to
  - **invitar a** — to invite to
  - **forzar a** — to force to
- **Trato de luchar contra la discriminación.**
  I try to fight against discrimination.

Key Point

When reading or listening, remember to use the context to help you work out meaning. These topics are quite emotive and there will often be indications of positive or negative emotions to aid comprehension. Also, look out for cognates, e.g. **la deforestación**, which help understanding.

Quick Test

1. Translate into English: **El cambio climático me preocupa mucho.**
2. Create a sentence in Spanish using **ayudar a**.
3. In Spanish, give five examples of global environmental problems.
4. What are the two Spanish adjectives that mean 'worrying'?

Holiday Plans

You must be able to:

- Say where you are going on holiday
- Talk about your holiday plans
- Say what you want to buy in the souvenir shop.

Countries and Destinations

- **Normalmente paso mis vacaciones en...**   I usually spend my holidays in...

Alemania	Germany
Escocia	Scotland
España	Spain
Estados Unidos	United States
Europa	Europe
Francia	France
Inglaterra	England
Irlanda (del Norte)	(Northern) Ireland
Italia	Italy
Gales	Wales
Gran Bretaña	Great Britain
Grecia	Greece
Las Islas Canarias	The Canary Islands
Londres	London
El Mediterráneo	The Mediterranean

- **Suelo ir de vacaciones a España porque mis padres tienen una casa allí.**
  I usually go on holiday to Spain because my parents have a house there.
- **Este año he decidido ir de vacaciones a Italia con mis amigos.**
  This year I have decided to go on holiday to Italy with my friends.

Nationalities

- Note that nationalities in Spanish do not have a capital letter:
- **¿De dónde eres?**   Where are you from?
- **Soy... /Es...**   I am.../He/She is...

alemán/alemana	German	**francés/francesa**	French
británico/a	British	**galés/galesa**	Welsh
escocés/escocesa	Scottish	**griego/a**	Greek
español/a	Spanish	**inglés/inglesa**	English
italiano/a	Italian	**(nor)irlandés/**	(Northern) Irish
norteamericano/a	North American	**(nor)irlandesa**	

- Make sure you know the difference between the country and the nationality. Don't say that you went on holiday to Spanish (**español**); say that you went to Spain (**España**)! This is a common mistake to make.

Key Point

The language spoken in the country is usually the same as the masculine nationality. For example, in Spain they speak **español**; in Germany they speak **alemán**.
Hablo francés e italiano.
(I speak French and Italian.)

Useful Verbs

- **De vacaciones se puede...** On holiday, you (one) can...

bañarse	(to) swim/bathe	**ir de excursión**	(to) go on an excursion
broncearse	(to) get a sun tan	**nadar**	(to) swim
comprar recuerdos	(to) buy souvenirs	**pasar (una quincena)**	(to) spend (a fortnight)
dar un paseo	(to) go for a walk	**practicar los deportes acuáticos/de invierno**	(to) practise water sports/ winter sports
descansar	(to) rest		
esquiar	(to) ski		
hacer turismo	(to) go sightseeing		
hacer la maleta	(to) pack your suitcase	**sacar fotos**	(to) take photos
		tomar el sol	(to) sunbathe
hacer una visita guiada	(to) go on a guided tour	**viajar**	(to) travel
		volar	(to) fly

- **Durante mis vacaciones voy a tomar el sol en la playa y hacer turismo en el pueblo.**
  During my holiday, I am going to sunbathe on the beach and go sightseeing in the town.

- **Cuando estoy de vacaciones me encantar ir de excursión, sobre todo a los lugares antiguos.**
  When I am on holiday I love to go on an excursion, particularly to old places.

Shopping for Souvenirs

- **¿Qué desea?** — What would you like?
- **Quisiera estas dos postales, por favor.** — I'd like these two postcards, please.

el abanico	fan
la bandera	flag
la bufanda	scarf
la camiseta	T-shirt
el collar	necklace
la crema solar	suncream
el folleto	leaflet, pamphlet
la guía	guidebook
la muñeca	doll
los pendientes	earrings
la sombrilla	sunshade, parasol
la sudadera	sweatshirt

> ### Key Point
>
> Vary your sentence structure by using **antes de +** infinitive to say 'before doing something' or **después de +** infinitive to say 'after doing something': **Después de esquiar en las montañas, voy a pasar una semana en la playa.** After skiing in the mountains, I'm going to spend a week at the beach.

Quick Test

1. Translate into Spanish:
   I usually go on holiday to the Mediterranean with my family.
2. In Spanish, ask for five things in the souvenir shop.
3. How do you say the following languages in Spanish?
   a) English **b)** French **c)** German **d)** Greek
4. Translate into English:
   En España voy a hacer una visita guiada y sacar muchas fotos.

Holiday Accommodation

You must be able to:

- Book your accommodation
- Inquire about a campsite
- Talk about problems with your accommodation.

Talking about Accommodation

- Here are some useful words for talking about accommodation:

el aire acondicionado	air conditioning
el albergue juvenil	youth hostel
el alojamiento	accommodation
el aparcamiento	car park
el apartamento	apartment
el ascensor	lift
el aseo	toilet
el balcón	balcony
el hotel	hotel
la habitación individual	single room
la habitación doble	double room
el huésped	guest
la llave	key
la media pensión	half board
la pensión	guesthouse
la pensión completa	full board
el parador	state-owned hotel (in Spain)
la vista al mar	view of the sea
alojarse	to stay, lodge
alquilar	to hire, rent
quedarse	to stay
reservar	to reserve

Organising Accommodation

- **Quisiera reservar una habitación doble con cuarto de baño y vistas al mar para dos noches.**
  I'd like to reserve a double room with a bathroom and sea views for two nights.
- **¿Tiene habitaciones libres desde el tres hasta el diez de mayo?**
  Do you have any vacant rooms from the 3rd to the 10th of May?
- **¿Cuánto es por noche por persona?**
  How much is it per night per person?
- **Quisiera un apartamento con aparcamiento y aire acondicionado, por favor.**
  I'd like an apartment with parking and air conditioning, please.
- **¿A qué hora se sirve el desayuno?**
  What time is breakfast served?

> ### Key Point
>
> When talking about holiday dates, use **desde** to mean 'from' and **hasta** to mean 'until':
> - **Voy a pasar una semana en España desde el tres hasta el diez de mayo.**
>
> You can also use **de** and **a**:
> - **Voy a pasar una semana en España del tres al diez de mayo.**

At the Campsite

- Here are some useful words for talking about going camping:

el agua caliente	hot water
el agua potable	drinking water
el bloque sanitario	toilet block
el camping	campsite
la caravana	caravan
el saco de dormir	sleeping bag
el sitio	a place
la tienda (de campaña)	tent
montar la tienda	to pitch the tent

- **¿Hay sitio para una tienda para tres noches?**
  Is there space for a tent for three nights?
- **¿Hay agua potable aquí?**
  Is there drinking water here?
- **Somos dos adultos y dos niños y tenemos un coche y una caravana.**
  There are two adults and two children and we have a car and a caravan.

Talking about Problems

- **El ascensor/el aseo/la ducha/la luz no funciona.**
  The lift/toilet/shower/light doesn't work.
- **He perdido mi bolso/la llave/el monedero/el pasaporte.**
  I have lost my handbag/key/purse/passport.
- **No hay papel higiénico/jabón/toallas.**
  There isn't/aren't any toilet paper/soap/towels.
- **La habitación y la cama están sucias.**
  The room and the bed are dirty.
- **Nos quedamos en un camping muy bonito al lado de un río con vistas preciosas del campo. Había un bloque sanitario y un parque infantil. Pero no había ni agua caliente ni papel higiénico. ¡Qué horror!**
  We stayed on a very pretty campsite by a river with beautiful views of the countryside. There was a toilet block and a children's play area. But there was no hot water or toilet paper! How awful!

> **Key Point**
>
> Add more depth to your work by giving specific detail rather than just a basic description.

> **Quick Test**
>
> 1. Translate into Spanish:
>   I'd like a double room with a balcony, please.
> 2. Ask in Spanish if there is room for a caravan saying how many nights you would like to stay and how many people there are.
> 3. Practise dates saying the following in Spanish:
>   a) From the 5th to the 12th of August
>   b) From the 10th to the 24th of July
>   c) From the 1st to the 7th of May
> 4. Translate into English:
>   **El cuarto de baño está sucio y no hay papel higiénico.**

Holiday Activities

You must be able to:

- Say what you did on holiday
- Talk about the weather on holiday
- Use sequencers and connectives to extend sentences.

Useful Holiday Verbs

- **De vacaciones me gusta…**   On holiday, I like…
  bailar en la discoteca   to dance at the disco/nightclub
  cenar en un restaurante   to eat in a restaurant
  dar una vuelta en bici   to go for a bike ride
  mejorar mi español   to improve my Spanish
  montar a caballo   to go horse-riding
  pasar   to spend (time)
  practicar el idioma   to practise the language
  relajarme (relajarse)   to relax
  ver lugares de interés   to see interesting places
  ver fiestas típicas   to watch traditional festivals
  visitar…   to visit…
  volver…   to return…

- **Suelo ir de vacaciones con mi familia y a veces viene un amigo también.**
  I usually go on holiday with my family and sometimes a friend comes as well.

- **Normalmente visito muchos sitios de interés porque me gusta enterarme de culturas diferentes.**
  I usually visit lots of interesting places because I like to find out about different cultures.

- **Por la noche, a veces cenamos en un restaurante y comemos platos típicos. Otras veces me gusta dar una vuelta por el pueblo y hablar con gente para practicar el idioma.**
  In the evening, sometimes we dine in a restaurant and eat traditional food. Other times I like to go for a walk in the town and speak to people to practise the language.

- **El año pasado fui a Kenya con mi familia. Viajamos en avión y el vuelo duró ocho horas. ¡Fue muy emocionante!**
  Last year I went to Kenya with my family. We travelled by plane and the flight lasted eight hours. It was really exciting!

- **Visitamos muchos lugares bonitos y un día fuimos de safari.**
  We visited lots of lovely places and one day we went on safari.

- **Vimos muchos animales impresionantes y lo pasé fenomenal. Me encantaría volver algún día.**
  We saw lots of amazing animals and I had a brilliant time. I'd love to go back some day.

> ### Key Point
>
> When speaking or writing, order what you want to say using sequencers such as: **primero…** first; **antes…** before; **después…** afterwards; **luego…** then; **entonces…** then/so; **finalmente/por fin…** finally, etc.
> <u>Primero</u> visitamos **Buenos Aires. Dimos un paseo por el centro** y <u>luego</u> **comimos en un restaurante típico.** <u>Después</u> **visitamos un museo.**

Talking about the Weather in the Past Tense

- To talk about the weather in the past tense, we can use the imperfect of **estar** and **hacer**.
  - **¿Qué tiempo hacía?**
    What was the weather like?
  - **Hacía sol/frío/calor/buen tiempo/mal tiempo.**
    It was sunny/cold/hot/fine weather/bad weather.
  - **Estaba nublado/lloviendo/nevando.**
    It was cloudy/raining/snowing.
- If you wanted to refer to a specific day or occasion, you would use the preterite:
  - **Un día hizo calor.**
    One day it was hot.
  - **El domingo hubo niebla.**
    On Sunday it was foggy.

Conjunctions or Connectives

- Always try to use a variety of conjunctions or connectives to extend your sentences rather than using short phrases all of the time. This will help you to gain more marks.
- Here are the most useful connectives:

a pesar de	in spite of	**por eso**	therefore
además	besides	**porque**	because
así que	so that/therefore	**pues**	then
aunque	although	**salvo que**	except
como	as/like	**si**	if
cuando	when	**sin embargo**	however
entonces	then	**tal vez**	maybe
lo primero	first	**también**	also
mientras	while/meanwhile	**tan pronto como**	as soon as
o/u	or	**y/e**	and
pero	but	**ya que**	since

> ### Key Point
>
> Make a list of some useful phrases, such as conjunctions or sequencers, which can be used over and over again in all topics. Refer to the list often and you will start to remember the phrases more easily.

- **Fuimos a la playa como a mí me gusta tanto.**
  We went to the beach as I like it so much.
- **Visitamos muchos lugares pero hacía mal tiempo.**
  We visited lots of places but it was bad weather.
- **Primero, nos relajamos porque estábamos muy cansados.**
  First, we relaxed because we were very tired.

> ### Quick Test
>
> 1. Translate into English:
>   **Vi muchos lugares de interés.**
> 2. In Spanish, say what the weather was like on your holiday.
> 3. Translate into Spanish:
>   I went horse-riding and I ate in a restaurant.
> 4. In Spanish, talk about your holiday activities using two sequencers and a connective.

Review Questions

Relationships with Family and Friends & Marriage and Partnerships

1 Study the family tree and then say whether each of the following sentences is **true** or **false**.

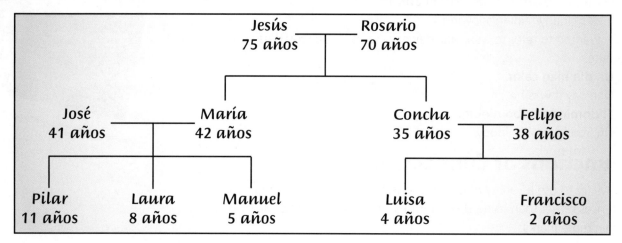

a) El hermano de Laura se llama Manuel. ....

b) José es el abuelo de Pilar. ....

c) María es la madre de Laura. ....

d) El tío de Pilar se llama Francisco. ....

e) La hermana de Concha se llama María. ....

f) La abuela de Luisa se llama Rosario. ....

g) Francisco es el primo de Manuel. ....

h) Laura es hija única. .... [8]

2 Draw lines between the boxes to match the people on the left with the descriptions on the right.

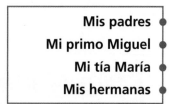

Mis padres •	• está casado.
Mi primo Miguel •	• están casadas.
Mi tía María •	• están separados.
Mis hermanas •	• está divorciada.

[4]

3 Translate into Spanish: My brother's name is Jacob. He has brown eyes and brown hair.

....

.... [2]

Social Media

1 Draw lines between the boxes to match the two halves of the sentences about social media.

A mí me gusta ●	● para descargar música.
Suelo usar ●	● sociales para buscar información sobre mi región.
Siempre uso mi portátil ●	● mucho navegar por internet.
Me encanta chatear ●	● unas fotos de mi cumpleaños en mi muro.
Utilizo las redes ●	● las redes sociales como Facebook y Twitter.
Esta noche voy a colgar ●	● con mis amigos todos los días en las salas de chat.

[6]

2 Match the descriptions **A**, **B**, **C**, **D**, **E** and **F** with the images **1–6**.

1

2

3

4

5

6

A Yo uso mi móvil para mandar correos electrónicos todos los días. ☐

B Suelo usar mi móvil sobre todo para jugar a los videojuegos. ☐

C El problema es que hay mucho ciberacoso con la tecnología. ☐

D Me gusta usar mi móvil para descargar música. ☐

E A mí me gusta comunicarme con mis amigos usando tecnología. ☐

F Lo que suelo hacer es usar la tecnología para ayudarme con los deberes. ☐

[6]

Review Questions

Music and Free Time & Cinema and Television

1 Match the descriptions **A**, **B**, **C**, **D**, **E** and **F** with the activities **1–6**.

1 Watching a film
2 Watching a play
3 Watching a TV programme
4 Listening to music
5 Reading
6 Playing an instrument

A **María fue al cine la semana pasada.**

B **Hoy voy a ver las noticias.**

C **Mi música preferida es la música pop.**

D **Anoche fuimos al teatro y fue fenomenal.**

E **Sé tocar las castañuelas y también la flauta.**

F **Me encanta leer revistas y tebeos.** [6]

2 Match the film reviews **A**, **B**, **C**, **D**, **E** and **F** with the film genres **1–6**.

1 **Una película de ciencia-ficción**
2 **Una película de amor**
3 **Una película de guerra**
4 **Una película de aventura**
5 **Una película policíaca**
6 **Una comedia**

A **¡Qué diversión! ¡Una película que te hace reír como un loco!**

B **¡Qué acción! ¡El héroe tiene que luchar para rescatar a la reina secuestrada!**

C **¡Los efectos especiales son estupendos – el mundo en el 2099!**

D **¿Quién ha cometido el crimen? ¿Pueden resolverlo antes de que sea demasiado tarde?**

E **¡Qué argumento más romántico! Los personajes principales son buenísimos.**

F **Esta película relata la historia de la segunda guerra mundial de una manera sensible y sensata.** [6]

Food, Eating Out, Sport & Customs and Celebrations

1 Match the descriptions **A**, **B**, **C**, **D**, **E**, **F** and **G** with the images **1–7**.

1   2   3   4

5   6   7

A   ¡Qué calor tengo! Me apetece un helado de frambuesa.

B   Yo quiero un trozo de esa tarta, ¡qué rica!

C   ¡Qué sed tengo! Necesito un vaso de agua muy fría.

D   Yo tengo mucha hambre. Creo que voy a tomar el bistec.

E   A mí me apetece algo caliente, un café por favor.

F   Quiero comer algo bastante ligero, un bocadillo de queso para mí.

G   ¡Feliz cumpleaños! Toma, un vaso de vino.

[7]

2 Match the descriptions **A**, **B**, **C**, **D**, **E**, **F**, **G** and **H** with the sports **1–8**.

1   El fútbol   2   La natación   3   El ciclismo   4   La pesca
5   El esquí   6   El atletismo   7   El windsurf   8   El footing

A   Mi nueva bici va muy rápido.

B   La semana pasada gané la carrera de cien metros.

C   Me encanta estar en el río. ¡Qué tranquilidad!

D   Tenemos un partido todos los sábados.

E   Voy a la piscina los fines de semana.

F   Las montañas son preciosas cubiertas de nieve.

G   Salgo a correr todas las mañanas antes de ir al colegio.

H   Hace falta viento para practicar este deporte.

[8]

Practice Questions

House and Home, Neighbourhood and Town & My Region

1   Match the descriptions **A**, **B**, **C**, **D**, **E** and **F** below about your local area with the images **1–6**.

1    **2**    **3**

4    **5**    **6**

A   Vivo en las afueras de la ciudad. Es muy limpio y tranquilo y me gusta mucho. ☐

B   Se puede salir a cenar con amigos en muchos restaurantes y bares bonitos. ☐

C   Vivo en el centro de la ciudad. Es muy ruidoso y sucio a causa del tráfico. ☐

D   Hay unos monumentos históricos y sitios de interés en mi pueblo, como el castillo antiguo. ☐

E   Se puede hacer la compra en los mercados diarios en la ciudad. ☐

F   Hay mucho que hacer en la ciudad como ir al teatro o al cine. ☐   [6]

2   Draw lines between the boxes to match the rooms with the activities.

La cocina	Mañana dormiré hasta muy tarde aquí.
El salón	Anoche preparé la cena con mi madre aquí.
El garaje	Aquí puedo usar el ordenador y todos mis libros del colegio.
El comedor	Siempre veo la tele aquí con mi familia.
El cuarto de baño	Aquí metemos muchas cosas incluyendo el coche y mi bici.
El dormitorio	Voy a ducharme aquí antes de salir.
El estudio	Ayer comí aquí con toda la familia.

[7]

Charity and Voluntary Work, Healthy Living & Unhealthy Living

1 Rearrange the words into the correct order to make sentences giving advice in Spanish.

a) dieta evitar que malsana una hay.

....

b) temprano que acostarte tienes.

....

c) tres a deporte la debes semana practicar el veces.

....

d) ni drogas no fumar tomar debes.

....

e) tratar hay el de estrés que evitar.

....

f) leer música debes o para escuchar relajarte.

....   [6]

2 Match the questions **A**, **B**, **C**, **D**, **E**, **F** and **G** with the answers **1–7**.

1 Para mí, el tabaco es asqueroso y perjudicial para el cuerpo.
2 Voy a seguir una dieta más saludable y hacer más deporte.
3 Suelo leer, escuchar música o hablar con mis amigos.
4 Es muy peligroso y siempre hay un riesgo de adicción.
5 Se debe comer una dieta equilibrada, o sea carne, pescado, fruta y verduras.
6 Hago ejercicio tres veces a la semana y voy al colegio a pie.
7 Tienes que evitar demasiadas golosinas y comida rápida.

A ¿Qué haces para mantenerte en forma? ☐

B ¿Qué hay que comer para estar en forma? ☐

C ¿Qué hay que evitar? ☐

D ¿Qué piensas de fumar? ☐

E ¿Qué haces para relajarte? ☐

F ¿Cuáles son los riesgos de tomar drogas? ☐

G ¿Qué piensas hacer en el futuro para estar en forma? ☐   [7]

Practice Questions

Local Environment & Global Issues

1 Read the headlines below and match them to the subjects that follow.

A 'Es esencial que luchemos contra el efecto invernadero.'

B '80% de las personas sin hogar son hombres.'

C 'He pasado el mejor año de mi vida ayudando a mucha gente – y ¡no me pagan nada!'

D '67 muertos y 29 heridos en la capital, después de una noche horrorosa.'

E 'Somos todos iguales y tenemos el derecho de vivir juntos con dignidad.'

F 'No quiero salir por la noche por si me intimidan o me abusan.'

1 Life as a volunteer ☐

2 Terrorism ☐

3 Against discrimination ☐

4 Global warming ☐

5 Crime and delinquency ☐

6 Homelessness ☐

[6]

2 Match the descriptions **A**, **B**, **C**, **D** and **E** with the images **1–5**.

1 2 3 4 5

A Para mejorar el medio ambiente, se debe andar o usar el transporte público en vez de coger el coche. ☐

B Se puede reciclar todo lo posible, como por ejemplo, el papel y el vidrio. ☐

C No se debe malgastar agua cuando nos lavamos los dientes o nos bañamos. ☐

D Se puede prohibir los vehículos en el centro de las ciudades para reducir la contaminación. ☐

E Se debe usar gasolina sin plomo si hay que usar el coche. ☐

[5]

Holiday Plans, Holiday Accommodation and Holiday Activities

1 Draw lines between the boxes to match each question with the relevant answer.

¿Tiene habitaciones libres? •	• Están al lado de la piscina.
¿El desayuno está incluido? •	• Somos dos adultos y dos niños.
¿Cuánto es por noche por persona? •	• Sí, reservamos una habitación doble con ducha.
	• Hasta el día trece, por favor.
¿Cuántos son? •	• Sí, todavía nos quedan tres habitaciones libres.
¿Hizo una reserva, señor? •	• Cuesta treinta euros los adultos y quince euros los niños por noche.
¿Hasta cuándo quiere quedarse? •	
¿Dónde están los servicios? •	• No, cuesta cinco euros por persona.

[7]

2 Match the descriptions **A**, **B**, **C**, **D**, **E** and **F** with the images **1–6**.

1

2

3

4

5

6

A   Me encanta visitar ciudades diferentes, son muy bonitas y emocionantes.

B   Yo prefiero estar en la playa relajándome y tomando el sol.

C   Lo más interesante para mí es visitar los monumentos históricos.

D   Como me encantan los deportes de invierno, yo voy a la montaña.

E   A mí me gusta mucho ver sitios más exóticos para ver cómo vive la gente allí.

F   Yo prefiero estar en el campo haciendo senderismo con mi familia.

[6]

School Life

You must be able to:

- Describe different aspects of your school
- Describe your uniform and give opinions
- Talk about school rules.

School

- Here are some useful words for talking about school:

el/la alumno/a	pupil	**la página**	page
el aula (f)	classroom	**el pasillo**	corridor
el bachillerato	school leaving exam	**el patio**	playground
		la pizarra (interactiva)	(smart) board
el colegio (mixto)	(mixed) school		
los deberes	homework	**la pregunta**	question
el/la director/a	headteacher	**el/la profesor/a**	teacher
la escuela	school	**la prueba**	test
el/la estudiante	student	**el recreo**	break
los estudios	studies	**la regla**	rule, ruler
el examen	exam	**la respuesta**	answer
la evaluación	assessment	**la sala de profesores**	staffroom
el gimnasio	gym		
el instituto	secondary school	**el salón de actos**	hall
		el taller	workshop
el intercambio	school exchange	**los vestuarios**	changing rooms
la lección	lesson	**el vocabulario**	vocabulary
la nota	mark		

> **Key Point**
>
> Although there is a lot of vocabulary associated with school, there are quite a number of near-cognates (words that are very like the English). For example:
> - **el laboratorio**
> - **el estudiante**
> - **el vocabulario**
> - **el examen**
> - **la clase**

Talking about School

- **¿Cómo es tu instituto?**
  What's your school like?
- **Mi instituto es bastante antiguo con unos novecientos alumnos.**
  My school is quite old with about 900 pupils.

- **Me gusta mi colegio porque tiene muchas instalaciones buenas como un gimnasio grande, cinco laboratorios modernos, una cantina muy buena y cuatro salas de informática.**
  I like my school because it has lots of good facilities such as a big gym, five modern labs, a really good canteen and four ICT rooms.
- **Las clases empiezan a las ocho y media y tenemos un recreo a las once menos cuarto.**
  Classes start at eight thirty and we have a break at quarter to eleven.
- **Me gustan muchos de los profesores en mi colegio porque son amables y explican bien.**
  I like lots of the teachers in my school because they are friendly and they explain things well.

- **Sin embargo me cae fatal a mi profesora de matemáticas porque es muy estricta y no me ayuda mucho.**
  However, I can't stand my maths teacher because she's very strict and she doesn't help me very much.

School Uniform

- **Tenemos que llevar uniforme escolar en mi colegio y diría que realmente me gusta.**
  We have to wear school uniform at my school and I would say that, in truth, I like it.

- **Creo que es mejor llevar uniforme porque así todo el mundo parece igual y es más elegante.**
  I think that it's better wearing a uniform because then everyone looks the same and it is smarter.

- **Llevamos...**   We wear...
  una falda   a skirt
  unos pantalones   trousers
  una camisa blanca   a white shirt
  un jersey   a jumper
  una corbata   a tie
  unos zapatos negros   black shoes
  una chaqueta   a blazer
  una camiseta   a T-shirt
  una blusa   a blouse

School Rules

- **Se debe respetar a los demás.**
  You must respect others.
- **No se permite comer chicle en clase.**
  You must not eat chewing gum in class.
- **Se debe hacer los deberes.**
  You must do your homework.
- **No se debe llevar maquillaje.**
  You must not wear make-up.
- **Solo se puede usar el móvil durante la hora de comer y nunca en clase.**
  You can only use your mobile phone at lunchtime and never in class.

> ### Key Point
>
> When describing your uniform with colours, make sure your adjectives agree:
> - **los pantalones grises** (grey trousers)
> - **la camisa blanca** (white shirt)
>
> However, when a colour is made up of two words (e.g. light blue), it doesn't agree:
> - **la camisa rojo oscuro** (dark red shirt)

> ### Quick Test
>
> 1. Translate into Spanish: I don't like chemistry because we always have lots of assessments.
> 2. In Spanish, describe your school uniform with colours.
> 3. Which sentence does not make sense?
>   a) **Me encanta mi uniforme porque es muy bonito.**
>   b) **Detesto mi uniforme porque es muy incómodo.**
>   c) **No me gusta mi uniforme porque es muy bonito.**
> 4. Translate into English: **En mi escuela primaria llevaba uniforme pero ahora no es obligatorio.**

School Studies

You must be able to:

- Say which subjects you like and dislike
- Give opinions about your school subjects
- Justify your opinions.

School Subjects

- **Estudio...**   I study...

las asignaturas	subjects	**la física**	physics
el alemán	German	**el francés**	French
el arte dramático	drama	**la geografía**	geography
la biología	biology	**la historia**	history
las ciencias	sciences	**los idiomas**	languages
las ciencias económicas	economics	**la informática**	ICT
		el inglés	English
la cocina	food technology	**las matemáticas**	maths
el comercio	business studies	**la música**	music
el dibujo	art	**la química**	chemistry
la educación física	PE	**la religión**	RE
el español	Spanish	**la tecnología**	technology

- **Estudio nueve asignaturas en total y mi asignatura preferida es la geografía.**
  I study nine subjects altogether and my favourite subject is geography.
- **No me gustan las ciencias porque son muy difíciles.**
  I don't like science because it is very difficult.

Useful Verbs

- Here are some useful verbs for talking about school subjects:

aburrirse	to be bored	**estudiar**	to study
aprender	to learn	**explicar**	to explain
comenzar	to begin	**interesar**	to interest
comprender	to understand	**odiar**	to hate
contestar	to answer	**olvidarse de**	to forget
corregir	to correct	**opinar**	to think, give an opinion
deber	to have to		
deletrear	to spell	**preferir**	to prefer
dibujar	to draw	**repasar**	to revise
enseñar	to teach	**sacar buenas/ malas notas**	to get good/bad marks
entender	to understand		
escuchar	to listen	**suspender**	to fail
escribir	to write		

Key Point

Don't forget that when talking about a subject that is plural in Spanish (e.g. **las ciencias**), the adjective needs to be plural as well. For example:

- **Creo que las matemáticas son prácticas.**

Giving and Justifying Opinions

- Use these phrases to give your opinion:

Me gusta(n)	I like
No me gusta(n)	I don't like
Me encanta(n)	I love
Me interesa(n)	I'm interested in

- Use these adjectives to give positive and negative opinions:

Positive Opinions		Negative Opinions	
creativo/a	creative	**aburrido/a**	boring
divertido/a	fun	**complicado/a**	complicated
entretenido/a	entertaining/amusing	**difícil**	difficult
fácil	easy	**injusto**	unfair
interesante	interesting	**inútil**	useless
práctico	practical		
útil	useful		

- **A mi hermano le interesan mucho las matemáticas pero para mí, son muy difíciles.**
  My brother is really interested in maths but I find it very difficult.
- **Opino que el español es muy interesante y divertido.**
  I think that Spanish is very interesting and fun.
- **Me encantan las ciencias porque son prácticas.**
  I love science because it's practical.
- **Preferiría estudiar la educación física porque es divertida y práctica.**
  I would prefer to study PE because it's fun and practical.
- **El año pasado estudié la informática pero la dejé porque era muy aburrida.**
  Last year I studied ICT but I dropped it because it was very boring.
- **No aprendo mucho en la clase de música porque la encuentro muy difícil.**
  I don't learn much in my music lesson because I find it very difficult.

> **Key Point**
>
> When using one of the impersonal verbs, such as **gustar**, you must use the definite article (**el/la/los/las**). For example:
> - **Me gusta el inglés.**
>   I like English.
> - **Te gustan las ciencias.**
>   You like science.

> **Key Point**
>
> You will get more marks if you justify your opinions:
> - **Mi asignatura preferida es la historia porque el profesor es muy interesante.**
>   My favourite subject is history because the teacher is very interesting.

> **Quick Test**
>
> 1. Are these subjects masculine or feminine?
>   **a) inglés   b) informática   c) matemáticas   d) religión**
> 2. Complete these sentences using the correct definite article:
>   **Me gusta _____ geografía.**
>   **No me gustan nada _____ ciencias.**
>   **Me interesa mucho _____ tecnología.**
> 3. Translate the following into English:
>   **No me gusta la física porque no entiendo nada.**
> 4. Translate the following into Spanish:
>   I hate science because it's complicated, but I am interested in maths.

School Pressures

You must be able to:

- Talk about pressures and problems at school
- Give your thoughts on bullying
- Use 'fillers' when speaking.

Useful School Vocabulary

- Here are some useful words for talking about the pressures at school:

el acoso (escolar)	(school) bullying
el apoyo	support
el ataque físico	physical attack
la ayuda	help
el comportamiento	behaviour
la conducta	behaviour
los deberes	homework
la disciplina	discipline
el estrés	stress
el éxito	success
el fracaso	failure
la intimidación	bullying
la nota	mark
la presión	pressure
el ruido	noise
la víctima	victim

Useful School Verbs

- Here are some useful verbs for talking about the pressures at school:

aprobar	to pass (an exam)
atacar	to attack
callarse	to stop talking/keep quiet
castigar	to punish
comportarse	to behave
concentrarse	to concentrate
dar igual	to not mind
dar miedo	to scare/frighten
estar estresado/a	to be stressed
estar harto/a de	to be fed up with
faltar	to be absent
fastidiar	to annoy
fracasar	to fail
golpear	to hit
gritar	to shout
insultar	to insult
intimidar	to intimidate
justificar	to justify
molestar	to bother

Key Point

Aim high in speaking and writing by changing tense within a sentence, to add complexity:

- **El año pasado suspendí la informática y creo que voy a suspenderla otra vez este año.**
  Last year I failed ICT and I think that I'm going to fail it again this year.

sacar buenas/malas notas	to get good/bad marks
suspender	to fail (an exam)
tener éxito	to be successful
traducir	to translate

Academic Pressures

- **Estoy harto de pasar todo mi tiempo libre haciendo los deberes. ¡No es justo!**
  I am fed up with spending all of my free time doing homework. It's not fair!

- **Para poder ir a la universidad, tengo que aprobar todos mis exámenes con buenas notas.**
  To be able to go to university, I have to pass all of my exams with good marks.

- **Tengo miedo de suspender los exámenes y no puedo concentrarme muy bien.**
  I am scared of failing my exams and I can't concentrate very well.

- **Los cursos son muy exigentes, aún con el apoyo de los profes.**
  The courses are very demanding, even with the support of the teachers.

- **El año pasado aprobé las matemáticas pero creo que voy a suspenderlas este año.**
  Last year I passed mathematics but I think I'm going to fail it this year.

Bullying

- **Hay unos estudiantes mayores en mi cole que intimidan a los más jóvenes y les quitan el dinero. ¡Es insoportable!**
  There are some older students in my school who intimidate the younger ones and take their money. It's unbearable!

- **Creo que el problema del acoso escolar existe en todos los institutos hasta cierto punto.**
  I think that the problem of bullying exists in all schools to some degree.

- **No aguanto a los estudiantes que maltratan a otros, pero yo me callo porque me dan miedo a mí también.**
  I can't stand students who abuse others, but I keep quiet because they scare me as well.

Using Fillers When Speaking

- When speaking, use 'fillers' to give you time to think of what you want to say:
  - **pues...**   well...
  - **a ver...**   let's see...
  - **un momento...**   one moment...
  - **bueno...**   well...

 Quick Test

1. Translate into English:
   El acoso escolar ocurre bastante en mi colegio.
2. Which is the odd one out?
   a) **aprobar**   b) **suspender**   c) **fracasar**
3. In Spanish, give your opinion of exams, starting your sentence with a filler.
4. Translate into Spanish:
   You have to study a lot to pass your exams.

Further Education and Part-time Jobs

You must be able to:

- Talk about your future education
- Give your thoughts on work experience
- Discuss part-time jobs.

Choices

- **Quiero…**   I want…
conseguir un aprendizaje	to get an apprenticeship
estudiar el bachillerato	to study for A-levels
hacer experiencia laboral	to do work experience
hacer formación (profesional)	to do vocational training
ir a la universidad	to go to university
seguir estudiando	to continue studying
seguir una carrera	to pursue a career
tomar un año sabático	to take a gap year
trabajar a tiempo completo/parcial	to work full-time/part-time

- **Después de terminar los exámenes, voy a buscar trabajo a tiempo parcial.**
  After finishing my exams, I am going to look for a part-time job.
- **Me gustaría conseguir un aprendizaje para ser electricista.**
  I would like to get an apprenticeship to be an electrician.
- **Estoy pensando en tomar un año sabático antes de estudiar en la universidad.**
  I am thinking about taking a gap year before studying at university.

- **Voy a intentar hacer experiencia laboral con una compañía porque me gustaría estudiar el comercio en la universidad.**
  I am going to try to do work experience with a company because I would like to study business at university.

Talking about Work Experience

- Work experience is a good topic to discuss in a speaking exam, or to mention in writing.
- **Hice mis prácticas laborales en una tienda/oficina/escuela/fábrica/banco.**
  I did my work experience in a shop/office/school/factory/bank.
- **Todos los días trabajaba en la oficina. Contestaba llamadas telefónicas y escribía en el ordenador y era bastante interesante, aunque un poco monótono a veces, en mi opinión.**
  I worked in the office every day. I answered phone calls and typed on the computer and it was quite interesting, although a little monotonous at times, in my opinion.
- **Me gustaron mucho mis prácticas. Trabajé como profesor en una escuela primaria. Era muy divertido y útil y ahora sé que me gustaría ser profesor en el futuro.**
  I really liked my work experience. I worked as a teacher in a primary school. It was a lot of fun and useful and now I know that I would like to be a teacher in the future.

> ### Key Point
>
> Use both the preterite tense (completed actions in the past) and the imperfect tense (repeated/incomplete actions in the past) to talk about what you did on your work experience:
> - **Aprendí mucho.**
>   I learnt a lot. (preterite)
> - **Trabajaba ocho horas cada día.**
>   I worked (was working) eight hours every day. (imperfect)

Part-time Jobs

- **Los sábados, trabajo en una tienda como dependienta.**
  On Saturdays, I work in a shop as a sales assistant.
- **Los fines de semana suelo hacer de canguro y está bien.**
  At weekends I usually babysit and it's good.
- **Reparto periódicos todas las mañanas antes de ir al colegio. Me paga bastante bien.**
  I deliver newspapers every morning before going to school. I get quite well paid.
- **Yo tengo que hacer tareas domésticas para ganar un poco de dinero.**
  I have to do housework to earn a little money.

Connectives for Expressing Opinions

- Here are some useful connectives for linking your statements when giving opinions:

a causa de	because of
a pesar de	in spite of
aparte de	apart from
claro que	of course
dado que	given that
en cuanto a	regarding
en lugar de	instead of
es decir	that is (to say)
sin duda	without doubt

- **No tengo trabajo a tiempo parcial a causa de tener tantos deberes.**
  I don't have a part-time job because of having so much homework.
- **Espero ir a la universidad a pesar de tener que trabajar muchísimo para aprobar los exámenes.**
  I hope to go university in spite of having to work very hard to pass my exams.

Key Point

Use the gerund with the preterite or the imperfect to talk about something that you did repeatedly in the past:

- **Trabajaba como camarero y pasaba mi tiempo sirviendo a los clientes, limpiando las mesas y trabajando en la caja.**
  I worked as a waiter and I spent my time serving customers, cleaning the tables and working on the till.

Quick Test

1. Translate into English:
   Quiero conseguir un trabajo y ganar mucho dinero.
2. Put these words in the correct order to talk about work experience:
   horas tenía largas trabajar me que pero gustó
3. Translate into Spanish:
   I would like to do work experience abroad.
4. Which connective fits better in this sentence: **a pesar de** or **en lugar de?**
   _____ seguir estudiando, voy a buscar un trabajo a tiempo completo.

Career Choices and Ambitions

You must be able to:

- Talk about your future career and ambitions
- Give your thoughts on different jobs
- Discuss future intentions.

Jobs and Careers

- Here are some useful words for talking about jobs and careers:

el albañil	bricklayer, building worker
el/la abogado/a	lawyer
el actor/la actriz	actor/actress
el/la auxiliar de vuelo	flight attendant
la azafata	air hostess
el/la bombero/a	firefighter
el/la cajero/a	cashier
el/la cartero/a	postman/postwoman
el/la contable	accountant
el/la dentista	dentist
el/la dependiente/a	sales assistant
el/la enfermero/a	nurse
el/la fontanero/a	plumber
el/la ingeniero/a	engineer
el/la mecánico/a	mechanic
el/la médico/a	doctor
el/la peluquero/a	hairdresser
el/la periodista	journalist/reporter
el/la policía	policeman/woman
el/la profesor/a	teacher
el/la programador/a	computer programmer
el/la secretario/a	secretary
el/la soldado	soldier
el/la veterinario/a	vet

- **Quiero ser veterinario porque me encantan los animales.**
  I want to be a vet because I love animals.
- **Quiere ser médico para poder ayudar a la gente.**
  He wants to be a doctor so that he can help people.

Advantages and Disadvantages of Jobs

- **Para mí, lo más importante es tener un sueldo elevado. ¡Quiero ganar mucho dinero!**
  For me, the most important thing is having a high salary. I want to earn lots of money!
- **Me gustaría hacerme médico para ayudar a la gente.**
  I'd like to become a doctor to help people.
- **Yo quiero trabajar con niños y tener responsabilidades en mi trabajo.**
  I want to work with children and have responsibility in my job.

> ### Key Point
>
> When talking about what jobs people do, the article is not needed:
> - **Soy peluquera.**
>   I am a hairdresser.
> - **Mi padre es médico.**
>   My father is a doctor.
> - **Quiero ser dentista.**
>   I want to be a dentist.

- **Trabajo bien como parte de un equipo y soy muy trabajador entonces quiero ser bombero.**
  I work well as part of a team and I am very hard-working so I want to be a fireman.
- **Sueño con casarme, tener una familia y ser ama de casa.**
  I dream of getting married, having a family and being a housewife.
- **Me gustaría ser policia porque quiero hacer algo útil en la vida.**
  I would like to be a policeman because I'd like to do something useful in life.

Ways of Expressing the Future

- Apart from using the future tense, there are other ways to express the future:

- **Querer** + infinitive:
  - **Quiero ir a la universidad el año que viene.**
    I want to go to university next year.
- **Esperar** + infinitive:
  - **Espero encontrar un trabajo interesante.**
    I hope to find an interesting job.
- **Tener la intención de** + infinitive:
  - **Tengo la intención de seguir estudiando.**
    I intend/plan to continue studying.
- **Pensar** + infinitive:
  - **Pienso viajar por el mundo.**
    I'm thinking of travelling around the world.
- Conditional tense:
  - **Me gustaría trabajar en el extranjero.**
    I would like to work abroad.

> ### Key Point
>
> Try to use different parts of the verb when speaking or writing; don't just stick to 'I':
> - **Mi hermano es electricista y mis padres son médicos.**
>   My brother is an electrician and my parents are doctors.
> - **Mi amiga y yo tenemos la intención de ir a la universidad.**
>   My friend and I intend to go to university.

Quick Test

1. Translate into Spanish: I want to do a fun job.
2. In Spanish, say what your plans are for the future.
3. Is the following statement positive or negative?
   Para mí, ser contable no sería muy interesante.
4. Translate into English: **Tengo la intención de viajar con mi hermana.**

Gender, Plurals and Articles

You must be able to:

- Identify the correct articles for masculine and feminine nouns
- Make a singular word plural
- Know when to use definite and indefinite articles.

Genders

- When you learn a Spanish noun, you have to learn whether it is masculine or feminine:

- **un**   a (for masculine nouns)
  - **un gato**   a cat
  - **un hombre**   a man

- **una**   a (for feminine nouns)
  - **una casa**   a house
  - **una mujer**   a woman

- **el**   the (for masculine nouns)
  - **el gato**   the cat
  - **el hombre**   the man

- **la**   the (for feminine nouns)
  - **la casa**   the house
  - **la mujer**   the woman

Rules and Exceptions

- Words ending in **-o, -or, -ón, -és** and many ending in **-ma** are masculine, except:

la mano	hand
la radio	radio
la cama	bed
la pluma	feather

- Words that end in **-a, -sión, -ción, -dad, -tad, -tud, -umbre** are usually feminine, except:

el día	day
el mapa	map
el planeta	planet
el sofá	sofa

- A few nouns may change their article in the singular if the first syllable is a stressed **-a** or **-ha**:

el agua	water, but **las aguas** (feminine, plural)
el hambre	hunger
el ama de casa	housewife

Key Point

When using impersonal verbs such as **gustar**, the definite article must also be used:

- **Me gustan las películas de terror.**
- **No me gustan las comedias.**

Plurals

- To make a noun plural, you need to apply the following rules:
  - Add an **-s** onto a vowel.
  - Add an **-es** onto a consonant.
  - If the noun ends in **-ón** or **-ión**, drop the accent before adding **-es**.
  - If the noun ends in **-z**, change the **z** to **c** and then add **-es**.
- Remember that the article must also become plural:

unos	some (for masculine plural nouns)
unos gatos	some cats
unas	some (for feminine plural nouns)
unas casas	some houses
los	the (for masculine plural nouns)
los gatos	the cats
las	the (for feminine plural nouns)
las casas	the houses

Using Articles

- The definite article is sometimes used in Spanish where we wouldn't use it in English:

  El español es genial.   Spanish is great.
  Me gusta el inglés.   I like English.

- The indefinite article is sometimes not used in Spanish where we would use it in English:

  Soy profesor.   I am a teacher.
  No tengo boli.   I don't have a pen.

- Where a job title is qualified by an adjective, the indefinite article is used, e.g.
  - **Es un buen actor.**   He's a good actor.

> **Quick Test**
>
> 1. Are the following words masculine or feminine?
>   natación   bolígrafo   ciudad   salchichón   universidad
> 2. Make the following words plural:
>   manzana   cristal   pez   dormitorio   profesor
> 3. Make the following words singular:
>   marrones   actrices   perros   televisiones   flores

Adjectives

You must be able to:

- Recognise an adjective
- Make appropriate changes to an adjective when it is feminine, feminine plural and masculine plural
- Use comparatives and superlatives to compare people and things.

Adjectives

- When describing something in Spanish the adjective must agree with the noun. The spelling of the adjective changes depending on whether the noun is masculine, feminine, singular or plural.
- Here is the pattern for regular adjectives:

Masculine Singular	Feminine Singular	Masculine Plural	Feminine Plural	English
bonito	bonita	bonitos	bonitas	pretty
amable	amable	amables	amables	friendly
trabajador	trabajadora	trabajadores	trabajadores	hard-working
azul	azul	azules	azules	blue

- Most adjectives come after the noun that they are describing, for example:
  - **Es una mujer graciosa.** She is a funny woman.
  - **Es un hombre tímido.** He is a shy man.

Some Exceptions

- Some adjectives come before the noun. When this happens, the masculine singular form ending in **-o**, is shortened (e.g. **bueno** becomes **buen**). The feminine form does not change:
  - **Es un buen actor.** He is a good actor. (masculine)
  - **Es una buena amiga.** She is a good friend. (feminine)
- The following adjectives follow this pattern:

bueno	good	**segundo**	second
malo	bad	**alguno**	some/any
primero	first	**ninguno**	none

- Adjectives of quantity almost always come before the noun:
  - **poco** few
    Hay muy poca gente. There are very few people.
  - **mucho** many/a lot
    Hay muchas manzanas. There are a lot of apples.
- **Grande** is shortened before both a masculine noun and a feminine noun to **gran**. It also changes meaning depending on its position in the sentence. Before a noun it means 'great' and after a noun, it means 'big':

Un gran hombre.	A great man.
Una gran mujer.	A great woman.
Un hombre grande.	A big man.
Una mujer grande.	A big woman.

Key Point

When using adjectives, always double-check that your adjective agrees with the noun, where necessary, in both gender and number, for example:

- **una casa bonita**
- **unas flores preciosas**
- **un chico alto**

Comparatives and Superlatives of Adjectives

- To compare things or people, use the following words (plus an adjective where indicated '...'):

más ... que	more ... than
menos ... que	less ... than
mejor que	better than
peor que	worse than
tan ... como	as ... as

- **Mi padre es más divertido que mi hermana.**
  My dad is *more* fun *than* my sister.
- **Los programas musicales son mejores que las emisiones deportivas.**
  Music programmes are *better than* sports programmes.
- To say that something or someone is the best, the worst, the most/least interesting, etc., you use the superlative, by putting **el, la, los, las** in front of **más/menos:**
  - **Las películas de terror son las más emocionantes.**
    Horror films are the most exciting.
- Common irregulars are:

el/la mejor	the best
el/la peor	the worst
el/la mayor	the biggest/oldest
el/la menor	the youngest

- To form the absolute superlative of an adjective, add **-ísimo** to the end of the adjective after removing the final vowel:
  - **La película es aburridísima.**   The film is extremely boring.

Indefinite Adjectives

- Indefinite adjectives, such as **cada, otro, todo, mismo, alguno** and **ninguno** can sometimes cause a problem:
- The word **cada** never changes: **Cada noche me acuesto a las diez.** (Every night I go to bed at 10.)
- Do not use the indefinite article when using the adjective **otro**, and make it agree with the noun: **Vamos a otra fiesta el sábado.** (We are going to another party on Saturday.)
- **Todo** and **mismo** also agree with the noun: **Todos los años celebramos mi cumpleaños en el mismo restaurante**. (Every year we celebrate my birthday in the same restaurant.)
- **Alguno** and **ninguno** lose their final **-o** if they are placed in front of a masculine singular noun: **Algún día iré a Sudamérica.** (Some day, I will go to South America.)

> **Quick Test**
>
> 1. Translate into Spanish:
>   a) The big dog.   b) The pretty city.   c) The hard-working boys.
> 2. Translate into English:
>   a) **Las chicas inteligentes.** b) **Un gran problema.** c) **El primer año.**
> 3. Complete the sentences:
>   a) **Mi hermana es más alta _____ yo.**
>   b) **Soy la _____ graciosa.**
>   c) **Mi hermano es ____ mayor.** (eldest)
> 4. Say in Spanish that the film is extremely good.

Adverbs, Interrogatives, and Por and Para

You must be able to:

- Recognise an adverb and how to form one
- Be able to use adverbial phrases in writing and speaking
- Know when to use **por** and when to use **para**.

Adverbs

- Adverbs describe verbs, e.g. 'quickly', 'badly', 'always'. They often end in **-ly** in English.
- In Spanish, adverbs are formed by adding **-mente** onto the feminine form of the adjective:
  - **lento/a**   slow   →   **lentamente**   slowly
  - **probable**   probable   →   **probablemente**   probably
- Some irregulars don't follow the same pattern:

ahora	now	**demasiado**	too/too much
allí	there	**deprisa**	fast
a menudo	frequently	**mal**	badly
aquí	here	**mucho**	a lot
algunas veces	sometimes	**muchas veces**	often
bastante	enough	**siempre**	always
bien	well	**ya**	already

  - **¡Mi padre siempre habla lentamente!** My dad always talks slowly!

Adverbial Phrases

- Use adverbial phrases to make your writing and speaking more interesting:
  - **muchas veces**   often
  - **dentro de poco**   soon
  - **por todas partes**   everywhere
  - **en otra parte**   elsewhere
  - **con entusiasmo**   enthusiastically
  - **de manera sorprendente** surprisingly

Comparatives and Superlatives of Adverbs

- Comparatives and superlatives of adverbs are formed in the same way as comparatives and superlatives of adjectives, using **más... que, menos... que**, etc:
  - **Mi padre habla más lentamente que mi madre.**
    My dad talks more slowly than my mum.
  - **Compro fruta en el mercado más a menudo que en el supermercado.**
    I buy fruit in the market more often than in the supermarket.

Position of Adverbs

- Adverbs usually follow the verb they describe:
  - **Andamos lentamente.** We walk slowly.
- Sometimes they come before the verb to add emphasis:
  - **Siempre hacemos eso.** We always do that.

Interrogatives

- There are two ways of forming a question in Spanish: using intonation and question words.
- Take a straightforward sentence and then use intonation by raising your voice at the end to turn it into a question:
  - **¿El perro es grande?** Is the dog big?
- You can also form a question by using a question word or interrogative word. Here are the most common:

  - **¿Adónde?** Where?
  - **¿Cómo?** What/How?
  - **¿Cuál(es)?** What/Which (one)?
  - **¿Cuándo?** When?
  - **¿Cuánto?** How much?
  - **¿Para qué?** What for?/For what reason?

  - **¿Cuántos?** How many?
  - **¿Dónde?** Where?
  - **¿Por qué?** Why?
  - **¿Qué?** What?
  - **¿Quién?** Who?

Key Point

Interrogative words always have an accent:
- **¿dónde?**
- **¿cuándo?**

However, when these words are used as relative pronouns in a sentence, the accent is not used:
- **El chico que habla es mi hermano**.
  The boy who is talking to my brother.
  (Relative pronouns are explained on page 87).

Por and Para

- **Por** and **para** can both mean 'for' but are used in different situations:

Por can mean...	Para can mean...
– 'for' or 'in' when talking about time: **Salí con mis amigos por la noche.** I went out with my friends at night. – 'through' when talking about locations: **Doy un paseo por el pueblo.** I go for a walk through the town. – 'in exchange for': **Le di 40 euros por la chaqueta.** I gave him 40 euros for the jacket. – 'on behalf of' **Lo hizo por ti.** He did it for you.	– 'by' or 'in time for': **Tengo que terminarlo para mañana.** I have to finish it by tomorrow. – 'in order to' followed by the infinitive: **Reciclo mucho para proteger el medio ambiente.** I recycle a lot (in order) to protect the environment. – 'for' a purpose or recipient: **Lo compró para su amiga.** She bought it for her friend. – 'in my opinion': **Para mí es muy importante ahorrar agua.** In my opinion it's really important to save water. – 'for what reason': **¿Para qué quieres el boli?** What do you want the pen for?

Quick Test

1. What do the following adverbs mean in English?
   lentamente   rápidamente   correctamente   saludablemente
2. Change the following adjectives into adverbs:
   feliz fácil posible frecuente
3. What does the following question mean? **¿Dónde vives?**
4. Would you use **por** or **para** in the following sentences?
   a) _____ ir al instituto, tengo que coger el autobús.
   b) Vamos a pasar _____ el parque _____ llegar al centro comercial.

Pronouns 1

You must be able to:

- Recognise different types of pronouns
- Use the correct pronoun in a given phrase
- Correctly place a pronoun into a phrase.

Subject Pronouns

- Subject pronouns (I, you, etc.) are not used as often in Spanish as they are in English. In Spanish, the verb ending shows who is doing the action. Subject pronouns are normally used to add emphasis to a sentence.

yo	I	**nosotros/as**	we
tú	you (informal, singular)	**vosotros/as**	you (informal, plural)
él	he/it	**ellos**	they (masculine or mixed masculine and feminine)
ella	she/it	**ellas**	they (feminine)
usted	you (formal, singular, often abbreviated to **Vd.**)	**ustedes**	you (formal, plural, often abbreviated to **Vds.**)

Examples:

- **Quiero un café.**   I want a coffee.
- **Yo quiero un café.**   *I* want a coffee.
- **¿Qué piensas?**   What do you think?
- **¿Qué piensas tú?**   What do *you* think?

Direct and Indirect Object Pronouns

- Pronouns replace nouns to avoid repetition. Direct object pronouns are used to say 'it', 'me' or 'them'. Indirect pronouns mean 'to me', 'to you' or 'to them'. For example:

- **Me gusta la falda. ¿La tiene en azul?**
  I like the skirt. Do you have *it* in blue? ⟵ — 'it' = direct object pronoun

- **¿Me puede dar la falda roja?**
  Can you give *(to) me* the red skirt? ⟵ — 'me' = indirect object pronoun

Direct Object Pronouns				Indirect Object Pronouns			
me	me	**nos**	us	**me**	to/for me	**nos**	to/for us
te	you	**os**	you	**te**	to/for you	**os**	to/for you
le/lo	him/it	**les/las**	them (people)	**le**	to/for him/it	**les**	to/for them
la	her/it	**los**	them (objects)	**le**	to/for her/it	**les**	to/for them
le/la	you (Vd.)	**les/las**	you (Vds.)	**le**	to/for you (Vd.)	**les**	to/for you (Vds.)

- Note that the pronoun must agree with the noun that it replaces. For example:
  - **¿Tiene estas botas en negro? Sí, las tengo en negro y en marrón.**
    Do you have these boots in black? Yes I have *them* in black and in brown.
- If an indirect and a direct object pronoun are used together, the indirect object pronoun goes first:
  - **Mi madre me la dio**.
    My mum gave me it/gave it to me.

- Object pronouns usually go before the verb, as above. However, with the immediate future or the present continuous, they come either before the verb or attached to the end of the verbal phrase.
  - **Los voy a comprar./Voy a comprarlos.** I'm going to buy *them*.
  - **Los estoy comprando./Estoy comprándolos.** I am buying *them*.
- This also works for verbs such as **quiero** + infinitve:
  - **Los quiero comprar./Quiero comprarlos.** I want to buy *them*.
- Pronouns are also attached to the end of an imperative:
  - **¡Cómpralos!** Buy them!

The Personal 'a'

- If the direct object of the sentence is a person, rather than a thing/object, the personal 'a' is added before the object:
  - **Veo la casa.**   I see the house. (thing/object)
  - **Veo *a* la niña.**   I see the girl. (person)

Disjunctive Pronouns

- A disjunctive pronoun is a pronoun that is used with a preposition, e.g. for me.
- The disjunctive pronouns are shown in the table:

mí	me	**nosotros/as**	us
ti	you (informal, singular)	**vosotros/as**	you (informal, plural)
él	him/it	**ellos**	them (masculine)
ella	her/it	**ellas**	them (feminine)
usted	you (formal, singular)	**ustedes**	you (plural, formal)

- **Mí** has an accent but **ti** does not. This is to distinguish the pronoun **mí** (me) from the possessive adjective **mi** (my).
  - **Es para mí**.   It is for me.
  - **Vamos sin él**.   We are going without him.
- After **con,** the pronouns **mí** and **ti** are joined to the preposition to form one word:
  - **¿Vienes conmigo?**   Are you coming with me?

Reflexive Pronouns

- Reflexive verbs describe an action that you do to yourself. They are accompanied by a reflexive pronoun. An example is **lavarse** – to wash (oneself)/to get washed:

  me lavo   I wash (myself)
  te lavas   you wash (yourself – **tú**)
  se lava   he/she/it washes (him/her/itself)/you wash (yourself) **(Vd.)**
  nos lavamos   we wash (ourselves)
  os laváis   you wash (yourselves) **(vosotros)**
  se lavan   they wash (themselves)/you wash (yourselves) **(Vds.)**
  - **Me lavo siempre en el cuarto de baño.**
    I always get washed (wash myself) in the bathroom.

Quick Test

1. How do you say the following subject pronouns in English?
   nosotros   ellos   él   vosotros   tú
2. Translate into English: **Me gustan los pantalones. ¿Los tiene en marrón?**
3. Translate into Spanish: I want to go with you **(tú)**.

House and Home, Neighbourhood and Town & My Region

1 Match descriptions **A**, **B**, **C**, **D**, **E** and **F** below with the correct images **1–6**.

1  **2**  **3**

4  **5**  **6**

A Vivo en un chalé muy grande en un pueblo.

B Prefiero tomar una ducha por la mañana.

C Nuestra casa tiene un jardín precioso con muchas flores y árboles.

D Siempre comemos juntos en la mesa grande.

E Tengo una cama muy cómoda en mi habitación.

F La puerta está a la derecha del armario.

[6]

2 For each of the directions below, use the map to say where you would end up.

a) Siga todo recto. ....

b) Tome la primera calle a la derecha. ....

c) Tome la segunda a la izquierda. ....

d) Tome la tercera a la derecha. ....

e) Tome la primera calle a la izquierda. ....

f) Tome la tercera a la izquierda. ....

g) Tome la segunda a la derecha. ....

[7]

Charity and Voluntary Work, Healthy Living & Unhealthy Living

1 Choose the correct words from the options given to complete the following sentences.

ayudar a　　　**ponernos a**　　　**debe**　　　**empezar a**　　　**acabo de**

a) Voy a _____ mandar dinero a una caridad benéfica.

b) Hay que _____ trabajar juntos para luchar contra la discriminación.

c) _____ hacerme voluntario para ayudar a los demás.

d) El gobierno _____ crear oportunidades de trabajo para los parados.

e) Yo quiero _____ mejorar la situación social donde vivo.　　[5]

2 These people are saying how they stay fit and healthy. Match the descriptions **A, B, C, D, E, F** and **G** with the images **1–7**.

1　　2　　3　　4　

5　　6　　7　

A　Para mantenerme en forma practico el deporte cuatro veces a la semana.　☐

B　No fumo porque es muy malo para la salud.　☐

C　Para relajarme me gusta leer.　☐

D　No bebo nunca el alcohol, es muy malsano.　☐

E　Intento beber mucha agua mineral todos los días.　☐

F　Me acuesto bastante temprano y duermo por lo menos ocho horas.　☐

G　Como mucha fruta y verduras.　☐　[7]

Review Questions

Local Environment & Global Issues

1   Match the descriptions **A**, **B**, **C**, **D** and **E** with the images **1–5**.

1

2

3

4

5

A   Me preocupa que haya personas que viven en la calle, los sin techo.   ☐

B   Creo que no hay suficientes servicios de reciclaje en todos los pueblos.   ☐

C   Lo que a mí me preocupa mucho es que las selvas se estén desapareciéndose a un ritmo alarmante.   ☐

D   El gobierno necesita tratar de ayudar más a los parados.   ☐

E   En muchos países del tercer mundo hay todavía mucha pobreza y mucha gente vive en casitas muy básicas.   ☐

[5]

2   Say whether each of the following opinions is **positive** (**P**) or **negative** (**N**). Write **P** or **N** for each.

a)   Mi pueblo es precioso con muchas zonas verdes.   _____

b)   El reciclaje, para mí, es una buena idea.   _____

c)   Mi ciudad está sucia, no me gusta.   _____

d)   Vivo en una región muy industrial y hay mucha contaminación.   _____

e)   Mi pueblo es muy limpio y tranquilo.   _____

f)   Muchas personas no cuidan del barrio.   _____

[6]

Holiday Plans, Holiday Accommodation and Holiday Activities

1 For each of the descriptions **A**, **B**, **C**, **D**, **E** and **F**, choose a suitable room **1–6**.

1 Una habitación doble con baño para cuatro noches en el barrio viejo.
2 Una habitación grande con vistas al mar para una semana.
3 Una habitación individual sin baño para una noche.
4 Una habitación grande con vistas de la montaña para dos semanas.
5 Una habitación con dos camas individuales para tres noches.
6 Una habitación con pensión completa para dos semanas.

A La familia Blanco y su hijo quieren una habitación grande donde quedarse durante sus vacaciones de esquí. ☐

B Isabel no tiene mucho dinero y sólo necesita pasar una noche en un hotel. ☐

C Jorge y Carmen necesitan una quincena en un hotel sin hacer nada más que relajarse. ☐

D María y su hermana quieren visitar la ciudad durante unos días. ☐

E La familia Jerez quiere pasar una semana en la playa. ☐

F Luis y Leticia quieren ver los monumentos en la ciudad y estar allí cuatro noches. ☐ [6]

2 Read the passage below and then say whether the following statements are **True (T)**, **False (F)** or **Not Known (?)**. Write the correct responses in the boxes provided.

Ángel: Solemos ir de vacaciones a la playa pero el año pasado decidimos hacer algo diferente y fuimos a la montaña para practicar los deportes de invierno. ¡A mí me encantó! Practicaba el esquí casi todos los días y un día hice senderismo en la nieve con mi padre. Subimos una montaña y fue estupendo. Me encantaría volver el año próximo pero creo que vamos a volver a la playa otra vez, porque a mi madre no le gustó el frío.

a) Ángel usually spends his holidays by the beach. ☐

b) Last year they did water sports on holiday. ☐

c) Ángel is good at skiing. ☐

d) He skied every day. ☐

e) He went hiking in the snow. ☐ [5]

Practice Questions

School Life, School Studies & School Pressures

1 Match descriptions **A**, **B**, **C**, **D**, **E** and **F** below about school life with the correct images **1–6**.

1

2

3

4

5

6

A   Durante el recreo me divierto con mis amigos.

B   Hay setecientos cincuenta alumnos en mi colegio.

C   Mi asignatura preferida es la educación física.

D   Lo que no me gusta es el uniforme escolar.

E   Estudio en la biblioteca durante la hora de comer.

F   En general los profesores son muy buenos.

[6]

2 Choose the correct verb from the options given to complete the sentences about school.

repetir   repasar   aprobar   sacar   enseñar   aprender

a) ¡Qué pesado! Tengo que _____ cada noche a causa de los exámenes.

b) Quiero _____ buenas notas en todas las asignaturas, pero es difícil.

c) Tengo que _____ bien el nuevo vocabulario en la clase de francés.

d) En el futuro me gustaría _____ geografía.

e) En la clase de español, tenemos que _____ las nuevas frases.

f) Espero _____ el examen de biología porque quiero ser médico.

[6]

Further Education and Part-time Jobs & Career Choices and Ambitions

1 Draw lines between the boxes to match the definitions with the jobs.

Preparo la comida en un restaurante italiano. Soy…	…azafata.
Doy clases de geografía en un instituto. Soy…	…mujer de negocios.
Trabajo en aviones sirviendo a la gente. Soy…	…cocinero.
Yo escribo novelas de intriga. Soy…	…criada.
Limpio casas y hago tareas domésticas todos los días. Soy…	…soldado.
Trabajo en un comercio en el centro de la ciudad. Soy…	…escritor.
Yo trabajo con un periódico, escribiendo reportajes. Soy…	…profesora.
Tengo que ir a las guerras a luchar. Soy…	…periodista.

[8]

2 Choose the correct future tense verbs from the options given to complete the sentences.

hablaré   trabajará   conseguiré   encontrarán   estudiaré   repasaremos

a) El año próximo _____ los idiomas en el colegio.

b) Mi amigo dice que en el futuro _____ en Francia.

c) Mañana _____ con mi profesor de inglés sobre los deberes.

d) Mis amigos creen que _____ un trabajo más interesante en la ciudad.

e) Esta noche mi amiga y yo _____ la geografía porque mañana tenemos un examen.

f) Si estudio mucho ahora _____ un buen trabajo en el futuro.   [6]

Practice Questions

Gender, Plurals and Articles & Adjectives

1 Put the following nouns into the correct column to say whether they are masculine or feminine.

color   problema   mano   día   lección   lápiz   libro   pared

Masculine	Feminine

[8]

2 Translate the following sentences into Spanish.

a) My dog is bigger than your dog.

_____

b) Your brother is less stupid than your sister.

_____

c) My TV is as good as your TV.

_____

d) The new James Bond film is worse than the previous one.

_____   [4]

3 Choose the correct adjective from the options given to complete each sentence.

precioso   contaminado   bonita   aislado

a) Hay mucha industria y mucho tráfico en el centro y por eso, es muy _____.

b) Es muy bonito aquí en el campo pero a veces puede ser bastante _____.

c) Mi pueblo está lleno de edificios antiguos e interesantes. Para mí es un pueblo _____.

d) Hay mucho que ver en mi ciudad como una iglesia antigua y una plaza de toros _____.   [4]

Adverbs, Interrogatives, Por and Para & Pronouns 1

1 Choose either **por** or **para** to complete these sentences about daily routine.

a) _____ la mañana me levanto temprano.

b) Bajo a la cocina _____ desayunar.

c) Voy al instituto en autobús y pasamos _____ el centro del pueblo.

d) El lunes, me quedo un rato después del instituto _____ practicar deporte.

e) Esta noche tengo que hacer mis deberes _____ mañana.

f) A mi amiga, le gusta mucho la historia pero _____ mí es muy aburrida.

g) Muchas gracias _____ ayudarme en la cocina Javier.

h) No vamos a salir esta noche _____ el frío que hace.

i) Voy a diseñar una tarjeta de cumpleaños _____ mi hermana.

j) Me gusta acostarme tarde _____ la noche. [10]

2 Draw lines between the boxes to match the questions with the answers.

¿Tienes las llaves?
¿Tienes el libro de español?
¿Quieres comprar la camiseta?
¿Para quién compraste los pantalones?
¿Has probado el chocolate?
¿Dónde me viste?

Los compré para mi madre.
No, no lo tengo.
Te vi en el parque.
No, lo voy a comer ahora.
Sí, las tengo aquí.
Sí, pero la quiero en azul.

[6]

Pronouns 2

You must be able to:

- Recognise different types of pronouns
- Use the correct pronoun in speaking and writing
- Improve fluency by using the correct relative pronoun.

Possessive Adjectives and Pronouns

- The table below shows possessive adjectives and pronouns.
- **¿De quién es?** Whose is it/Who does it belong to?

Adjectives		Pronouns	Masc. Sing.	Fem. Sing.	Masc. Plural	Fem. Plural
My	**mi/mis**	Mine	**mío**	**mía**	**míos**	**mías**
Your	**tu/tus**	Yours **(tú)**	**tuyo**	**tuya**	**tuyos**	**tuyas**
His/Her/Its/ Your **(Vd.)**	**su/sus**	His/Hers/Its Yours **(Vd.)**	**suyo**	**suya**	**suyos**	**suyas**
Our	**nuestro/a/ os/as**	Ours	**nuestro**	**nuestra**	**nuestros**	**nuestras**
Your	**vuestro/a/ os/as**	Yours **(vosotros)**	**vuestro**	**vuestra**	**vuestros**	**vuestras**
Their/Your **(Vds.)**	**sus/sus**	Theirs/Yours **(Vds.)**	**suyo**	**suya**	**suyos**	**suyas**

- **¿De quién es este móvil? ¿Es tuyo?**
  Whose is this mobile phone? Is it yours?
  Sí, es mío. Sí, es mi móvil.
  Yes, it's mine. Yes, it's my mobile.
- When the possessive pronoun does not follow the verb **ser**, you need to add the relevant definite article **(el/la/los/las)** in front of the pronoun:
  - **En cuanto a los móviles, el mío es más nuevo que el tuyo.**
    As for mobiles, mine is newer than yours.

Demonstrative Adjectives and Pronouns

- Words such as 'this', 'that', 'these' or 'those' are demonstrative adjectives. They must agree with the noun.
- There are two words for 'that': **ese** and **aquel**. The difference is that **aquel** refers to something further away:
  - **ese supermercado**   that supermarket
  - **aquel supermercado**   that supermarket over there
- For example:
  - **esta falda**   this skirt
  - **esa falda**   that skirt
  - **aquella falda**   that skirt over there

Masc. Sing.	Fem. Sing.	Masc. Plu.	Fem. Plu.	
este	esta	estos	estas	this/these
ese	esa	esos	esas	that/those
aquel	aquella	aquellos	aquellas	that/those… over there

- By adding an accent to the demonstrative adjectives, they become demonstrative pronouns and can stand alone to mean 'this one' or 'that one':
  - **¿Qué banco – éste, ése o aquél?**
    Which bank – this one, that one or that one over there?
- **Esto, eso** and **aquello** refer to an idea, or anything that isn't specifically mentioned by name:
  - **¿Quién ha hecho esto?**   Who did this?
  - **Y ¿esto, qué es?**   And what is this?

Indefinite Pronouns

- When referring to an unspecified thing you should use the word **algo**; when referring to an unspecified person you should use the word **alguien**:
  - **Quiero comprar algo.**   I want to buy something.
  - **¿Alguien me puede ayudar?**   Can anybody help me?

Relative Pronouns

- Relative pronouns relate back to something or someone previously mentioned in the sentence.
- The most common relative pronoun in Spanish is **que**, which translates as 'that', 'which', or 'who'. This is sometimes left out in English, but must be used in Spanish:
  - **El libro que lee es mío.** The book (that) he is reading is mine.
  - **La chica que habla es mi hermana.** The girl who is talking is my sister.
- The pronouns **el que**, **la que**, **los que**, **las que** are usually used after prepositions:
  - **El asunto del que hablamos, es muy serio.**
    The subject about which we are talking is very serious.
- **El cual**, **la cual**, **los cuales** and **las cuales** are used in the same way, but tend to be more formal:
  - **El asunto del cual hablamos, es muy serio.**
- **Lo que** refers to an abstract concept and often translates as 'what':
  - **Lo que más me molesta, es que muchas personas no tengan trabajo**.
    What bothers me the most is that many people don't have a job.
- **Quien** and **quienes** (plural) are only used when referring to people and usually after a preposition:
  - **El profesor con quien hablaba es mi profesor de música.**
    The teacher that I was talking to (to whom I was talking) is my music teacher.

> **Key Point**
>
> Demonstrative and possessive adjectives and pronouns agree with the noun, not the person:
> - **Esta regla es mía. Y los zapatos son míos también.**
>   This ruler is mine. And the shoes are mine as well.

In this example, the preposition **de** is joined with **el** to make **del**.

> **Quick Test**
>
> 1. Translate into English: **¿La mochila es tuya?**
> 2. Translate into Spanish: Whose are the books? Are they yours? **(tú)**
> 3. Which demonstrative pronoun would you use to talk about the following?
>   **a)** This one (skirt)   **b)** That one (biro)   **c)** Those over there (apples)

The Present Tense, Infinitives and Negatives

You must be able to:

- Conjugate regular verbs in the present tense
- Use infinitives correctly
- Make verbs negative.

The Present Tense

- Use the present tense to talk about what you are doing now, e.g. 'I am eating my lunch' or what you usually do, e.g. 'I eat my lunch every day'.

-ar Verbs

Hablar (To speak)

hablo	I speak	**hablamos**	we speak
hablas	you speak **(tú)**	**habláis**	you speak **(vosotros)**
habla	he/she/it speaks/you speak **(Vd.)**	**hablan**	they speak/you speak **(Vds.)**

- **Hablo francés y español. ¿Y tú?**
  I speak French and Spanish. And you?
- **Mis padres hablan inglés y alemán.**
  My parents speak English and German.
- **Hablamos todos los días por teléfono.**
  We speak on the phone every day.

-er Verbs

Comer (To eat)

como	I eat	**comemos**	we eat
comes	you eat **(tú)**	**coméis**	you eat **(vosotros)**
come	he/she /it eats/you eat **(Vd.)**	**comen**	they eat/you eat **(Vds.)**

- **¿Siempre coméis en el comedor?**
  Do you always eat in the dining room?
- **Come a la una y media todos los días.**
  He eats at half past one every day.

-ir Verbs

Vivir (To live)

vivo	I live	**vivimos**	we live
vives	you live **(tú)**	**vivís**	you live **(vosotros)**
vive	he/she/it lives/you live **(Vd.)**	**viven**	they live/you live **(Vds.)**

- **Vivimos en el sur de Inglaterra.**
  We live in the south of England.
- **Mis amigos viven en Perú.**
  My friends live in Peru.

Key Point

Make sure that you use the correct part of the verb to show who is doing the action, as the personal pronouns (I, you, etc.) are not often used:

- **Bebo**   I drink
- **Estudian** They study

Irregular First Persons

- Some verbs are irregular in the first person (the **yo**) form. The rest of the verb follows the patterns shown opposite:

dar → **doy** (I give)	**ver** → **veo** (I see)	**conducir** → **conduzco** (I drive)	
hacer → **hago** (I do/make)	**salir** → **salgo** (I go out)	**conocer** → **conozco** (I know (person))	
poner → **pongo** (I put)	**saber** → **sé** (I know (fact))	**traer** → **traigo** (I bring)	

Infinitives

- Infinitives translate as 'to …' in English, for example, **ver** – to look, and **comer** – to eat.
- Infinitives are used after phrases such as '**me gusta**' (I like) and after modal verbs such as **poder** (to be able), **querer** (to want) and **preferir** (to prefer).
  - **Puedo charlar con mis padres sobre cualquier tema.**
    I can chat to my parents about any topic.
  - **Prefiero jugar al fútbol en mi tiempo libre.**
    I prefer to play football in my free time.

Negatives

- To make a verb negative in Spanish, put **no** before the verb:
  No hablo francés.
  I *don't* speak French.
- Sometimes the negatives are in two parts and sometimes just one. When in two parts, the negatives come before and after the verb:
  - **Nunca veo la tele por la noche.**
  - **No veo nunca la tele por la noche.** } I never watch TV at night.
  - **Tampoco leo el periódico.**
  - **No leo el periódico tampoco.** } I don't read the newspaper either.
- Here are some more negative expressions:

– **No... nadie**	no one/nobody
– **No... nunca/jamás**	never
– **No... ni... ni**	neither... nor
– **No... ninguno**	no/not any/none

> **Quick Test**

1. How would you say the following in English?
   beben   **hacemos**   **charlas**   **estudio**
2. How would you say the following in Spanish?
   I take   We do/make   He cooks   They receive
3. What are the infinitives of the following verbs?
   hago   **comemos**   **salgo**   **estudias**
4. Make the following sentence negative:
   Siempre comemos pescado los lunes.

Radical Changing Verbs

You must be able to:

- Recognise which parts of the verb change their stem
- Understand the spelling changes that take place.

Radical Changing Verbs

- Radical changing verbs, also known as 'stem-changing verbs' have changes to the vowel(s) in the stem or root of the verb, as well as the normal changes to the endings.
- In the present tense, the changes occur in the **I, you** (singular), **he/she** and **they** parts.
- There are three common groups: **e → ie**; **o → ue**; and **e → i**.

The e → ie Group

- The verb **querer** (to want) is an example of a radical changing verb in the 'e → ie' group:

quiero	I want
quieres	you want **(tú)**
quiere	he/she/it wants/you want **(Vd.)**
queremos	we want
queréis	you want **(vosotros)**
quieren	they want/you want **(Vds.)**

- The following verbs also change in this way:

cerrar	to close	**encender**	to light	**preferir**	to prefer
comenzar	to start/begin	**entender**	to understand	**sentir**	to feel
despertar(se)	to wake (up)	**perder**	to lose	**venir**	to come
empezar	to begin	**tener**	to have		
nevar	to snow	**sentarse**	to sit down		
pensar	to think	**divertirse**	to amuse oneself		

- Note that **tener** and **venir** are irregular in the first person singular – **tengo** (I have) and **vengo** (I come).
- Examples:
  - **¿Quieres té o café?**   Do you want tea or coffee?
  - **Prefiero el rojo.**   I prefer the red one.
  - **¿A qué hora empieza la película?**   What time does the film start?
  - **Nieva mucho en el invierno.**   It snows a lot in winter.

The o → ue Group

- The verb **volver** (to return) is an example of a radical changing verb in the 'o → ue' group:

vuelvo	I return		**volvemos**	we return
vuelves	you return **(tú)**		**volvéis**	you return **(vosotros)**
vuelve	he/she/it returns/you return **(Vd.)**		**vuelven**	they return/you return **(Vds.)**

> ### Key Point
>
> Radical changing verbs are often known as '1,2,3,6 verbs', which corresponds to the parts of the verb that have a stem change.

- The following verbs also change in this way:

almorzar	to have lunch	devolver	to give back/to return
contar	to tell/count	doler	to hurt
costar	to cost	llover	to rain
encontrar	to meet/find	poder	to be able
mostrar	to show	soler	to be accustomed to
probar	to have a go/to try	acordarse	to remember
recordar	to remember	dormir	to sleep
volar	to fly	morir	to die

- Note that **jugar** (to play) follows the pattern, changing the **u** to **ue**.
- Examples:
  - **¡Cuéntame lo que pasó!**   Tell me what happened!
  - **Los helados no cuestan mucho.**   The ice-creams don't cost a lot.
  - **Normalmente, almuerzo a las dos y media.**   I usually have lunch at half past two.

The e → i Group

The verb **pedir** (to ask for) is an example of a radical changing verb in the
'e → i' group:

pido	I ask
pides	you ask **(tú)**
pide	he/she/it asks/you ask **(Vd.)**
pedimos	we ask
pedís	you ask **(vosotros)**
piden	they ask/you ask **(Vds.)**

- The following verbs also change in this way:

decir	to say
despedirse de	to say goodbye to
medir	to measure
reír	to laugh
repetir	to repeat
seguir	to follow
servir	to serve
vestirse	to dress oneself

- Note that **decir** and **seguir** are irregular in the first person singular – **digo** (I say) and **sigo** (I follow).
- Examples:
  - **El profesor repite la pregunta.**   The teacher repeats the question.
  - **Yo siempre pido postre.**   I always order a dessert.
  - **Miden la distancia.**   They measure the distance.

> **Quick Test**
>
> 1. Translate into English: **comienzo**   **piensas**   **muestran**   **puedo**
> 2. Translate into Spanish:
>   I fly   You (singular) follow   We have   You (**vosotros**) remember
> 3. What does the following sentence mean? **Suelo comer a las dos.**

Ser and Estar, Continuous Tenses and Conjunctions

You must be able to:

- Recognise when to use **ser** and **estar**
- Use the continuous tense to talk about what you are/were doing
- Extend sentences using a variety of conjunctions.

Ser and Estar

- **Ser** and **estar** both mean 'to be' but they are used in different ways.
  - **Ser** is used for describing a permanent quality or state of something.
  - **Estar** is used to describe temporary situations, including mood and location.
- Both verbs are shown below in full:

Ser	To be	Estar	To be
soy	I am	estoy	I am
eres	you are **(tú)**	estás	you are **(tú)**
es	he/she/it is/you are **(Vd.)**	está	he/she/it is/you are **(Vd.)**
somos	we are	estamos	we are
sois	you are **(vosotros)**	estáis	you are **(vosotros)**
son	they are/you are **(Vds.)**	están	they are/you are **(Vds.)**

- **Ser** is used to refer to:
  - a person's profession, e.g. **Soy abogado**. (I'm a lawyer.)
  - a person's nationality, e.g. **Es español/española**. (He/She is Spanish.)
  - permanent characteristics, e.g. **Mi madre es baja**. (My mother is small.)
  - relationships, e.g. **Somos amigos**. (We are friends.)
  - the time, e.g. **Son las tres**. (It's three o'clock.)
  - who owns something, e.g. **La casa es mía**. (The house is mine.)
- **Estar** is used to refer to:
  - place or position, e.g. **¿Dónde está tu casa?** (Where is your house?)
  - temporary states, e.g. **El agua está fría**. (The water is cold.)
  - feelings, emotions, e.g. **Estoy contento/a**. (I am happy.)
  - marital status, e.g. **Estoy casado**. (I am married.)
  - continuous tenses, e.g. **Estoy trabajando**. (I am working.)

The Present Continuous Tense

- The present continuous tense is used to describe what is happening at this moment.
- It is formed using the appropriate part of the verb **estar** in the present tense and adding the gerund. The gerund is formed by adding **-ando** (-ar) or **-iendo** (-er/-ir) onto the stem of the verb:
  - **Estoy hablando.** I am speaking.
  - **Estamos viendo una película.** We are watching a film.

> ### Key Point
>
> Stem-changing **-ir** verbs have an irregular gerund:
> - o → ue
>   **dormir → durmiendo** (sleeping)
> - e → i
>   **pedir → pidiendo** (asking)
>
> Here are a few other irregular gerunds:
> - **caer → cayendo**
> - **leer → leyendo**
> - **oír → oyendo**
> - **poder → pudiendo**
> - **reír → riendo**

The Imperfect Continuous Tense

- The imperfect continuous tense describes what *was* happening at a particular moment in the past.
- It is formed with the appropriate part of **estar** and the gerund, with **estar** being in the imperfect tense:
  - **¿Qué estabas haciendo?**
    What were you doing?
  - **Estaba escribiendo un ensayo.**
    I was writing an essay.

(For more information on the imperfect tense, see page 95.)

Conjunctions

- Conjunctions are words and phrases that can be used to improve the flow of your language:
  - **Fuimos a la playa como a mí me gusta tanto.**
    We went to the beach as I like it so much.
  - **No visitamos un museo porque es muy aburrido.**
    We didn't visit a museum because it's boring.
- 'And' is **y** unless it is followed by a word beginning with **i** or **hi**, in which case it changes to **e**:
  - **Aprendo español e inglés.**
    I study Spanish and English.
- 'Or' is **o** unless it is followed by a word beginning with **o** or **ho**, in which case it changes to **u**:
  - **Normalmente desayuno a las siete u ocho.**
    I usually have breakfast at seven or eight.
- Some other examples of conjunctions are shown below:

a pesar de	in spite of	**así que**	so that/therefore
aunque	although	**como**	as/like
cuando	when	**pero**	but
por eso	therefore	**porque**	because
pues	then	**salvo quo**	except
si	if	**sin embargo**	however
tal vez	maybe	**también**	also
además	besides	**ya que**	since

Quick Test

1. Would you use **ser** or **estar** in the following sentences?
   a) I am in the garden.
   b) My brother is very tall.
2. Translate into English:
   Los niños están jugando al fútbol.
3. Translate into Spanish:
   I was talking to my mum.
4. Join these sentences together with conjunctions:
   Tengo una hermana. Tiene 10 años. Me gustan las manzanas. No me gustan los plátanos. No me gusta mi pueblo. Voy a vivir en Londres en el futuro.

The Preterite Tense

You must be able to:

- Recognise when to use the preterite tense
- Use regular and irregular forms of the preterite tense
- Recognise spelling changes and radical changing verbs in the preterite tense.

The Preterite Tense

- The preterite tense is also known as the 'simple past' and is used to talk about completed actions in the past: 'I went', 'You ate', etc.
- There are two sets of endings for regular verbs in the preterite: **-ar** and **-er/-ir**.

-ar Verbs

Hablar (To speak)

hablé	I spoke	**hablamos**	we spoke
hablaste	you spoke **(tú)**	**hablasteis**	you spoke **(vosotros)**
habló	he/she/it spoke/you spoke **(Vd.)**	**hablaron**	they spoke/you spoke **(Vds.)**

- **Hablé español en México.** I spoke Spanish in Mexico.
- **Hablaron por teléfono.** They spoke on the phone.

-er Verbs and **-ir** Verbs

Comer (To eat)

comí	I ate	**comimos**	we ate
comiste	you ate **(tú)**	**comisteis**	you ate **(vosotros)**
comió	he/she/it ate/you ate **(Vd.)**	**comieron**	they ate; you ate **(Vds.)**

- **¿Comiste mucho pescado?** Did you eat lots of fish?
- **Comí platos típicos en España.** I ate traditional dishes in Spain.
- **Vivimos en un piso en el centro.** We lived in a flat in the centre of town.

Radical Changing Verbs in the Preterite Tense

- There are no **-ar** or **-er** radical changing verbs in the preterite tense.
- There are two types of changes for **-ir** verbs: **-e** to **-i** and **-o** to **-u** in the third person singular **(él, ella, usted)** and third person plural **(ellos, ellas, ustedes)**.

-e > -i

Pedir (To ask for)

pedí	I asked for	**pedimos**	we asked for
pediste	you asked for **(tú)**	**pedisteis**	you asked for **(vosotros)**
p*i*dió	he/she/it asked for/you asked for **(Vd.)**	**p*i*dieron**	they asked for/you asked for **(Vds.)**

- Some other **–ir** verbs that follow this pattern are **preferir** (to prefer), **reír** (to laugh), **seguir** (to follow), **sentir** (to feel), **sonreír** (to smile), **vestirse** (to get dressed).
- **Prefirió viajar en avión.** He preferred to travel by plane.

-o > -u

Dormir (To sleep)

dormí	I slept	**dormimos**	we slept
dormiste	you slept **(tú)**	**dormisteis**	you slept **(vosotros)**
durmió	he/she/it slept/you slept **(usted)**	**durmieron**	they slept/you slept **(ustedes)**

- **Morir(se)** 'to die' also follows this pattern.

Irregular Verbs in the Preterite Tense

- The most common irregular verbs in the preterite tense are shown in the table:

	Ser/Ir (To be/To go)	Hacer (To do/To make)	Tener (To have)	Ver (To see)
(yo)	fui	hice	tuve	vi
(tú)	fuiste	hiciste	tuviste	viste
(él/ella/usted)	fue	hizo	tuvo	vio
(nosotros)	fuimos	hicimos	tuvimos	vimos
(vosotros)	fuisteis	hicisteis	tuvisteis	visteis
(ellos/ellas/ustedes)	fueron	hicieron	tuvieron	vieron
	Dar (To give)	**Poner (To put)**	**Poder (To be able)**	**Venir (To come)**
(yo)	di	puse	pude	vine
(tú)	diste	pusiste	pudiste	viniste
(él/ella/usted)	dio	puso	pudo	vino
(nosotros)	dimos	pusimos	pudimos	vinimos
(vosotros)	disteis	pusisteis	pudisteis	vinisteis
(ellos/ellas/ustedes)	dieron	pusieron	pudieron	vinieron

Irregular Spelling in the First Person Singular (Yo)

- The verbs below have irregular spellings in the first person singular form **(yo)**:

buscar	to look for	→	**busqué**	I looked for
sacar	to take out/get	→	**saqué**	I took out/got
tocar	to play (instrument)	→	**toqué**	I played
cruzar	to cross	→	**crucé**	I crossed
empezar	to start	→	**empecé**	I started
jugar	to play	→	**jugué**	I played
llegar	to arrive	→	**llegué**	I arrived

- **Leer** (to read) and **caer** (to fall) follow their own pattern:

leí	I read	**caí**	I fell
leíste	you read **(tú)**	**caíste**	you fell **(tú)**
leyó	he/she/it reads/you read **(Vd.)**	**cayó**	he/she/it fell/you fell **(Vd.)**
leímos	we read	**caímos**	we fell
leísteis	you read **(vosotros)**	**caísteis**	you fell **(vosotros)**
leyeron	they read/you read **(Vds.)**	**cayeron**	they fell/you fell **(Vds.)**

- Other verbs that follow this pattern are **construír** (to build), **creer** (to believe), **destruir** (to destroy) and **oír** (to hear).

Quick Test

1. Translate into English: **Bebieron una botella de agua.**
2. Translate into Spanish: I arrived   I visited   I saw   You **(tú)** ate   We drank
3. Translate into Spanish: I took lots of photos of the hotel.

Key Point

Irregular verbs in the preterite tense do not have accents. However, it is vital that accents are used correctly when writing, otherwise the meaning of the verb can change.

- **Hablo con el profesor.** I speak to the teacher.
- **Habló con el profesor.** He/She spoke to the teacher.

The Imperfect, Perfect and Pluperfect Tenses

You must be able to:

- Recognise when to use the imperfect tense
- Understand how to form the perfect and pluperfect tenses
- Recognise irregular past participles.

The Imperfect Tense

- The imperfect tense is used to describe:
  - what used to happen in the past
  - what someone or something was like
  - what was happening/what someone was doing.
- To form the imperfect, the following endings must be added to the verb stem:

-ar Verbs

Hablar	(To speak)
hablaba	I was speaking/used to speak
hablabas	you were speaking/used to speak **(tú)**
hablaba	he/she/it was speaking/you were speaking **(Vd.)**/used to speak
hablábamos	we were speaking/used to speak
hablabais	you were speaking/used to speak **(vosotros)**
hablaban	they were speaking/you were speaking **(Vds.)**/used to speak

- **Escuchaba la radio todos los días.** I used to listen to the radio every day.

-er /-ir Verbs

Comer	(To eat)
comía	I was eating/used to eat
comías	you were eating/used to eat **(tú)**
comía	he/she/it was eating/you were eating **(Vd.)**/used to eat
comíamos	we were eating/used to eat
comíais	you were eating/used to eat **(vosotros)**
comían	they were eating/you were eating **(Vds.)**/used to eat

- **Veíamos la tele todas las noches.**
  We used to watch TV every night.

- There are only three irregular verbs in the imperfect tense:

	Ir (To go)	Ser (To be)	Ver (To see)
(yo)	iba	era	veía
(tú)	ibas	eras	veías
(él/ella/usted)	iba	era	veía
(nosotros)	íbamos	éramos	veíamos
(vosotros)	ibais	erais	veíais
(ellos/ellas/ustedes)	iban	eran	veían

- Two useful verbs in the imperfect are **haber** (**hay** in the present) and **soler**:
  - **Había mucha gente allí.**
    There were a lot of people there.
  - **Solía salir con mis amigos los sábados.**
    I used to go out with my friends on Saturdays.

The Perfect Tense

- The perfect tense is used to say what someone *has* done or what *has* happened. For example: 'I have eaten', 'She has walked'.
- To form the perfect tense, use the present tense of the verb **haber** and add a past participle.

Haber (To have) – as an auxiliary verb		+ past participle, e.g.
he	I have	**hablado** (spoken)
has	you have **(tú)**	**comido** (eaten)
ha	he/she/it has/you have **(Vd.)**	**salido** (left/gone)
hemos	we have	
habéis	you have **(vosotros)**	
han	they have/you have **(Vds.)**	

For example:
- **He hablado con mi hermano esta mañana.**
  I have spoken to my brother this morning.
- **¡El perro ha comido la cena!** The dog has eaten dinner!

- As usual, there are a number of irregular past participles. Common ones are:

abrir	to open	→	**abierto**	opened
decir	to say	→	**dicho**	said
descubrir	to discover	→	**descubierto**	discovered
escribir	to write	→	**escrito**	written
hacer	to do/make	→	**hecho**	done/made
morir	to die	→	**muerto**	died
poner	to put	→	**puesto**	put
romper	to break	→	**roto**	broken
ver	to see	→	**visto**	seen
volver	to return	→	**vuelto**	returned

Key Point

To form the past participle of regular verbs, simply remove the infinitive endings (-ir, -er and -ar) and add the following:
- ado (-ar verbs)
- ido (-ir and -er verbs)

- Nothing comes between **haber** and the past participle. All pronouns and negatives come before **haber**:
  - **¡Yo no he dicho nada!** I haven't said anything!
  - **No he visto a mi madre hoy.** I haven't seen my mother today.
  - **Me he levantado muy temprano.** I have got up very early.

The Pluperfect Tense

- The pluperfect tense describes what *had* happened or what someone *had* done.
- Like the perfect, it is formed by using the verb **haber** + past participle, but this time, **haber** is in the *imperfect* tense:
  - **Había hablado con mi hermano.** I had spoken to my brother.
  - **Cuando Miguel llegó a casa, María había comido ya.**
    When Miguel arrived home, María had already eaten.

Key Point

To say 'I have just + past participle' in Spanish, you do not use the perfect tense: you use **acabar de** + infinitive, for example: **Acabo de terminar** (I have just finished).

Quick Test

1. Translate into English: **Cuando era joven, tocaba la trompeta.**
2. Translate into Spanish:
   We used to go to the swimming pool on Saturday mornings.
3. Say in Spanish:
   a) I have opened the door.　　b) They have broken the window.

The Future and Conditional Tenses

You must be able to:

- Understand how to form the future tense and the conditional tense
- Recognise how to form the irregulars
- Use the future and conditional tenses in a variety of structures.

The Future Tense

- The future tense can be expressed in two ways: the immediate future and the simple future.
- The immediate future tense describes what is *going to* happen. It is formed by using the verb **ir** (to go) in the present tense + **a** + infinitive:
  - **Voy a hablar español.**
    I am going to speak Spanish.
- The simple future tense describes what *will* happen or what someone *will* do. It is formed by adding the following set of endings onto the infinitive of all regular **-ar, -er** and **-ir** verbs:

Hablar	(To speak)
hablaré	I will speak
hablarás	you will speak **(tú)**
hablará	he/she/it will speak/you will speak **(Vd.)**
hablaremos	we will speak
hablaréis	you will speak **(vosotros)**
hablarán	they will speak/you will speak **(Vds.)**

- **¡Mañana hablaré español!**
  Tomorrow I will speak Spanish!
- **Comeremos a las dos y media.**
  We will eat at half past two.

- The following verbs have irregular stems:

decir	→	dir-	diré	I will say
hacer	→	har-	haré	I will do
poder	→	podr-	podré	I will be able to
poner	→	pondr-	pondré	I will put
querer	→	querr-	querré	I will want
saber	→	sabr-	sabré	I will know
salir	→	saldr-	saldré	I will go out
tener	→	tendr-	tendré	I will have
venir	→	vendr-	vendré	I will come
hay (haber)	→	habr-	habrá	there will be (3rd person singular)

- For example: **Saldré mañana por la noche.** (I will go out tomorrow night.)
- Note that the future tense is used in constructions with **si** (if) + present + future:
  - **Si saco buenas notas, podré ir a la universidad.**
    If I get good grades, I will be able to go to university.

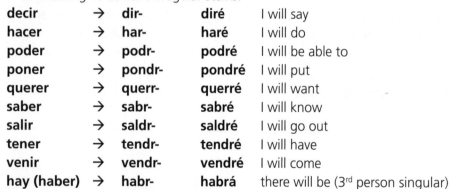

The Conditional Tense

- The conditional tense is used to talk about what someone *would* do or what *would* happen in the future.
- Just like the future tense, there is only one set of endings for all verbs -**ar**, -**er**, and -**ir**. As with the future tense, the endings are added to the end of the infinitive:

Hablar	(To speak)
hablaría	I would speak
hablarías	you would speak **(tú)**
hablaría	he/she/it would speak/you would speak **(Vd.)**
hablaríamos	we would speak
hablaríais	you would speak **(vosotros)**
hablarían	they would speak/you would speak **(Vds.)**

- **Yo iría mañana.**
  I would go tomorrow.
- **Haría muchas cosas**.
  I would do lots of things.

- Verbs that have an irregular stem in the future tense have the same irregular stem in the conditional. As with the future tense, the endings are regular:

decir	→	dir-	diría	I would say
hacer	→	har-	haría	I would do
poder	→	podr-	podría	I would be able to
poner	→	pondr-	pondría	I would put
querer	→	querr-	querría	I would want
saber	→	sabr-	sabría	I would know
salir	→	saldr-	saldría	I would go out
tener	→	tendr-	tendría	I would have
venir	→	vendr-	vendría	I would come
hay (haber)	→	habr-	habría	there would be

Key Point

The conditional tense endings are the same as the -**er/-ir** endings for the imperfect tense. When using the conditional, make sure that you add the ending onto the infinitive – it should have the **–r** at the end:
- **Comería**
  I would eat (conditional)
- **Comía**
  I ate/used to eat (imperfect)

Quick Test

1. Translate into English:
   iré   visitaremos   sabrán   harás
2. Translate into Spanish:
   I will swim   He will think   We will work
3. What do the following mean?
   tendrían   hablarías   comeríamos   estudiaríais
4. Translate into English:
   ¿Podrías salir esta noche?

The Subjunctive, Imperative and Passive

You must be able to:

- Recognise the subjunctive and understand how it is formed
- Recognise imperatives and negative imperatives
- Understand how to use the passive.

The Present Subjunctive

- The subjunctive is rarely used in English, but it is used quite often in Spanish, generally when the main verb is in the present tense. It occurs in the following situations:
  - In formal positive commands and all negative commands (see page opposite):

¡Coma!	Eat! **(Vd.)**
¡No comas!	Don't eat! **(tú)**

  - After **cuando** when talking about a future event:

    Cuando sea mayor, voy a ser profesor.
    When I am older, I'm going to be a teacher.
  - When asking/wanting/ordering someone else to do something:

    Quiero que vayas al banco. I want you to go to the bank.
  - When expressing feelings or emotions about something:

    Es una pena que no puedas ir a la fiesta.
    It's a pity you can't go to the party.
  - After **para que**, 'so that', 'in order that':

    Es para que lo leas. It's for you to read.
  - To express doubt or uncertainty:

    No creo que vaya. I don't think that he's going.

- To form the present subjunctive, take the first person singular **yo**, remove the final **o** and add the endings shown in the table:

	Hab<u>lar</u>	Co<u>mer</u>	Vi<u>vir</u>
yo	hable	coma	viva
tú	hables	comas	vivas
el/ella/Vd.	hable	coma	viva
nosotros	hablemos	comamos	vivamos
vosotros	habléis	comáis	viváis
ellos/ellas/Vds.	hablen	coman	vivan

- If a verb has an irregular first person singular in the present continuous (also known as present indicative), the subjunctive will take the same form:

hacer (hago)	→	haga
decir (digo)	→	diga

- There are also a number of irregular present subjunctive verbs that have to be learnt, for example:

Ir	→	vaya, vayas, vaya, etc.
Ser	→	sea, seas, sea, etc.

The Imperfect Subjunctive

- **Quisiera** (I would like) is commonly used in shopping situations and to express future desires, e.g. **Quisiera un kilo de manzanas por favor.** (I would like a kilo of apples, please.)
- The imperfect subjunctive is used in the same situations as the present subjunctive but generally when the main verb is in the preterite or imperfect tense.
- It is also used in 'if' clauses in the past:
  - **Si tuviera mucho dinero, compraría un Ferrari.**
    If I had a lot of money, I would buy a Ferrari.
  - **Si ganase la lotería, viajaría por el mundo.**
    If I won the lottery, I would travel the world.

Imperatives

- Imperatives are instructions or commands. The endings change depending on whether you are addressing the person(s) as **tú/vosotros** (familiar) or **usted/ustedes** (formal):

	Familiar		Formal		
	tú	**vosotros**	**usted**	**ustedes**	
	(sing.)	(plural)	(sing.)	(plural)	
-ar	baja	bajad	baje	bajen	go down!
-er	come	comed	coma	coman	eat!
-ir	sube	subid	suba	suban	go up!

- These verbs have irregular imperatives in the **tú** form:
  - **decir** → **di** (say)   **poner** → **pon** (put)
  - **hacer** → **haz** (do)   **salir** → **sal** (go/get out)
  - **ir** → **ve** (go)   **tener** → **ten** (have)
  - **oír** → **oye** (hear)   **venir** → **ven** (come)
- **¡Ven aquí! ¡Haz lo que te digo!** Come here! Do what I say!

Negative Imperatives

- When giving a negative command, the subjunctive is used in the appropriate person for all four forms:
  - **¡No hables!**   Don't speak! **(tú)**
  - **¡No cruce aquí!**   Don't cross here! **(usted)**

The Passive

- In Spanish, the passive is not used as much as in English, but you may need to recognise it in a listening or reading exam.
- The passive is formed by using the correct part of the verb 'to be' – either **ser** or **estar** – and the past participle. Because of the use of **ser** or **estar**, the past participle must agree with the subject:
  - **La contaminación será reducida bastante.**
    Pollution will be reduced considerably.

> **Quick Test**

1. Translate into English: **Es importante que vayas conmigo**.
2. Translate into Spanish: I want you to speak in Spanish!
3. Translate into Spanish: If I had more time, I would practise more sport.
4. Make these commands negative:
   a) **¡Habla!**   b) **¡Comed!**   c) **¡Escriba!**

Review Questions

School Life, School Studies & School Pressures

1 Draw lines between the boxes to link the sentence parts and create full sentences.

Me encanta la informática porque creo que es
Para mí las ciencias son muy
En mi opinión el francés es muy interesante
Yo odio la educación física porque es
En general diría que los profesores son
No me gusta nada el dibujo porque no es
Odio los exámenes porque son siempre

divertido y para mí es inútil.
divertida y muy útil para el futuro.
muy complicados y poco prácticos.
muy simpáticos y sus clases son interesantes.
difíciles y no las entiendo mucho.
aburrida y el gimnasio es muy antiguo.
y aprendo mucho en esa clase.

[7]

2 Match the definitions **A**, **B**, **C**, **D**, **E** and **F** to the correct heading about school life **1–6**.

1 Journey to school

2 Lunchtime

3 School day

4 Extra-curricular activities

5 Lessons

6 Size of school

A El colegio empieza a las nueve menos cuarto y termina a las tres y veinte. ☐

B En mi instituto hay unos seiscientos alumnos y cincuenta y cinco profesores. ☐

C Durante la hora de comer voy a la cantina y charlo con mis amigos. ☐

D Normalmente voy al colegio en autobús o a veces voy andando. ☐

E Hay seis clases cada día y cada clase dura cincuenta minutos. ☐

F Los jueves practico el deporte después de las clases. ☐ [6]

Further Education and Part-time Jobs & Career Choices and Ambitions

1 Draw lines between the boxes to complete the sentences about future choices.

En el futuro, quiero	con mis estudios para seguir una carrera en medicina.
Después de terminar mis	ir a la universidad.
Me gustaría conseguir un	experiencia laboral en una oficina.
Lo mejor para mí sería continuar	exámenes, voy a buscar un trabajo.
Creo que voy a intentar hacer	aprendizaje en la ingeniería.

[5]

2 Match descriptions **A**, **B**, **C**, **D**, **E**, **F** and **G** about jobs with the correct images **1–7**.

1  2  3  4

5  6  7

A Soy peluquera y trabajo en una peluquería en el centro.

B Soy cartero y reparto el correo por las mañanas.

C Trabajo en una tienda de regalos. Soy dependienta.

D Yo trabajo en un hospital muy grande, soy enfermera.

E Trabajo en la ciudad como taxista.

F Yo soy profesora y trabajo en un instituto.

G Me encantan los coches y por eso soy mecánico.

[7]

Review Questions

Gender, Plurals and Articles & Adjectives

1 Make each of the following nouns and their definite articles plural.

a) El hombre _____

b) La naranja _____

c) La mujer _____

d) El castillo _____

e) El planeta _____

f) El agua _____

g) La luz _____

h) La estación _____

[8]

2 Make each of the following nouns and their indefinite articles singular.

a) Unos bolígrafos _____

b) Unas habitaciones _____

c) Unos árboles _____

d) Unas catedrales _____

e) Unos cines _____

f) Unas motos _____

g) Unos autobuses _____

h) Unos balcones _____

[8]

3 Choose the correct adjectives from the options given to complete the following sentences.

gran   impacientes   graciosas   simpática   hablador   rubio

a) Mi madre es muy _____.

b) Mi hermano es muy _____.

c) Mis padres pueden ser muy _____.

d) En mi opinión, mis amigas son muy _____.

e) Mi amigo Raúl tiene el pelo _____.

f) Creo que mi padre es un _____ hombre.

[6]

Adverbs, Interrogatives, Por and Para & Pronouns 1

1 Match the interrogatives on the left with the correct endings of the questions on the right.

¿Cómo...	...es tu cumpleaños?
¿Cuál...	...quieres ir, en coche o en autobús?
¿Cuándo...	...significa eso?
¿Cuánto...	...es el mío, el rojo o el azul?
¿Cuántos...	...es aquella mujer, Señora Smith o Señora Brown?
¿Dónde...	...dices eso?
¿Por qué...	...está mi móvil?
¿Qué...	...cuesta la chaqueta?
¿Quién...	...años tienes?

[9]

2 Which of the following is the correct reflexive pronoun for the sentence? Tick the correct option.

a) Mi hermano siempre .... levanta muy tarde.

A me ☐   **B** nos ☐   **C** se ☐

b) Normalmente .... lavo antes de vestirme.

A me ☐   **B** os ☐   **C** se ☐

c) Mis padres .... duchan por la mañana.

A os ☐   **B** nos ☐   **C** se ☐

d) Nosotros .... vestimos en el uniforme escolar.

A me ☐   **B** nos ☐   **C** te ☐

e) ¿A qué hora .... acostáis el fin de semana?

A os ☐   **B** te ☐   **C** me ☐

f) ¿Y tú Lola, a qué hora .... despiertas durante la semana?

A me ☐   **B** os ☐   **C** te ☐

[6]

Practice Questions

Pronouns 2 & The Present Tense, Infinitives and Negatives

1 Choose the correct possessive adjective from the options given to complete the following sentences.

| tu | mi | nuestras | mis | vuestro | nuestra |

a) _____ **cortinas son bonitas.** (my)

b) _____ **dormitorio es pequeño.** (your – **vosotros**)

c) ¿**Cómo es** _____ **dormitorio?** (your – **tú**)

d) _____ **casa es bonita.** (our)

e) _____ **armario es moderno.** (my)

f) _____ **paredes son blancas.** (our)

[6]

2 Use the infinitive given to translate the following verbs into Spanish.

a) I eat **(comer)** _____

b) They drink **(beber)** _____

c) We are **(estar)** _____

d) You **(tú)** put **(poner)** _____

e) They know **(saber)** _____

f) I speak **(hablar)** _____

g) She listens **(escuchar)** _____

h) We study **(estudiar)** _____

[8]

Radical Changing Verbs & Ser and Estar, Continuous Tenses and Conjunctions

1   Choose the correct verbs from the options given to complete the following sentences.

entiendo   piensa   queréis   empiezan   queremos   prefiero   quieren   prefieres

a) Las clases en mi colegio _____ a las nueve menos cuarto.

b) Yo _____ los perros a los gatos.

c) Mi hermano _____ que las matemáticas son muy fáciles.

d) Mis amigas _____ ir al cine el jueves.

e) ¿Y cuál _____ tú, el verde o el azul?

f) El problema es que yo no _____ mucho el alemán.

g) ¿Qué _____ hacer vosotros?

h) Nosotros _____ escuchar música.   [8]

2   Choose the correct part of **ser** or **estar** from the options given to complete the following sentences.

estoy   estamos   son   estás   están   es   soy   está

a) ¿Dónde _____ tu casa exactamente?

b) Los caballos _____ blancos.

c) Los dormitorios _____ en la primera planta.

d) Yo _____ una persona muy organizada.

e) <<¡Mamá! ¿Dónde _____ ?>>

f) << _____ aquí Rafa, en el salón.>>

g) <<¡Y nosotros _____ aquí en el jardín!>>

h) Lo importante _____ terminar tus deberes.   [8]

Practice Questions

The Preterite Tense & The Imperfect, Perfect and Pluperfect Tenses

1   Translate the following sentences into Spanish.

a)   Yesterday I played football.

....

b)   Last week my parents spoke to my teacher.

....

c)   Last year we went to France.

....

d)   He preferred to travel by bus.

....

e)   I made the bed this morning.

....

f)   We had to eat in the dining room.

.... **[6]**

2   Choose the correct part of **haber** from the options given to complete the sentences.

he   **has**   **ha**   **hemos**   **habéis**   **han**

a) **Mis padres** .... **hablado con mi profesor de español.**

b) **Nosotros** .... **comido a las dos.**

c) **Yo** .... **visto la película antes.**

d) **Laura** .... **bebido el café.**

e) **¿Vosotros** .... **escrito a la abuela?**

f) **¿Tú** .... **ido al cine esta semana?**   **[6]**

The Future and Conditional Tenses & The Subjunctive, Imperative and Passive

1 Choose the correct conditional tense verbs from the options given to complete the sentences.

irías   comerían   tendrías   viviríamos   podría   iría   tendría   sería

a) Tú _____ que ir conmigo.

b) Yo _____ contigo pero no tengo tiempo.

c) Eso no _____ ningún problema.

d) ¿Por qué no _____ tú al cine con Miguel?

e) José _____ estar aquí para las siete.

f) Mi hermano nunca _____ bastante dinero.

g) Ellos _____ con nosotros pero van a llegar tarde.

h) Nosotros _____ en la capital pero cuesta demasiado.   [8]

2 Translate the following sentences into English.

a) Cuando vaya a la universidad, voy a estudiar español.

_____

b) Quiero que me traigas el pan de la panadería.

_____

c) Es una lástima que no haya una piscina en mi pueblo.

_____

d) Tienes que estudiar mucho para que apruebes los exámenes.

_____

e) No creo que vayamos a comer en el restaurante.

_____

f) ¡No hagas eso, por favor!

_____   [6]

Review Questions

Pronouns 2 & The Present Tense, Infinitives and Negatives

1 Choose the correct words from the options given to complete the sentences.

esta   eso   aquél   esos   aquella   aquellas   este   aquel

a) Me gusta mucho _____ falda roja.

b) _____ paquete aquí pesa más que ese.

c) Esas postales son más bonitas que _____.

d) Este supermercado aquí es mejor que _____.

e) Déjame ver _____ zapatos que compraste el otro día.

f) ¿Quién te ha dicho _____?

g) _____ panadería es buenísima.

h) _____ mercado en la plaza tiene cosas muy baratas. [8]

2 Which of the following is the correct present tense for the sentence? Tick the correct option.

a) Mi hermano siempre .... muy rápido.

A corro ☐   B corremos ☐   C corre ☐

b) Yo .... en una casa grande con mi familia.

A vivo ☐   B vives ☐   C viven ☐

c) Normalmente mi equipo .... el partido.

A ganáis ☐   B gana ☐   C gano ☐

d) Nosotros no .... animales en casa.

A tengo ☐   B tenemos ☐   C tienen ☐

e) <<¡Hola Marta! ¿Cómo ....?>>

A están ☐   B estáis ☐   C estás ☐

f) Mis hermanos nunca .... la mesa.

A pongo ☐   B ponen ☐   C pones ☐ [6]

Radical Changing Verbs & Ser and Estar, Continuous Tenses and Conjunctions

1 Translate the following verbs into English.

a) **Jugáis** ....

b) **Encuentro** ....

c) **Vuelan** ....

d) **Cuestan** ....

e) **Puedes** ....

f) **Llueve** ....

g) **Cuentan** ....

h) **Me acuerdo** ....

[8]

2 Draw lines between the boxes to complete the sentences.

Con respecto a mi madre, es muy graciosa…	…porque no trabaja mucho en el colegio.
En el futuro quiero ser dentista…	…y tres caballos.
Mi abuelo tiene noventa y cinco años…	…pero encuentro muy difíciles las matemáticas.
Mi hermana no es simpática…	…e inteligente.
En casa tenemos cinco gatos, dos ratones…	…que es muy viejo.
En mi opinión mi amiga Bea es muy perezosa…	…u ocho horas todos los días.
Al fin y al cabo hay que trabajar siete…	…o médico.
Me gustaría ser contable…	…sino desagradable.

[8]

Review Questions

The Preterite Tense & The Imperfect, Perfect and Pluperfect Tenses

1 Complete the following sentences with the correct form of the **preterite** tense. Tick the correct option.

a) Anoche mi amiga y yo .... en un restaurante en el centro.

A comemos ☐   B comimos ☐   C comeremos ☐

b) El lunes Antonio .... con Penélope por teléfono.

A hablo ☐   B hablaron ☐   C habló ☐

c) Mis padres .... a España para dos semanas.

A van ☐   B fui ☐   C fueron ☐

d) No .... contestar la pregunta.

A puedo ☐   B pude ☐   C podré ☐

e) ¿Vosotros .... la película ayer?

A visteis ☐   B vieron ☐   C vi ☐

f) Ayer, yo .... a las ocho.

A me visto ☐   B me vistí ☐   C me vestí ☐   [6]

2 Choose the correct imperfect tense verbs from the options given to complete the sentences.

esquiaba   hablaban   me gustaba   nadaba   veía   jugaba   comíamos   íbamos

a) Cuando era pequeño yo siempre _____ al fútbol en el jardín.

b) Yo _____ cada verano en el mar.

c) Cada invierno Pablo _____ en los Alpes.

d) Nosotros siempre _____ en el mismo restaurante.

e) _____ todos los años de vacaciones a España.

f) Ellos siempre _____ muy bien el francés.

g) Mi padre _____ el programa todos los sábados.

h) _____ mucho visitar a mis abuelos.   [8]

The Future and Conditional Tenses & The Subjunctive, Imperative and Passive

1 Rewrite the following future tense sentences and correct the mistake in each sentence.

a) Esta noche saliré con mis amigos al pueblo.

b) Mañana, después del instituto jugé al baloncesto en el gimnasio.

c) Para ayudar en casa, hoy poneré la mesa.

d) Mi hermano tenerá que estudiar mucho para aprobar sus exámenes.

e) Terminé mis estudios en junio.

f) Si saco buenas notas poderé ir a la universidad.

[6]

2 Match the imperative phrases with the correct English translation.

¡Háblame!	Talk to me! (formal)
Toma la primera a la derecha	Listen to me!
Escribid la fecha	Take the first on the left
Toma la primera a la izquierda	Write the date (singular)
¡Hábleme!	Talk to me! (informal)
Siga todo recto	Take the first on the right
Escribe la fecha	Write the date (plural)
¡Escúchame!	Go straight on

[8]

Mixed Exam-Style Questions

Section A: Questions and answers in **English**

1 Choose the correct adjectives from the options given to complete the following sentences.

buen	verdes	simpáticos	habladora	alto	guapas

a) Mi mejor amiga es muy _____.

b) Mi primo es muy _____.

c) Mi abuelo tiene los ojos _____.

d) En mi opinión, mis primas son muy _____.

e) Mi vecino Raúl es un _____ amigo.

f) Creo que mis abuelos son muy _____.

6 marks

2 Translate the following into English.

Tengo dieciséis años y mi cumpleaños es el veinticinco de enero. Nací en el año dos mil. En mi familia somos cuatro. Mi hermana se llama Laura y en mi opinión es muy graciosa. Me llevo muy bien con ella.

_____

_____

_____

9 marks

3 Read what these people say about relationships and then answer the questions that follow.

Hola, me llamo Natalia y tengo quince años. Mi novio Juan tiene dieciséis años y es muy simpático y gracioso. A veces puede ser un poco callado porque es bastante tímido pero nos llevamos muy bien. Nos gusta charlar durante el recreo en el instituto y de vez en cuando vamos al cine el fin de semana.

Hola, soy Nacho y tengo diecisiete años. Mis padres están divorciados y vivo con mi padre y su pareja Carmen. Me llevo bastante bien con mi padre pero me molesta mucho Carmen porque, en mi opinión, es muy perezosa. Prefiero salir con mis amigos que estar en casa.

Hola, me llamo María y mi hermana se llama Rosa. Tiene un novio que se llama Raúl y tiene veinticuatro años. Mi hermana piensa que Raúl es muy encantador y dice que se van a casar algún día, pero Raúl dice que no quiere casarse. Rosa quiere una boda muy grande pero Raúl está totalmente en contra de la idea. Por eso, a veces, discuten.

a) Who can be a bit quiet? _____

b) Who doesn't want to get married? _____

c) Who is funny? _____

d) Who is lazy? _____

e) Who argues with her boyfriend? _____

☐ 5 marks

4 Read the following blogs and answer the questions.

Ana	Hola, en mi tiempo libre lo que me gusta hacer es practicar el deporte. Juego al baloncesto tres veces a la semana en el colegio y los sábados voy a la piscina con mis amigos. Mi hermana practica la gimnasia pero para mí es aburrida. También soy miembro del equipo de atletismo y suelo entrenarme los lunes y los jueves.
Rafa	Yo soy futbolista y la semana pasada marqué dos goles para mi equipo. ¡Qué guay! Soy hincha del Real Madrid y voy a los partidos con mi padre. También, en mi tiempo libre suelo ir a casa de un amigo y jugamos con el ordenador o damos un paseo con su perro. No leo nunca porque prefiero ver la tele o escuchar música.
Manolo	A mí me encanta ir de pesca con mi hermano y mi padre. Hay un lago cerca de mi pueblo y normalmente pasamos los domingos allí. Es muy tranquilo y llevamos algo para comer y beber. A veces voy al centro para ver una película con mis amigos pero no vamos todas las semanas porque depende de si tenemos suficiente dinero.

a) What does Ana do three times a week?_____.

b) Who thinks gymnastics is boring?_____.

c) What does Rafa do with his father?_____.

d) Who goes swimming with friends?_____.

e) What does Ana do on Mondays and Thursdays?_____.

f) What does Manolo take when he goes fishing?_____.

g) Where does Manolo go fishing?_____.

h) Why doesn't Manolo go to the cinema every week?_____.

☐ 8 marks

5 Read the signs below.

A CORREOS

B BIBLIOTECA

C POLIDEPORTIVO

D BANCO

E MERCADO

F CASTILLO

Which sign would you follow in these situations? Put the correct letter in the answer box.

a) You want to do some sport.

b) You want to buy some fruit.

c) You need to post a parcel.

d) You want to borrow a book.

4 marks

6 Read the following opinions about school and say whether they are **Positive (P)**, **Negative (N)** or **Positive AND Negative (P+N)**. Put the correct letter(s) in the answer boxes.

Roberto	Me gusta estar con mis amigos en el colegio. Las clases no son muy interesantes y no como nunca en la cantina porque la comida es mala.
Clara	Me interesan mucho todas las clases en el colegio. Los profesores son buenos y explican bien y cada día es muy interesante.
Victoria	Para mí, ir al colegio es aburrido. No tengo muchos amigos allí y mis padres esperan demasiado.
Guillermo	El uniforme escolar en mi colegio es muy elegante. La clase de educación física es estupenda. Algunos profesores son aburridos y no nos escuchan.

Roberto

Clara

Victoria

Guillermo

4 marks

7 Read the sentences below and match them to the statements that follow.

A Vivo en un pueblo pequeño en el campo que es bonito, pero a veces puede ser bastante aislado.

B Para mí es muy residencial y no hay muchas instalaciones.

C Es muy fácil divertirse en mi pueblo a causa de las instalaciones que hay.

D Lo que ofrece es la tranquilidad y un paisaje precioso.

E Lo que pasa es que hay basura en las calles y contaminación de las fábricas.

F El castillo pintoresco y la catedral antigua merecen la pena visitar.

a) Lots to do ....

b) Historic sites ....

c) Pollution ....

d) Town is isolated ....

e) Positives of the countryside ....

f) Not a lot to do there ....

6 marks

8 Read what María has to say.

Me llamo María. Tengo muchos amigos que fuman cigarrillos cuando salimos los fines de semana pero yo no. No estoy ni a favor ni en contra de fumar porque creo que todo el mundo tiene que tomar sus propias decisiones.

Mis padres fumaban durante veinte años pero lo han dejado y ahora están bastante en forma. A mí me gusta mucho practicar la natación y también la gimnasia, y sé que para estar en forma no se debe fumar pero me da igual si quieren fumar mis amigos. Lo que no aguanto son las drogas.

According to María, which **three** of the following statements are true?

A	María smokes at the weekend.
B	She is neither for nor against smoking.
C	Her parents smoke.
D	María likes to go swimming.
E	She doesn't mind when her friends smoke.
F	She takes drugs.

☐ ☐ ☐

☐

3 marks

9 Read the following opinions about the environment.

| **Paco:** Yo sé que se debe hacer mucho esfuerzo para reciclar todo. Lo que pasa es que no tenemos espacio en nuestro piso para todos los contenedores y bolsas de reciclaje entonces solemos tirar mucha basura que, en realidad, deberíamos reciclar. También, mi padre me lleva al cole en coche porque me levanto demasiado tarde para poder coger el autobús. | **Mariela:** Creo que todo el mundo hace falta hacer algo para mejorar el medio ambiente. Yo siempre intento comprar productos sin mucho envase y uso mis propias bolsas cuando voy de compras. Estoy intentando usar el transporte público en vez de siempre ir en coche de mis padres. | **Cristina:** Lo que yo intento hacer es malgastar menos energía en casa. Siempre apago las luces y también mi portátil y la televisión cuando no los estoy usando. También me ducho en vez de bañarme e intento cerrar el grifo al cepillarme los dientes. La otra cosa que hago es mandar mi ropa al tercer mundo para que se use otra vez. |

Who do the following statements refer to? Put a cross (**X**) in the correct box.

		Paco	Mariela	Cristina
a)	Who thinks about packaging before purchasing something?			
b)	Who doesn't really do much to help the environment?			
c)	Who thinks about the amount of water they use?			
d)	Who travels by car instead of by bus?			
e)	Who recycles their clothes?			
f)	Who uses their own bags when shopping?			

☐

6 marks

10 Read this passage.

Ángel: ¡Hola! Estoy de vacaciones en Nueva York. ¡Es genial! Estamos visitando todos los lugares de interés y actualmente estoy de compras. El año pasado decidimos hacer algo diferente y fuimos a la montaña para practicar los deportes de invierno. ¡A mí me encantó! Practicaba el esquí casi todos los días y un día hice senderismo en la nieve con mi padre.

Me encantaría volver el año próximo pero creo que vamos a ir a la playa a tomar el sol porque a mi madre no le gusta el frío. En la montaña cenamos en el chalet pero aquí solemos cenar en restaurantes.

Which of Ángel's holidays do the following activities apply to?

- Write **P** for something that happened in the **past**.
- Write **N** for something that is happening **now**.
- Write **F** for something that is going to happen in the **future**.

Write the correct letter in each box.

a) Skiing ☐

b) Shopping ☐

c) Sunbathing ☐

d) Hiking ☐

e) Eating out ☐

☐

5 marks

11 Read the accounts below about pressures and problems at school and answer the questions that follow.

Ramón: Me siento muy estresado porque dentro de poco haré los exámenes. Creo que mis padres esperan demasiado y eso provoca mucho estrés. Intento estudiar mucho pero no tengo suficiente tiempo para repasar todas las asignaturas y tengo que sacar buenas notas si quiero ser veterinario en el futuro. Los cursos son muy exigentes.

Carolina: Lo que a mí me molesta es la disciplina en el colegio. En clase, ciertos estudiantes no escuchan y no puedo concentrarme bien a causa del ruido que hacen. Los profes deben ser más severos pero no comprenden el problema. Estoy muy estresada porque quiero tener éxito en mis exámenes.

a) What is the problem with Ramón's parents? ....

b) What problem does Ramón have with revising?

....

c) Why does Ramón want to get good grades? ....

d) What is causing a problem for Carolina? ....

e) What does Carolina think the teachers should do? ....

5 marks

12 Read the accounts below and then answer the questions that follow.

Diego	Yo soy muy bajo, pelirrojo con los ojos verdes. Afortunadamente soy inteligente, sin embargo el colegio para mí es un poco aburrido. Voy a cumplir dieciséis años dentro de dos días. ¡Qué bien! Mi madre dice que soy hablador pero en mi opinión ¡no es verdad!
Fernando	Tengo dieciséis años de momento pero cumpliré diecisiete años el mes que viene. Soy bastante alto y tengo el pelo corto, moreno y rizado. En mi opinión soy gracioso y bastante inteligente pero a veces soy muy perezoso y no me gusta mucho ir al instituto. Mi hermana dice que soy un poco raro.
Joaquín	Soy de estatura mediana con el pelo rubio y rizado. A veces puedo ser muy tímido y me falta confianza y por eso no tengo muchos amigos. Vivo en Madrid desde hace un año y me encanta el instituto porque es muy interesante.

a) Who is sixteen years old? ....

b) Who likes school? ....

c) Who has short hair? ....

d) Who is quite shy? ....

e) Whose sister thinks he is strange? ....

f) Who thinks that he is not talkative? ....

6 marks

13 Read the description and then answer the questions that follow.

Hola, me llamo Luisa. Llevo ocho años viviendo en una casa adosada en un pueblo bonito.
Me gusta mucho la casa, especialmente el jardín, que está detrás de la casa. Tiene un
césped y en medio hay un árbol muy bonito. También hay muchas flores. Entre la casa y
el césped hay una terraza donde pasamos mucho tiempo en el verano, sobre todo cuando
viene mi familia a pasar el día con nosotros.

Mi casa es bastante moderna con muebles bonitos pero desafortunadamente tengo que
compartir mi dormitorio con mi hermana. Me llevo bien con mi hermana pero no tenemos
mucho espacio para todas nuestras cosas.

¡Me encantaría tener mi propio dormitorio! Mi dormitorio ideal sería muy grande con
un escritorio para mi ordenador y con muebles muy modernos. También cambiaría la
moqueta y las cortinas y el color de las paredes porque de momento mi dormitorio está
pintado de rosa, que no me gusta nada. El color ideal para mi dormitorio sería el verde.

a) How long has Luisa lived in her house? ....

b) What does Luisa like most about where she lives? ....

c) Describe the garden. Give three details.

....

....

....

d) Where is the patio? ....

e) What is the problem with Luisa's bedroom?

....

f) What would Luisa's ideal room be like? Give three details.

....

....

....

g) What colour is Luisa's present bedroom? ....

11 marks

TOTAL

78

Section B: Questions and answers in **Spanish**

14 Lee la lista de adjetivos:

A gracioso   B antipático   C perezoso

D guapo   E trabajador   F tímido

Escoge el adjetivo correcto para describir a la gente de abajo. Escribe la letra correcta en cada casilla.

Ejemplo:

Mi amigo Raúl no habla mucho porque es… | F |

a) Yo estudio mucho en el cole porque soy… | |

b) Mi padre siempre nos hace reír porque es muy… | |

c) Mi hermano no hace nada en casa para ayudar porque es muy… | | | |

3 marks

15 Unos jóvenes hablan de su tiempo libre. Lee lo que dicen.

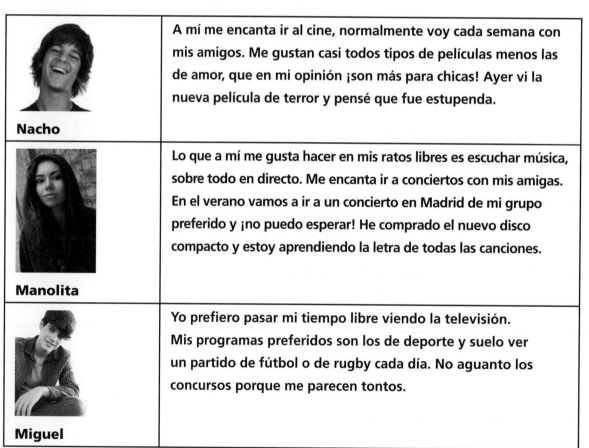

Nacho	A mí me encanta ir al cine, normalmente voy cada semana con mis amigos. Me gustan casi todos tipos de películas menos las de amor, que en mi opinión ¡son más para chicas! Ayer vi la nueva película de terror y pensé que fue estupenda.
Manolita	Lo que a mí me gusta hacer en mis ratos libres es escuchar música, sobre todo en directo. Me encanta ir a conciertos con mis amigas. En el verano vamos a ir a un concierto en Madrid de mi grupo preferido y ¡no puedo esperar! He comprado el nuevo disco compacto y estoy aprendiendo la letra de todas las canciones.
Miguel	Yo prefiero pasar mi tiempo libre viendo la televisión. Mis programas preferidos son los de deporte y suelo ver un partido de fútbol o de rugby cada día. No aguanto los concursos porque me parecen tontos.

Contesta a las preguntas en **español**.

a) ¿Qué le gusta hacer a Nacho con sus amigos? ....

b) i) ¿Qué tipo de películas no le gusta? ....

    ii) ¿Por qué? ....

c) ¿Cuál fue su opinión de la película que vio? ....

d) ¿Qué le gusta hacer Manolita en su tiempo libre? ....

e) ¿Qué va a hacer en Madrid? ....

f) ¿Qué tipo de programas le gusta a Miguel? ....

g) ¿Por qué no le gustan los concursos? ....

8 marks

16 Lee las descripciones de trabajos.

A	Trabajo con salario elevado y muchas oportunidades. Horas largas.
B	Trabajo al aire libre. Hay que andar mucho y a veces hablar con el público.
C	Hay que tener un buen nivel de lengua, escribir mucho y hacer entrevistas.
D	Hay que viajar mucho a países diferentes. Conocimiento de idiomas extranjeros beneficioso.
E	Hay que cuidar de la gente y ser amable. Horas largas y trabajo duro pero gratificante.

Escoge la descripción correcta y pon una X en la casilla correcta.

		A	B	C	D	E
a)	Cartero					
b)	Enfermera					
c)	Periodista					
d)	Auxiliar de vuelo					

4 marks

17 Eva escribe un blog sobre sus planes futuros.

Completa el texto usando palabras de la tabla.

Escribe la letra correcta en cada casilla.

Creo que me gustaría ☐ profesora en el futuro pero antes de ☐ a la universidad,

voy a ☐ por el mundo y conocer a gente nueva. ☐ estudiando tres idiomas y

¡quiero practicarlos!

A	ir	E	voy
B	visitar	F	viajar
C	estoy	G	soy
D	ser		

☐

4 marks

18 Escoge un adjetivo de la tabla para describir a la gente:

A	simpático	D	listo
B	divertido	E	deportivo
C	perezoso	F	reservado

a) Mi hermano menor no hace nada en casa y nunca quiere hacer los deberes. ☐

b) Mi padre me ayuda mucho y es muy comprensivo. ☐

c) Mi hermano mayor tiene un trabajo muy importante y tiene que saber mucho. ☐

d) Tengo un amigo que no habla mucho en el colegio y nunca quiere salir
con nosotros. ☐

e) A mí me encanta jugar al rugby y también voy mucho al gimnasio. ☐

f) Mi primo Miguel es muy extrovertido y gracioso. Me encanta salir con él. ☐

☐

6 marks

19 Lee lo que dice José y contesta a las preguntas en **español**.

José: Uno de los problemas más grandes para los jóvenes de hoy es el de estar 'a la moda'. Todas las chicas en el colegio hablan de sus actores o cantantes preferidos y lo guapos que son y no nos miran a nosotros, los compañeros, si no llevamos la última moda y si no somos guapos como los famosos. Yo lo encuentro muy difícil porque soy un chico bastante gordito y sé que a veces las chicas se ríen de mí. No tengo el dinero para estar siempre comprando nueva ropa y realmente prefiero conservar mi individualidad pero a veces me siento muy aislado. Creo que nunca encontraré novia y eso me molesta mucho.

a) Según José, ¿quién tiene un gran problema? ....

b) Dice que las chicas no les hacen caso a los chicos. ¿Por qué no?

....

....

c) A veces, ¿cómo reaccionan las chicas a José? ....

d) Aparte del dinero, ¿por qué no compra mucha nueva ropa?

....

e) ¿Cómo se siente? ....

6 marks

20 Lee la lista de asuntos medioambientales en la tabla.

1	Contaminación del tráfico	5	Clasificación de desechos
2	Suciedad	6	Deforestación
3	Contaminación industrial	7	Falta de agua
4	Transporte público	8	Recursos naturales

Empareja las descripciones **A–H** con el asunto correcto **1–8**. Escribe el número en la casilla correcta.

A   En mi ciudad, hay un problema de los desperdicios tóxicos de las fábricas, que contaminan el aire y los ríos.

B   Creo que hacen falta más contenedores de reciclaje en mi pueblo, porque se debe reciclar todo lo posible, el vidrio, el cartón, el plástico, el papel, la ropa ¡y mucho más!

C   A causa del efecto invernadero, algunos países tienen un problema enorme de sequía. Es algo que a mí me preocupa mucho.

D   Mi pueblo es muy bonito pero me molesta mucho que haya tanta circulación y eso causa mucho ruido y también contaminación del medio ambiente.

E   Para mí el problema medioambiental más grave es el de la desaparición de las selvas tropicales. En el Amazonas, por ejemplo, están tallando miles y miles de árboles todos los días.

F   En mi opinión el problema en mi pueblo es que las calles están sucias a causa de toda la basura en el suelo. Es una lástima porque es un pueblo bonito.

G   El problema del tráfico en mi ciudad es enorme. Hacen falta más autobuses y trenes para que la gente pueda dejar de usar el coche.

H   Debemos estar usando alternativas a los combustibles fósiles porque sabemos que ya se están acabando. El gobierno debe invertir más dinero a la energía renovable.

8 marks

21 Lee lo que dicen los jóvenes sobre la tecnología.

Ana	Suelo usar mi portátil para hacer mi trabajo de colegio porque es muy útil para encontrar información sobre cualquier tema. Lo único es que a veces paso muchas horas completando una tarea, porque hay tantos sitios web, que tarda mucho tiempo en leerlo todo.
Adolfo	Utilizo mi móvil sobre todo para jugar con los videojuegos. Siempre hay muchos juegos nuevos que me entretienen cuando viajo en autobús o durante el recreo. Paso muchas horas jugando con ellos. A veces me distrae de mi trabajo escolar e incluso pierdo mis programas favoritos porque estoy jugando.
Paula	Uso las redes sociales para mantenerme en contacto con todos mis amigos. A veces algunas personas las usan para hablar mal de la gente y han habido casos de cíberacoso en mi colegio. Para mí es muy fácil y rápido chatear con mis amigos porque lo puedo hacer en cualquier sitio con mi móvil o mí portátil.

Completa la tabla en **español**.

		Usa la tecnología para…	Positivo	Negativo
Ejemplo:	Ana	**hacer deberes/trabajo de colegio**	**útil para encontrar información**	**tarda mucho tiempo en leer todo pasa mucho tiempo haciendo tareas/ deberes**
a)	Adolfo	....	**le entretiene en el autobús/durante el recreo**	....
b)	Paula	**mantener el contacto con amigos (en las redes sociales)**	....	....

4 marks

TOTAL

43

Pronunciation Guide

Pronunciation of Letters

- Spanish pronunciation is quite straightforward. However, there are a few rules to follow:

Letters	Sounds like...	Examples
b and v	English **b** as in *big*	baile, vista, bebida, volver
j	**ch** as in Scottish *loch*	jugar, jamón
g	**j** when in front of **e** or **i**	gente, gimnasio
gu	**g** as in *get*	guerra, guitarra
h	always silent	hora, ahora
c	hard **th**, as in **th**eatre, when before **e** or **i** (in most of mainland Spain and Balearics) but soft **s** in the rest of Spanish-speaking world	centro, cine
z	hard **th**, as in **th**eatre, when before **e** or **i** (in most of mainland Spain and Balearics) but soft **s** in the rest of Spanish-speaking world	zona, zorro
r	slightly rolled (double r has a slightly longer roll)	pero, comer, perro
ll	*y*	llamar, lluvia
ñ	*n* followed by *y*	mañana, año

Stress

- For words ending in **n, s** or a **vowel,** the penultimate syllable is stressed:
  - recepcion*i*sta
  - pat*a*tas
  - c*e*nan
- For words ending in a consonant other than **n** or **s,** the last syllable is stressed:
  - com*er*
  - habl*ar*
  - ciud*ad*
- When the above rules do not apply, an acute accent appears over the stressed syllable:
  - recepción
  - inglés
  - marrón

Additional Vocabulary

- Here are some additional items of vocabulary for the topic areas.

Theme 1: Identity and Culture

Me, My Family and Friends

agradable	pleasant
amable	kind
animado/a	lively
antipático/a	unfriendly
comprensivo/a	understanding
débil	weak
desagradable	unpleasant
duro/a	hard/harsh
egoísta	selfish
honrado/a	honest
maduro/a	mature
muerto/a	dead
rico/a	wealthy
serio/a	serious
valiente	bold, brave
la familia numerosa	large family

el archivo	file
arroba	@
el buscador	search engine
el buzón	mailbox
la contraseña	password
el correo basura	spam
el disco duro	hard drive
el guión	hyphen
el guión bajo	underscore
inalámbrico	wireless
el internauta	Internet user
el navegador	browser
el ordenador	computer
la pantalla	screen
punto	full stop
punto com	.com
el usuario	user

Free-time Activities

apetecer	to feel like/fancy
los cereales	cereal
los churros	fritter/doughnut
las galletas	biscuits
el huevo	egg
la mantequilla	butter
la mermelada	jam
la mermelada de naranja	marmalade
la miel	honey
la nuez	nut, walnut
el pan	bread
el pan tostado/la tostada	toast
el panecillo	bread roll
pedir	to order/ask for
el plato (combinado)	(set) dish
la propina	tip
saber	to taste
el yogur	yogurt

el/la atleta	athlete
el campeón	champion
la campeona	champion
la carrera	race
el/la ciclista	cyclist
el equipo	team
el/la espectador/a	spectator
el/la futbolista	footballer
el/la jugador/a	player
el/la tenista	tennis player
el campo	pitch/field
la cancha (de tenis)	(tennis) court
el estadio	stadium
el piragüismo	canoeing
la piscina	swimming pool
la pista	ski-slope
la pista de hielo	ice-rink
el polideportivo	sports centre
el premio	prize

Theme 2: Local, National, International and Global Areas of Interest

Environment and Social Issues

la aspiradora	vacuum cleaner
el balcón	balcony
la butaca	armchair
la calefacción	heating
el cepillo de dientes	toothbrush
la chimenea	fireplace
el congelador	freezer
la ducha	shower
los electrodomésticos	household appliances
el equipo de música	music system
la estantería	shelves
el fregadero	sink
el hogar	home
el horno	oven
el lavabo	washbasin
la lavadora	washing machine
el lavaplatos	dishwasher
el microondas	microwave
la nevera	fridge
la papelera	waste-paper bin
la pasta de dientes	toothpaste
las persianas	shutters, blinds
el plato	plate/dish
la silla	chair
el televisor	television
el aparcamiento	car park
el bosque	woods/forest
el lago	lake

encontrarse bien/mal	to feel well/ill
el entrenamiento	training
entrenarse	to train
tener dolor de	to have a pain in
la encuesta	poll, survey
el ladrón	thief
la ley	law
los necesitados	needy people
el pájaro	bird
la pila	battery
recoger	to collect, gather, pick up

Travel and Tourism

la avería	breakdown, fault
averiado	broken down
el bañador	swimming costume
el bonobús	bus pass
el castellano	Castillian, Spanish spoken in Spain
decepcionar	to disappoint
detener(se)	to stop
DNI	ID card
durar	to last
hacer transbordo	to change, to transfer
la insolación	sunstroke
el motor	engine
la queja	complaint
quejarse	to complain
rueda	wheel

Theme 3: Current and Future Studies and Employment

Studies and Employment

los trabajos manuales	handicrafts	**encargarse (de)**	to be in charge of
el trimestre	term	**estar en huelga**	to be on strike
el aprendiz	apprentice	**la expectativa**	hope, prospect
calificado	competent, skilled, qualified	**el gerente**	manager
		rellenar	to fill in
el intercambio	exchange	**solicitar**	to apply
lograr	to achieve	**la solicitud**	(job) application
la perspectiva	prospects, outlook, future developments		

Answers

Pages 4-5 Review Questions

1. a) 37
    b) 65
    c) 41
    d) 78
    e) 99
    f) 125
    g) 740
    h) 582
    i) 1300
    j) 473

2. Son las ocho y diez – 08:10
    Son las nueve y cuarto – 09:15
    Son las once menos cuarto – 10:45
    Son las tres y veinticinco – 03:25
    Son las cuatro menos cinco – 03:55
    Es la una y veinte – 01:20
    Son las siete menos
    veinticinco – 06:35
    Son las dos y cinco – 02:05

3. a) False
    b) False
    c) True
    d) True
    e) False
    f) False
    g) False
    h) True
    i) False
    j) True

4. A 5
    B 7
    C 3
    D 1
    E 2
    F 6
    G 4
    H 8

Pages 6–25 Revise Questions

Page 7 Quick Test
1. Example: Me llamo Erica y tengo quince años.

2. ¿Cómo te llamas? ¿Cuántos años tienes?

3. la hermanastra

4. Hi. I am called Carmen and I am 13 years old. My birthday is the 12th of August and I will soon be 14 (years old). I have two sisters called Laura and Elena and they are 8 and 5 years old.

Page 9 Quick Test
1. Soy muy alto/a y tengo el pelo rubio y corto.

2. Mi hermana es bastante <u>alta</u> y es <u>bonita</u>.

3. Either: No me llevo bien con mi madre. Or Me llevo mal con mi madre.

4. En mi opinión, me llevo bastante bien con mis hermanos porque son muy divertidos y siempre charlamos mucho.

Page 11 Quick Test
1. Mis padres están separados.

2. La pareja es encantadora.

3. el matrimonio

4. Mi madre es <u>animada</u>. Mis padres son <u>cariñosos</u>.

Page 13 Quick Test
1. Navego la red cada día.

2. correo electrónico

3. Uso mi móvil para hacer mis deberes.

4. I like to chat with my friends.

Page 15 Quick Test
1. Prefiero escuchar la música pop.

2. Sé tocar la batería.

3. Me encanta charlar con mis amigos.

4. Salir con amigos es muy divertido.

Page 17 Quick Test
1. Me encantan <u>las</u> películas románticas.
    No me gustan nada <u>los</u> programas musicales.

2. Me gusta ver dibujos animados.

3. I think that soaps are more fun than news programmes/the news.

4. Me encantan los documentales.

Page 19 Quick Test
1. comer/almorzar

2. Me encantan las coles de bruselas.

3. I'll have 150 grams of ham.

4. d) los guisantes

Page 21 Quick Test
1. Example: **De primero quiero/quisiera la sopa y de segundo la paella de mariscos.**

2. No me gustan las albóndigas.

3. a) el café

Page 23 Quick Test
1. a) el esquí

2. Voy de pesca con mi hermano el domingo./Voy a ir de pesca con mi hermano el domingo.

3. Juego al rugby todos los sábados/ cada sábado.

4. It is the wrong verb. It should be: Hago/Practico el footing todos los días.

Page 25 Quick Test
1. Me encanta celebrar la Noche Buena.

2. Decoramos/Adornamos la casa.

3. Espero con ilusión Los San Fermines.

4. My mum cooked a delicious dinner/ supper.

Pages 26-29 Practice Questions

Page 26

1. a) se llama   [1]
    b) eres   [1]
    c) tengo   [1]
    d) es   [1]
    e) son   [1]
    f) somos   [1]
    g) tiene   [1]

2. a) Mi prima tiene el pelo castaño y rizado.   [1]
    b) Soy bastante alto y tengo los ojos azules.   [1]
    c) Mi padre es de estatura mediana.   [1]
    d) Mis hermanos son bastante bajos y delgados.   [1]

3. a) P   [1]
    b) P   [1]
    c) N   [1]

Page 27

1. a) enviar   [1]
    b) mando   [1]
    c) descargué   [1]
    d) utilizar   [1]
    e) navegar   [1]
    f) cargar   [1]

2. a) N   [1]
    b) P   [1]
    c) P   [1]

Page 28

1. a) C   [1]
    b) A   [1]
    c) C   [1]
    d) B   [1]

e) B [1]
f) C [1]

2. A 5 [1]
   B 4 [1]
   C 2 [1]
   D 3 [1]
   E 1 [1]

Page 29

1. a) 3 bottles of white wine [1]
   b) 1 bottle of red wine [1]
   c) 2 kilos of bananas [1]
   d) 1 kilo of oranges [1]
   e) Half a kilo of grapes [1]
   f) 2 kilos of onions [1]
   g) 1 lettuce [1]
   h) Half a kilo of cured pork
      sausage [1]

2. A 3 [1]
   B 1 [1]
   C 6 [1]
   D 2 [1]
   E 5 [1]
   F 4 [1]

Pages 30–51 Revise Questions

Page 31 Quick Test

1. Example: Mi casa es bastante grande con ocho habitaciones en total. Abajo hay el salón, el comedor y una cocina grande. También hay un pequeño cuarto de baño. Arriba tenemos 3 dormitorios, el dormitorio de mis padres, el dormitorio de mi hermano, que es bastante grande y mi dormitorio, que es muy acogedor. Tenemos un jardín y un garaje.

2. Mi dormitorio está al lado <u>del</u> cuarto de baño.
El garaje está detrás <u>de la</u> casa.
El salón está enfrente <u>del</u> comedor.

3. Mi piso está en la primera planta.

4. In my bedroom there is a big bed.

Page 33 Quick Test

1. a) Hay mucho que hacer como el cine, las tiendas y muchos restaurantes.

2. Future

3. Me gusta ir en autobús porque es rápido.

Page 35 Quick Test

1. En mi región se puede ir a la playa.

2. La catedral está cerca <u>del</u> mercado.
El ayuntamiento está lejos <u>de la</u> plaza.

3. The good thing about my region is the scenery.

4. Positive

Page 37 Quick Test

1. Example. Creo que la violencia es un problema serio que existe en muchos sitios.

2. To give two sides of an argument: On the one hand… on the other hand…

3. If we work together we will improve the community.

4. Example: Voy a hacerme voluntario en una tienda solidaria para ayudar a los demás.

Page 39 Quick Test

1. c) Nunca hago ejercicio y como muchas golosinas.

2. Eating a lot of fat is very harmful for your health.

3. Example: Para ser más sano, se debe evitar demasiada comida rápida y comer más verduras y fruta. También hay que hacer ejercicio con frecuencia.

4. a) De momento - present
   b) En el pasado - past
   c) La semana que viene - future

Page 41 Quick Test

1. I am totally against taking drugs.

2. Para llevar una vida más sana, no se debe/no debes fumar.

3. Debes practicar deporte tres veces a la semana.

4. Example: No estoy ni a favor ni en contra de beber alcohol. Yo bebo un poco y no veo nada mal en eso.

Page 43 Quick Test

1. Examples: La contaminación de la atmósfera; los desechos tóxicos de las fábricas; atascos en las ciudades; basura en las calles; una falta de reciclaje

2. My city is very polluted.

3. Examples: Hay que reducir el consumo de energía; Se debe usar el transporte público en vez del coche.

4. Debemos consumir menos energía.

Page 45 Quick Test

1. Climate change worries me a lot.

2. Example: Hay que ayudar a la gente para mejorar la situación.

3. Examples: el consumo de combustibles fósiles; las inundaciones; el calentamiento global; la deforestación; las mareas negras

4. Inquietante, preocupante

Page 47 Quick Test

1. Suelo ir de vacaciones al Mediterráneo con mi familia.

2. Example: Quisiera un abanico, una muñeca, tres postales, una sombrilla y una botella de crema solar, por favor.

3. a) el inglés
   b) el francés
   c) el alemán
   d) el griego

4. In Spain, I'm going to go on a guided tour and take lots of photos.

Page 49 Quick Test

1. Quisiera una habitación doble con balcón, por favor.

2. Example: ¿Hay sitio para una caravana para tres noches para cinco personas?

3. a) Del cinco al doce de agosto.
   b) Desde el diez hasta el veinticuatro de julio.
   c) Del primero al siete de mayo.

4. The bathroom is dirty and there isn't any toilet paper.

Page 51 Quick Test

1. I saw lots of interesting places.

2. Example: Hacía sol y calor todos los días.

3. Hice equitación/Monté a caballo y comí en un restaurante.

4. Example: Primero visité el pueblo y luego dimos un paseo por la playa.

Pages 52–55 Review Questions

Page 52

1. a) True [1]
   b) False [1]
   c) True [1]
   d) False [1]
   e) True [1]
   f) True [1]
   g) True [1]
   h) False [1]

2. Mis padres – están separados. [1]
Mi primo Miguel – está casado. [1]
Mi tía María – está divorciada. [1]
Mis hermanas – están casadas. [1]

Answers

3. Mi hermano se llama Jacob. **[1]** Tiene los ojos marrones y el pelo moreno. **[1]**

Page 53

1. A mí me gusta – mucho navegar por internet. **[1]**
Suelo usar – las redes sociales como Facebook y Twitter. **[1]**
Siempre uso mi portátil – para descargar música. **[1]**
Me encanta chatear – con mis amigos todos los días en las salas de chat. **[1]**
Utilizo las redes – sociales para buscar información sobre mi región. **[1]**
Esta noche voy a colgar – unas fotos de mi cumpleaños en mi muro. **[1]**

2. A 5 **[1]**
B 1 **[1]**
C 6 **[1]**
D 2 **[1]**
E 3 **[1]**
F 4 **[1]**

Page 54

1. A 1 **[1]**
B 3 **[1]**
C 4 **[1]**
D 2 **[1]**
E 6 **[1]**
F 5 **[1]**

2. A 6 **[1]**
B 4 **[1]**
C 1 **[1]**
D 5 **[1]**
E 2 **[1]**
F 3 **[1]**

Page 55

1. A 5 **[1]**
B 2 **[1]**
C 1 **[1]**
D 7 **[1]**
E 6 **[1]**
F 4 **[1]**
G 3 **[1]**

2. A 3 **[1]**
B 6 **[1]**
C 4 **[1]**
D 1 **[1]**
E 2 **[1]**
F 5 **[1]**
G 8 **[1]**
H 7 **[1]**

Pages 56-59 **Practice Questions**

Page 56

1. A 6 **[1]**
B 3 **[1]**

C 2 **[1]**
D 1 **[1]**
E 5 **[1]**
F 4 **[1]**

2. La cocina – Anoche preparé la cena con mi madre aquí. **[1]**
El salón – Siempre veo la tele aquí con mi familia. **[1]**
El garaje – Aquí metemos muchas cosas incluyendo el coche y mi bici. **[1]**
El comedor – Ayer comí aquí con toda la familia. **[1]**
El cuarto de baño – Voy a ducharme aquí antes de salir. **[1]**
El dormitorio – Mañana dormiré hasta muy tarde aquí. **[1]**
El estudio – Aquí puedo usar el ordenador y todos mis libros del colegio. **[1]**

Page 57

1. a) Hay que evitar una dieta malsana. **[1]**
b) Tienes que acostarte temprano. **[1]**
c) Debes practicar el deporte tres veces a la semana. **[1]**
d) No debes fumar ni tomar drogas. **[1]**
e) Hay que tratar de evitar el estrés. **[1]**
f) Para relajarte debes leer o escuchar música. **[1]**

2. A 6 **[1]**
B 5 **[1]**
C 7 **[1]**
D 1 **[1]**
E 3 **[1]**
F 4 **[1]**
G 2 **[1]**

Page 58

1. A 4 **[1]**
B 6 **[1]**
C 1 **[1]**
D 2 **[1]**
E 3 **[1]**
F 5 **[1]**

2. A 3 **[1]**
B 1 **[1]**
C 4 **[1]**
D 5 **[1]**
E 2 **[1]**

Page 59

1. ¿Tiene habitaciones libres? – Sí, todavía nos quedan tres habitaciones libres. **[1]**
¿El desayuno está incluido? – No, cuesta cinco euros por persona. **[1]**
¿Cuánto es por noche por persona? – Cuesta treinta euros los adultos y quince euros los niños por noche. **[1]**

¿Cuántos son? – Somos dos adultos y dos niños. **[1]**
¿Hizo una reserva, señor? – Sí, reservamos una habitación doble con ducha. **[1]**
¿Hasta cuándo quiere quedarse? – Hasta el día trece, por favor. **[1]**
¿Dónde están los servicios? – Están al lado de la piscina. **[1]**

2. A 4 **[1]**
B 1 **[1]**
C 6 **[1]**
D 2 **[1]**
E 5 **[1]**
F 3 **[1]**

Pages 60–77 **Revise Questions**

Page 61 Quick Test

1. No me gusta la química porque siempre tenemos muchas evaluaciones.

2. Example: Llevo uniforme escolar y consiste en una falda negra o pantalones negros, una camisa blanca, una corbata amarilla y una chaqueta negra. También tenemos que llevar medias o calcetines grises y zapatos negros.

3. c) No me gusta mi uniforme porque es muy bonito.

4. I used to wear a uniform in my primary school, but now it's not compulsory.

Page 63 Quick Test

1. a) el inglés (masculine)
b) la informática (feminine)
c) las matemáticas (feminine)
d) la religión (feminine)

2. Me gusta la geografía.
No me gustan nada las ciencias.
Me interesa mucho la tecnología.

3. I don't like physics because I don't understand anything.

4. Odio las ciencias porque son complicadas, pero me interesan las matemáticas.

Page 65 Quick Test

1. Bullying happens quite a lot in my school.

2. a) aprobar

3. Example: Pues, los exámenes son muy difíciles y causan mucho estrés en mi opinión.

4. Tienes que estudiar mucho para aprobar los exámenes.

Page 67 Quick Test

1. I want to get a job and earn lots of money.

2. Tenía que trabajar largas horas pero me gustó.

3. Me gustaría hacer experiencia laboral en el extranjero.

4. En lugar de seguir estudiando, voy a buscar un trabajo a tiempo completo.

Page 69 Quick Test

1. Quiero hacer un trabajo divertido.

2. Example: Tengo la intención de seguir estudiando y luego espero conseguir un trabajo interesante.

3. Negative

4. I intend/plan to travel/go travelling with my sister.

Page 71 Quick Test

1. feminine; masculine; feminine; masculine; feminine

2. manzanas; cristales; peces; dormitorios; profesores

3. marrón; actriz; perro; televisión; flor

Page 73 Quick Test

1. a) El perro grande
   b) La ciudad bonita
   c) Los chicos trabajadores

2. a) The intelligent girls.
   b) A great problem.
   c) The first year.

3. a) que
   b) más/menos
   c) el

4. La película es buenísima.

Page 75 Quick Test

1. slowly; quickly; correctly; healthily

2. felizmente; fácilmente; posiblemente; frecuentemente

3. Where do you live?

4. a) para
   b) por; para

Page 77 Quick Test

1. we; they; he/it; you (pl); you (sing)

2. I like the trousers. Do you have them in brown?

3. Quiero ir contigo.

Page 78

1. A 2   [1]
   B 5   [1]
   C 1   [1]
   D 6   [1]
   E 3   [1]
   F 4   [1]

2. a) Correos   [1]
   b) La Biblioteca   [1]
   c) El Cine   [1]
   d) La Piscina   [1]
   e) El Banco   [1]
   f) La Estación de Trenes   [1]
   g) La Plaza de Toros   [1]

Page 79

1. a) empezar a   [1]
   b) ponernos a   [1]
   c) acabo de   [1]
   d) debe   [1]
   e) ayudar a   [1]

2. A 4   [1]
   B 1   [1]
   C 6   [1]
   D 2   [1]
   E 7   [1]
   F 5   [1]
   G 3   [1]

Page 80

1. A 5   [1]
   B 3   [1]
   C 1   [1]
   D 4   [1]
   E 2   [1]

2. a) P   [1]
   b) P   [1]
   c) N   [1]
   d) N   [1]
   e) P   [1]
   f) N   [1]

Page 81

1. A 4   [1]
   B 3   [1]
   C 6   [1]
   D 5   [1]
   E 2   [1]
   F 1   [1]

2. a) T   [1]
   b) F   [1]
   c) ?   [1]
   d) F   [1]
   e) T   [1]

Page 82

1. A 6   [1]
   B 3   [1]
   C 5   [1]
   D 4   [1]
   E 1   [1]
   F 2   [1]

2. a) repasar   [1]
   b) sacar   [1]
   c) aprender   [1]
   d) enseñar   [1]
   e) repetir   [1]
   f) aprobar   [1]

Page 83

1. Preparo la comida en un restaurante italiano. Soy… – …cocinero. [1]
   Doy clases de geografía en un instituto. Soy… – …profesora. [1]
   Trabajo en aviones sirviendo a la gente. Soy… – …azafata. [1]
   Yo escribo novelas de intriga. Soy… – …escritor. [1]
   Limpio casas y hago tareas domésticas todos los días. Soy… – …criada. [1]
   Trabajo en un comercio en el centro de la ciudad. Soy… – …mujer de negocios. [1]
   Yo trabajo con un periódico, escribiendo reportajes. Soy… – …periodista. [1]
   Tengo que ir a las guerras a luchar. Soy… – …soldado. [1]

2. a) estudiaré   [1]
   b) trabajará   [1]
   c) hablaré   [1]
   d) encontrarán   [1]
   e) repasaremos   [1]
   f) conseguiré   [1]

Page 84

1.

Masculine	Feminine
color	mano
problema	lección
día	pared
lápiz	
libro		[8]

2. a) Mi perro es más grande que tu perro. [1]
   b) Tu hermano es menos estúpido/tonto que tu hermana. [1]
   c) Mi tele es tan buena como tu tele. [1]

Answers

d) La nueva película de James Bond
es peor que la anterior. **[1]**

3. a) contaminado **[1]**
   b) aislado **[1]**
   c) precioso **[1]**
   d) bonita **[1]**

Page 85

1. a) por **[1]**
   b) para **[1]**
   c) por **[1]**
   d) para **[1]**
   e) para **[1]**
   f) para **[1]**
   g) por **[1]**
   h) por **[1]**
   i) para **[1]**
   j) por **[1]**

2. ¿Tienes las llaves? – Sí, las tengo
aquí. **[1]**
¿Tienes el libro de español? – No, no
lo tengo. **[1]**
¿Quieres comprar la camiseta? – Sí,
pero la quiero en azul. **[1]**
¿Para quién compraste los
pantalones? – Los compré para mi
madre. **[1]**
¿Has probado el chocolate? – No, lo
voy a comer ahora. **[1]**
¿Dónde me viste? – Te vi en el
parque. **[1]**

Pages 86–101 Revise Questions

Page 87 Quick Test
1. Is the backpack yours?

2. ¿De quién son los libros? ¿Son tuyos?

3. a) ésta
   b) ése
   c) aquéllas

Page 89 Quick Test
1. they drink; we do/make; you chat; I
study

2. tomo; hacemos; cocina; reciben

3. hacer; comer; salir; estudiar

4. Nunca comemos pescado los lunes./No
comemos nunca el pescado los lunes.

Page 91 Quick Test
1. I begin; You think; They show; I can/
am able

2. vuelo; sigues; tenemos; recordáis

3. I usually eat at 2 o'clock./I am
accustomed to eating at 2 o'clock.

Page 93 Quick Test
1. a) estar
   b) ser

2. The children are playing football.

3. Estaba hablando con mi madre.

4. Tengo una hermana _y_ tiene 10 años.
Me gustan las manzanas _pero_ no me
gustan los plátanos. No me gusta mi
pueblo _por eso/así que_ voy a vivir en
Londres en el futuro.

Page 95 Quick Test
1. They drank a bottle of water.

2. llegué; visité; vi; comiste; bebimos

3. Saqué muchas fotos del hotel.

Page 97 Quick Test
1. When I was young, I used to play the
trumpet.

2. El sábado por la mañana íbamos a la
piscina.

3. a) He abierto la puerta.
   b) Han roto la ventana.

Page 99 Quick Test
1. I will go; We will visit; They will know;
You will do

2. Nadaré; Pensará; Trabajaremos

3. They would have; You would speak;
We would eat; You (pl) would study

4. Could you go out tonight?/Would you
be able to go out tonight?

Page 101 Quick Test
1. It's important that you go with me.

2. ¡Quiero que hables en español!

3. Si tuviera más tiempo, practicaría más
deporte.

4. a) ¡No hables!
   b) ¡No comáis!
   c) ¡No escriba!

Pages 102–105 Review Questions

Page 102

1. Me encanta la informática porque
creo que es – divertida y muy útil
para el futuro. **[1]**
Para mí las ciencias son muy – difíciles
y no las entiendo mucho. **[1]**
En mi opinión el francés es muy
interesante – y aprendo mucho en
esa clase. **[1]**

Yo odio la educación física porque
es – aburrida y el gimnasio es muy
antiguo. **[1]**
En general diría que los profesores son
– muy simpáticos y sus clases
son interesantes. **[1]**
No me gusta nada el dibujo porque
no es – divertido y para mí es inútil. **[1]**
Odio los exámenes porque son
siempre – muy complicados y poco
prácticos. **[1]**

2. A 3 **[1]**
   B 6 **[1]**
   C 2 **[1]**
   D 1 **[1]**
   E 5 **[1]**
   F 4 **[1]**

Page 103

1. En el futuro, quiero – ir a la
universidad. **[1]**
Después de terminar mis –
exámenes, voy a buscar un trabajo. **[1]**
Me gustaría conseguir un –
aprendizaje en la ingeniería. **[1]**
Lo mejor para mí sería continuar –
con mis estudios para seguir una
carrera en medicina. **[1]**
Creo que voy a intentar hacer –
experiencia laboral en una oficina. **[1]**

2. A 5 **[1]**
   B 1 **[1]**
   C 6 **[1]**
   D 2 **[1]**
   E 7 **[1]**
   F 3 **[1]**
   G 4 **[1]**

Page 104

1. a) Los hombres **[1]**
   b) Las naranjas **[1]**
   c) Las mujeres **[1]**
   d) Los castillos **[1]**
   e) Los planetas **[1]**
   f) Las aguas **[1]**
   g) Las luces **[1]**
   h) Las estaciones **[1]**

2. a) Un bolígrafo **[1]**
   b) Una habitación **[1]**
   c) Un árbol **[1]**
   d) Una catedral **[1]**
   e) Un cine **[1]**
   f) Una moto **[1]**
   g) Un autobús **[1]**
   h) Un balcón **[1]**

3. a) simpática **[1]**
   b) hablador **[1]**

c) impacientes [1]
d) graciosas [1]
e) rubio [1]
f) gran [1]

Page 105

1. ¿Cómo… – …quieres ir, en coche o en autobús? [1]
¿Cuál… – …es el mío, el rojo o el azul? [1]
¿Cuándo… – …es tu cumpleaños? [1]
¿Cuánto… – …cuesta la chaqueta? [1]
¿Cuántos… – …años tienes? [1]
¿Dónde… – …está mi móvil? [1]
¿Por qué… – …dices eso? [1]
¿Qué…. – …significa eso? [1]
¿Quién… – …es aquella mujer, Señora Smith o Señora Brown? [1]

2. a) C [1]
b) A [1]
c) C [1]
d) B [1]
e) A [1]
f) C [1]

Pages 106-109 Practice Questions

Page 106

1. a) mis [1]
b) vuestro [1]
c) tu [1]
d) nuestra [1]
e) mi [1]
f) nuestras [1]

2. a) como [1]
b) beben [1]
c) estamos [1]
d) pones [1]
e) saben [1]
f) hablo [1]
g) escucha [1]
h) estudiamos [1]

Page 107

1. a) empiezan [1]
b) prefiero [1]
c) piensa [1]
d) quieren [1]
e) prefieres [1]
f) entiendo [1]
g) queréis [1]
h) queremos [1]

2. a) está [1]
b) son [1]
c) están [1]

d) soy [1]
e) estás [1]
f) estoy [1]
g) estamos [1]
h) es [1]

Page 108

1. a) Ayer jugué al fútbol. [1]
b) La semana pasada mis padres hablaron con mi profesor(a). [1]
c) El año pasado fuimos a Francia. [1]
d) Prefirió viajar por autobús. [1]
e) Hice la cama esta mañana. [1]
f) Tuvimos que comer en el comedor. [1]

2. a) han [1]
b) hemos [1]
c) he [1]
d) ha [1]
e) habéis [1]
f) has [1]

Page 109

1. a) tendrías [1]
b) iría [1]
c) sería [1]
d) irías [1]
e) podría [1]
f) tendría [1]
g) comerían [1]
h) viviríamos [1]

2. a) When I go to university, I'm going to study Spanish. [1]
b) I want you to bring me the bread from the baker's. [1]
c) It's a shame that there isn't a swimming pool in my town. [1]
d) You have to study a lot so that you pass your exams. [1]
e) I don't think that we're going to eat in the restaurant. [1]
f) Don't do that, please! [1]

Pages 110–113 Review Questions

Page 110

1. a) aquella/esta [1]
b) este [1]
c) aquellas [1]
d) aquél [1]
e) esos [1]
f) eso [1]
g) esta/aquella [1]
h) aquel [1]

2. a) C [1]
b) A [1]
c) B [1]
d) B [1]
e) C [1]
f) B [1]

Page 111

1. a) You play [1]
b) I meet/find [1]
c) They fly [1]
d) They cost [1]
e) You can/are able [1]
f) It rains [1]
g) They count/tell [1]
h) I remember [1]

2. Con respecto a mi madre, es muy graciosa… – …e inteligente. [1]
En el futuro quiero ser dentista… – …o médico [1]
Mi abuelo tiene noventa y cinco años… – …que es muy viejo. [1]
Mi hermana no es simpática… – …sino desagradable. [1]
En casa tenemos cinco gatos, dos ratones… – …y tres caballos. [1]
En mi opinión mi amiga Bea es muy perezosa… – …porque no trabaja mucho en el colegio. [1]
Al fin y al cabo hay que trabajar siete… – …u ocho horas todos los días. [1]
Me gustaría ser contable… – …pero encuentro muy difíciles las matemáticas. [1]

Page 112

1. a) B [1]
b) C [1]
c) C [1]
d) B [1]
e) A [1]
f) C [1]

2. a) jugaba [1]
b) nadaba [1]
c) esquiaba [1]
d) comíamos [1]
e) íbamos [1]
f) hablaban [1]
g) veía [1]
h) me gustaba [1]

Page 113

1. a) saldré [1]
b) jugaré [1]
c) pondré [1]
d) tendrá [1]

Answers

e) terminaré **[1]**
f) podré **[1]**

2. ¡Háblame! – Talk to me! (informal) **[1]**
Toma la primera a la derecha – Take the first on the right **[1]**
Escribid la fecha – Write the date (plural) **[1]**

Toma la primera a la izquierda – Take the first on the left **[1]**
¡Hábleme! – Talk to me! (formal) **[1]**
Siga todo recto – Go straight on **[1]**
Escribe la fecha – Write the date (singular) **[1]**
¡Escúchame! – Listen to me! **[1]**

Pages 114–126 **Mix it Up Questions**

Section A

1. **a)** habladora **[1]**
   b) alto **[1]**
   c) verdes **[1]**
   d) guapas **[1]**
   e) buen **[1]**
   f) simpáticos **[1]**

2.

	Key Idea	Accept	Reject	
Tengo dieciséis años y	I am 16 years old and	I am 16 and		**[1]**
mi cumpleaños es	my birthday is			**[1]**
el veinticinco de enero.	the twenty-fifth of January.	25th of January.	Any other month or number	**[1]**
Nací en	I was born in		Wrong tense	**[1]**
el año dos mil.	the year 2000.	2000.		**[1]**
En mi familia somos cuatro.	There are four/4 of us in my family.	There are four people in my family.	In my family we are four.	**[1]**
Mi hermana se llama Laura	My sister is called Laura			**[1]**
y en mi opinión es muy graciosa.	and in my opinion, (she) is very funny.			**[1]**
Me llevo muy bien con ella.	I get on very well with her.	I get on really well with her.		**[1]**

3. **a)** Juan **[1]**
   b) Raúl **[1]**
   c) Juan **[1]**
   d) Carmen **[1]**
   e) Rosa **[1]**

   c) Cristina **[1]**
   d) Paco **[1]**
   e) Cristina **[1]**
   f) Mariela **[1]**

   f) Any three from: Very big/It would have a desk for the computer/Modern furniture/It would be green. **[3]**
   g) Pink. **[1]**

4. **a)** Plays basketball **[1]**
   b) Ana **[1]**
   c) Goes to football matches **[1]**
   d) Ana **[1]**
   e) Athletics training **[1]**
   f) Something to eat/drink **[1]**
   g) To a lake (near the town) **[1]**
   h) It depends if he has enough money. **[1]**

10. **a)** P **[1]**
    b) N **[1]**
    c) F **[1]**
    d) P **[1]**
    e) N **[1]**

Section B

14. **a)** E **[1]**
    b) A **[1]**
    c) C **[1]**

11. **a)** They expect too much of him. **[1]**
    b) He doesn't have time to revise all subjects. **[1]**
    c) He wants to be a vet. **[1]**
    d) Discipline/noisy students at school. **[1]**
    e) They should be more strict. **[1]**

5. **a)** C **[1]**
   b) E **[1]**
   c) A **[1]**
   d) B **[1]**

15. **a)** ir al cine **[1]**
    b) i) las películas de amor **[1]**
       ii) piensa que son para las chicas **[1]**
    c) fue estupenda/le encantó **[1]**
    d) escuchar la música **[1]**
    e) ir a un concierto **[1]**
    f) programas de deporte **[1]**
    g) (piensa que) son tontos/le parecen tontos **[1]**

12. **a)** Fernando **[1]**
    b) Joaquín **[1]**
    c) Fernando **[1]**
    d) Joaquín **[1]**
    e) Fernando **[1]**
    f) Diego **[1]**

6. **Roberto** P+N **[1]**
   Clara P **[1]**
   Victoria N **[1]**
   Guillermo P+N **[1]**

7. **a)** C **[1]**
   b) F **[1]**
   c) E **[1]**
   d) A **[1]**
   e) D **[1]**
   f) B **[1]**

13. **a)** 8 years **[1]**
    b) Garden **[1]**
    c) Any three from: It's behind the house/It has a lawn/There's a tree in the middle of the lawn/It has lots of flowers. **[3]**
    d) In between the house and the lawn. **[1]**
    e) Any one from: She has to share it with her sister/There's not enough room for their things. **[1]**

16. **a)** B **[1]**
    b) E **[1]**
    c) C **[1]**
    d) D **[1]**

17. D - ser **[1]**
    A - ir **[1]**
    F - viajar **[1]**
    C - estoy **[1]**

8. B; D; E **[3]**

9. **a)** Mariela **[1]**
   b) Paco **[1]**

18. **a)** C (perezoso) **[1]**
    b) A (simpático) **[1]**
    c) D (listo) **[1]**
    d) F (reservado) **[1]**

e) E (deportivo) [1]
f) B (divertido) [1]

19. a) los jóvenes [1]
  b) si no llevan la última moda; si no son guapos (como los famosos) [2]
  c) se ríen de él [1]
  d) para/quiere conservar su individualidad [1]
  e) aislado [1]

20. A3 [1]
  B5 [1]
  C7 [1]
  D1 [1]
  E6 [1]
  F2 [1]
  G4 [1]
  H8 [1]

21. a)

Adolfo	jugar con los videojuegos **[1]**	**le entretiene en el autobús/durante el recreo**	(le) distraen de (su) trabajo escolar/sus estudios OR pierde (sus) programas (favoritos) **[1]**
b) Paula	**mantener el contacto con amigos (en las redes sociales)**	es fácil/rápido **[1]**	alguna gente habla mal de otros OR hay cíberacoso **[1]**

Notes

Notes

Index

Index

Collins

AQA GCSE Revision

Spanish

with Audio

with Audio

AQA GCSE

Workbook

Allison Macaulay

Contents

Theme 1: Identity and Culture

Theme 2: Local, National, International and Global Areas of Interest

Theme 3: Current and Future Studies and Employment

Practice Exam Papers

Visit our website at **www.collins.co.uk/collinsGCSErevision** to download the audio material for the Listening Paper on pages 177–189 of this workbook.

Me, My Family and Friends

1 Read the account below and then answer the questions that follow.

> Me llamo Elena y tengo 14 años. Voy a hablar de mi familia.
>
> Somos cinco en casa. Mi padre, Juan es italiano y trabaja en un hospital porque es médico. Creo que es muy gracioso y simpático. Mi madre se llama Dolores y es dentista. Es guapa e inteligente y muy trabajadora. Somos muy amigas.
>
> Tengo un hermano, Ramón. Es muy deportivo y es cocinero en un hotel. Me gusta mucho porque es muy amable y extrovertido. También tengo un hermanastro que se llama Pedro y es francés. Es mecánico pero en mi opinión, es muy perezoso. Tiene una novia, Charito que es bonita pero bastante antipática y no me gusta mucho.
>
> Finalmente, mi madre dice que soy habladora pero yo no estoy de acuerdo. Pienso que soy tímida. En el futuro quiero ser profesora aunque mis padres quieren que sea farmacéutica. ¡Ya veremos!

a) How does Elena describe her father? Give two details.

   i) ....

   ii) .... [2]

b) What is Elena's mother like? Give three details.

   i) ....

   ii) ....

   iii) .... [3]

c) What does Ramón do? .... [1]

d) Why doesn't Elena like Pedro's girlfriend very much? .... [1]

e) How does Elena describe herself? .... [1]

f) What does Elena want to be? .... [1]

2 Draw lines between the boxes to complete the sentences.

Creo que mi hermano es muy inteligente…	…estricto, pero también puede ser muy gracioso.
Mi madre tiene el pelo largo…	…practica deporte cinco veces a la semana.
En mi opinión mi padre es muy…	…porque aprobó todos sus exámenes.
Mi abuela es muy simpática y…	…y rizado con los ojos verdes.
Tengo dos hermanas que pueden ser…	…cariñosa y siempre me ayuda con todo.
Mi tía Paula es muy activa y…	…impacientes y a veces me molestan.

[6]

3 Read Nuria's account of relationships within her family.

> En mi familia somos cinco personas. Mis padres tienen cuarenta y cinco años los dos. Luego tengo un hermano mayor que tiene veinte años y también tengo una hermana mayor que tiene dieciocho años. Yo soy la pequeña con catorce años.
>
> Me llevo muy bien con mi padre porque es muy simpático y siempre hablo con él. También es muy comprensivo. En cuanto a mi hermana, no me llevo muy bien con ella porque, en mi opinión, es muy perezosa y nunca ayuda en casa. También a veces es bastante antipática.
>
> Creo que me parezco mucho a mi madre porque somos las dos de estatura mediana con el pelo castaño y rizado. Pero de carácter, somos muy diferentes, en eso soy más como mi padre.

Complete the sentences.

Write the correct letter in the boxes.

a) The youngest member of Nuria's family is…

A	her brother
B	Nuria
C	her sister

[1]

b) Nuria thinks that her sister is…

A	kind
B	lazy
C	funny

[1]

c) Nuria has hair like her…

A	sister
B	mum
C	dad

[1]

4 Your Spanish friend, Luisa, has answered this questionnaire from a magazine about technology. You read the questionnaire and look at the answers she has circled.

¿Cómo usas la Tecnología?

¡Puedes leer los resultados en la página 50!

1 ¿Cuántas veces al día usas tu móvil?

  A sobre unas cincuenta veces o quizás menos

  B más o menos cien veces

  C cada diez minutos e incluso durante las clases

2 ¿Para qué sueles usar tu móvil?

  A Para mandar mensajes y comunicarse con amigos y familia

  B Para navegar la red y buscar información

  C Para sacar fotos

3 Si dejas el móvil en casa y llegas al colegio sin él, ¿qué haces?

  A Llamas a tus padres que te traigan el móvil al colegio

  B Pasas el día sin el móvil

  C Vuelves a casa para recogerlo

4 ¿Piensas que las redes sociales son una cosa positiva?

  A Sí, son muy útiles para informarte de muchas cosas

  B No, porque puede haber gente engañosa que te pide cosas

  C Sí, si sabes usarlo de una manera segura, no hay problema

a) According to the circled answer, do you think that on average Luisa uses her mobile too much? Tick the correct box.

Yes ☐   No ☐

Give a reason for your answer.

.... [1]

b) According to the circled answer, for what purpose does Luisa use her phone most of the time?

.... [1]

c) According to the circled answer, do you think that Luisa is too dependent on her mobile?

Yes ☐   No ☐

Give a reason for your answer.

.... [1]

d) According to the circled answer, what is her opinion of social media?

.... [1]

5 You read a problem page in a Spanish magazine.

> Hola, soy Charro. Tengo dieciséis años y tengo un problema con mi madre y mi novio. Llevo dos años saliendo con Vicente y estamos muy enamorados. Él me quiere mucho y yo le quiero a él. Yo sé que me quiero casar con Vicente dentro de dos años. No me importa que solo tengamos dieciocho años entonces, porque él es el hombre de mi vida. Ya me ha comprado un anillo de compromiso pero no lo puedo enseñar a mi madre porque ella dice que somos demasiado jóvenes para hablar del matrimonio y piensa que somos muy niños todavía.
>
> He intentado explicarla como me siento, pero dice que no puedo casarme con Vicente. No quiero enfadarles a mis padres pero sé que no voy a cambiar mi manera de pensar. ¿Cómo puedo convencerlos que lo decimos en serio y que ya no somos niños? Vicente va a buscar un trabajo en cuanto termine el instituto.

Choose the four correct statements from the box below.

A	Vicente is 18 years old.
B	They love each other.
C	Charro wants to marry him.
D	Vicente said they would have to compromise.
E	They want to have children.
F	Charro's mum thinks they are too young to get married.
G	Charro doesn't want to upset her parents.
H	Vicente has a job.

Write the correct letters in the boxes.   ☐ ☐ ☐ ☐   [4]

6 Read the blog about Pablo's social media site and complete the text using words from the list.

Write the correct letter in the boxes.

Anoche colgué unas fotos en mi muro de Facebook. Me encanta ☐ cosas para que

las vean mis ☐ o mi familia. Para mí, es la mejor ☐ de mantenerme

en contacto con todo el mundo porque tengo, como mínimo, a ☐ amigos. Al principio

mis padres no estaban ☐ porque pensaban que las redes sociales eran muy tontas,

pero ahora ven que pueden ser útiles.

A	trescientos
B	buscar
C	colgar
D	contentos
E	familia
F	manera
G	amigos
H	página
I	aburridos

[5]

Free-time Activities

1 Choose the correct activity from the options given to complete the sentences about free time.

la cocina   los videojuegos   el rugby   las canciones

los deportes de invierno   la vela

a) A mí me gusta cantar, sobre todo _____ flamencas.

b) Para mí, lo que me encanta es hacer _____. ¡Siempre preparo dulces y pasteles!

c) Lo mejor es practicar _____ porque me gusta la nieve y el frío.

d) A mi hermano le gusta mucho _____ porque es un deporte muy físico.

e) A mí me gusta jugar con _____ en casa.

f) Prefiero estar en mi barco practicando _____. [6]

2 Read the blog about Enrique's Christmas celebrations and complete the text using words from the list. Write the correct letter in the boxes.

> Celebramos las Navidades el 24 y el 25 de diciembre. Normalmente el día 24, que es la Noche Buena, ☐ con la familia por la noche y vamos a la ☐ del gallo. Luego el día 25, abrimos los ☐ y pasamos mucho tiempo juntos ☐, cantando villancicos y comiendo mucho. A mí me encanta porque vemos mucho a mis tíos, abuelos y primos y todos lo ☐ bien juntos. Es muy especial.

[5]

A	jugando
B	puertas
C	comimos
D	cenamos
E	familia
F	misa
G	comer
H	pasamos
I	regalos

3 Read the accounts below of restaurant meals and then answer the questions that follow.

Ángel: Fui a un restaurante la semana pasada con mi familia para el cumpleaños de mi hermano. Yo comí mariscos con patatas y ensalada y estaba muy rica. De postre tomé el arroz con leche que a mí me encanta. Mis padres pagaron y me lo pasé bien.

Rosi: Yo salí a cenar con mi amiga en un restaurante cerca de mi casa. Su hermano es el camarero allí. Mi amiga pidió pollo con patatas fritas pero dijo que las patatas fritas estaban frías. Su hermano nos pidió otro plato y al final nos dieron un descuento. Tomamos las dos helado de chocolate y luego un café. Realmente no nos costó demasiado y lo pasamos bien.

Jaime: Cuando estaba de vacaciones el año pasado mi familia y yo fuimos a un restaurante mexicana donde comimos platos típicos de allí. El mío estaba demasiado picante y no pude comerlo. Los camareros eran bastante maleducados y tardaban mucho tiempo en atendernos. Pedí un café después pero estaba frío entonces tuve que pedir otro. Al final tuvimos que pagar mucho y salimos muy tarde del restaurante a causa del tiempo que teníamos que esperar.

a) Who loves rice pudding? ....

b) Whose food was very spicy? ....

c) Whose meal was reasonably priced? ....

d) Who was celebrating a special occasion? ....

e) Who had rude waiters? ....

f) Who had ice-cream? ....

g) Who paid a lot? ....

h) Who had seafood? ....

i) Who had slow service? ....

j) Whose coffee was cold? ....   [10]

4 Translate the text below into **English**.

> Me gusta mucho escuchar música y lo que más me gusta, es la música rock. Suelo escucharla en mi móvil cuando voy en autobús al colegio y también durante los recreos y por la noche en casa. La semana pasada fui a un concierto de mi grupo preferido. ¡Fue estupendo!

....

....

....

....

....

[9]

5 Lee lo que dice Javier sobre su tiempo libre.

Pues, en mi tiempo libre me gusta mucho practicar el deporte, me encanta ir al cine con mis amigos y a veces leo novelas de intriga también. Prefiero practicar la natación y entreno en la piscina tres veces a la semana. Para mí, el deporte no es sólo un pasatiempo, sino que también es una manera de mantenerme en forma, y eso es muy importante.

El fin de semana pasado fui a la piscina con mis primos y lo pasamos genial. Luego visité a mis abuelos que viven a media hora de mi casa. Por la noche fui al cine con mi familia para ver una nueva comedia. Yo prefiero ver una película en el cine porque es más emocionante que en casa, pero creo que es más divertido ir con mis amigos.

Este fin de semana voy a jugar al bádminton con mi mejor amigo en el polideportivo y después hemos quedado con cuatro compañeros para ir otra vez al cine.

Responde a las preguntas en **Español**.

a) ¿Cuáles son los tres pasatiempos preferidos de Javier?

....

....

.... [3]

b) ¿Por qué dice que el deporte es muy importante?

.... [1]

c) ¿A quién visitó Javier?

.... [1]

d) ¿Con quién prefiere ir al cine?

.... [1]

e) Javier y su mejor amigo van al cine el fin de semana, ¿Con quién van?

.... [1]

6 Re-order the sentences below by numbering them 1–10 so that they form a conversation at the market.

- ¿Cuánto cuestan las manzanas?
- Sí, déme un kilo de peras, por favor.
- No, nada más, gracias. ¿Cuánto es?
- ¿Qué desea?
- Dos euros el kilo.
- Aquí tiene, gracias, adiós.
- Aquí tiene. ¿Algo más?

Free-time Activities

- ¿Quiere algo más?
- Pues, un kilo de manzanas, por favor.
- Son tres euros cincuenta.

[10]

7 Match the sports to the descriptions below.

A	Es un deporte que se puede hacer en equipo o como individuo y hay que ser muy flexible.
B	Se juega en equipo con un balón, pero los pies no pueden ponerse en contacto con ello.
C	Deporte acuático que se puede hacer en un río, en el mar o en la piscina.
D	Deporte que se practica en un campo muy grande con una pequeña pelota dura y un palo.
E	Un deporte rápido que se hace con dos ruedas, o en equipo o como individuo. Hay que tener mucha fuerza.
F	Deporte individual que se practica en un cuadrilátero contra otra persona.

Write the letter in the box.

a) Golf   [1]

b) Boxing   [1]

c) Gymnastics   [1]

d) Diving   [1]

e) Basketball   [1]

f) Cycling   [1]

8 Draw lines between the boxes to match the Spanish to the English.

¿Perdone, dónde están los aseos?	Today, we're going to have lunch early.
¿Qué sabores hay?	How much do I owe you?
Perdone, falta un tenedor aquí.	Excuse me, where are the toilets?
Hoy, vamos a almorzar temprano.	The food here is really delicious.
¿Pedimos la cuenta?	What flavours are there?
¿Cuánto le debo?	Excuse me, there's a fork missing here.
La comida aquí es muy rica.	Shall we ask for the bill?

[7]

Environment and Social Issues

1 Read the article that your friend Manolo has written about his town.

Mi ciudad está en el suroeste de España y hay más de noventa mil habitantes. Me encanta porque está cerca de la costa, a dos kilómetros de la playa. En la ciudad hay mucho que hacer, por ejemplo se puede visitar museos, iglesias y la plaza antigua en el centro. También hay muchas tiendas y lo bueno es que hay varios lugares de ocio para los jóvenes, como la bolera. Lo único es que no tenemos muchos espacios verdes y tampoco hay polideportivo. Por la noche se puede comer en los restaurantes típicos o ir de copas a los bares en el centro.

Diría que las ventajas de vivir aquí son que siempre hay mucho que hacer y nunca se aburre. Al otro lado, las desventajas son que puede ser muy concurrido en el verano a causa de todos los turistas.

Actualmente no hay estación de trenes pero van a construir una el año próximo.

Now read the sentences below and choose the four sentences that are correct.

Write the letters in the boxes below.

A	There are nine thousand inhabitants in Manolo's town.
B	He lives on the coast.
C	There are lots of things for young people to do.
D	There aren't many parks.
E	There is a sports centre in the town.
F	You can go out to eat and drink in the evening.
G	It can be boring in the town.
H	It can get very busy because of the tourists.

☐ ☐ ☐ ☐   [4]

2 Translate the following text into **Spanish.**

I live in a small town in the country. I like it a lot because it is pretty. We have a church and some shops. Also, there is a park where I like to play football with my friends. In the future I would like to live in the mountains.

_____

_____

_____

_____

_____   [9]

Environment and Social Issues

3 Match the issues **A, B, C, D, E** and **F** to the newspaper headlines **1–6**.

1 ¡Qué pesadilla! La nueva reina de rock admite tener problemas con la comida y el peso...

2 LAS CIFRAS DE DESEMPLEO AUMENTAN OTRA VEZ A 5%.

3 *¡Qué disgusto! Empresa mundial no quiere mujeres: ¡Los hombres son los mejores!*

4 Otra amenaza de bomba en nuestra capital.

5 ¡La igualdad es mi derecho! Hombre marginalizado por su color...

6 *Cada vez más países se nuclearizan. ¿Por el bien o por el mal?*

A Racism ☐

B Sexism ☐

C Nuclear war ☐

D Anorexia/Bulimia ☐

E Unemployment ☐

F Terrorism ☐ [6]

4 Read Magdalena's account below and then answer the questions that follow.

> Magdalena nos habla de estar en forma: en mi opinión es muy importante mantenerte en forma para evitar el cansancio, la depresión y el estrés. Yo trato de comer una dieta equilibrada, realmente como un poco de todo menos el pescado que no me gusta. Practico el deporte cuatro veces a la semana, juego al hockey en el colegio y hago la natación en el polideportivo.
>
> Estoy en contra de las drogas porque hay muchos riesgos para la salud, aunque tengo unos amigos que las toman el fin de semana. Creo que les hace sentirse mayores. En el futuro no voy a beber alcohol porque puede causar la enfermedad.

a) According to Magdalena, what three things can keeping fit help to avoid?

....

.... [3]

b) What does Magdalena eat to maintain a healthy diet?

.... [1]

c) What does she do at the sports centre? .... [1]

d) Why is she against taking drugs?

.... [1]

e) According to Magdalena, why do her friends take them?

.... [1]

5 You read an article about alcohol.

Choose the correct summary for each person and write the correct letter in the box.

1 **En mi clase, la mayoría de los chicos beben alcohol y nos divertimos mucho cuando salimos juntos. No veo ningún problema.**

2 **Empecé a beber un poco con mis amigos los fines de semana en la calle o en el parque.**

3 **Conozco a gente que bebe porque los amigos lo hacen. Realmente no quieren hacerlo pero no quieren parecer aburridos.**

A Alcohol is dangerous for your health.

B Drinking alcohol is no big deal.

C My first drinking experiences.

D Alcohol is fine in small quantities.

E Peer pressure to drink.   [3]

6 Lee las frases.

¿Son **positivas** o **negativas**? Escribe **P** o **N** en las casillas.

a) **La deforestación es muy inquietante y es algo que nos afecta a todos.**

b) **Vivo en un pueblo pintoresco donde no existe contaminación.**

c) **En mi ciudad no hay problemas de basura ni de contaminación de los coches.**

d) **En mi pueblo hay mucho paro que es problemático para toda la región.**

e) **Si trabajamos juntos, podremos mejorar los problemas medioambientales.**

f) **Mucha gente es muy egoísta y no intenta proteger el mundo.**

g) **Hay una cantidad alarmante de gente sin techo en nuestras ciudades.**

h) **Hay cada vez más voluntarios para ayudar a los necesitados.**   [8]

7 Match the homes **A, B, C, D, E, F** and **G** with the people's requests **1–7**.

1 Señor and Señora Gutiérrez are looking for a house for themselves and their three children. It needs to have facilities close by.

2 Dolores works in the city and hates travelling to and from work every day.

3 Manuel and Irene want to live in the country with their dog.

4 Virginia and Nico want a house for themselves and their daughter near the sea.

5 María loves old buildings and is looking for somewhere to renovate.

6 The García family want a house where they can entertain family and friends.

7 Carlos is a painter and wants a house where he can work undisturbed by neighbours.

A   Una casa adosada en la costa a cinco minutos de la playa. ☐

B   Un chalé muy grande y moderno con diez habitaciones, un jardín grande
     y una terraza enorme. ☐

C   Una casa bastante grande en un pueblo bonito cerca de un colegio, un parque
     y unas tiendas. ☐

D   Un chalé pequeño en medio del campo. El pueblo más cercano está
     a tres kilómetros. ☐

E   Piso moderno en el centro de la ciudad cerca de la zona comercial
     y las tiendas. ☐

F   Una granja antigua. Hace falta mucho trabajo y modernización. ☐

G   Una casa adosada en el campo con un jardín enorme. ☐   [7]

8 Match descriptions **A, B, C, D, E** and **F** below with the correct images **1–6**.

1   **2**   **3**

4   **5**   **6**

A   Tenemos una cocina muy grande y moderna. ☐

B   Me gusta relajarme en el salón viendo la tele o escuchando música. ☐

C   Siempre comemos juntos en el comedor. ☐

D   Mi hermana pasa mucho tiempo en el cuarto de baño por la mañana. ☐

E   Prefiero hacer mis deberes en el estudio. ☐

F   Tengo un dormitorio muy acogedor con muebles bonitos. ☐   [7]

9 Translate the following sentences into Spanish using **usted**.

a) i) Excuse me, where is the post office, please?

                                                               [1]

  ii) Go straight on and it's opposite the market.

                                                               [1]

b) i) How do I get to the museum, please?

                                                               [1]

  ii) Take the first on the right and go straight on.

                                                               [1]

c) i) Excuse me, can you tell me where the main square is, please?

                                                               [1]

  ii) Yes, cross the bridge and go straight on. It's on the left.

                                                               [1]

d) i) Is the police station far?

                                                               [1]

  ii) No, it's five minutes on foot; go down the street and it's at the end, next to the cinema.

                                                               [1]

e) i) Can you help me, please? I can't find the market.

                                                               [1]

  ii) Cross the river and go straight on. It's in the main square.

                                                               [1]

Travel and Tourism

1 Choose the correct word from the options given to complete the sentences about accommodation.
Write the correct letter in each box.

A	desayuno
B	niños
C	vistas
D	junio
E	persona
F	habitación
G	pensión
H	tiendas

a) Buenos días, quisiera reservar una ☐ doble, por favor.

b) Habitación número diez, señor, con ☐ al mar y baño.

c) ¿Cuánto es por noche por ☐?

d) ¿A qué hora se sirve el ☐?

e) ¿Hay sitio para dos ☐?

f) Quisiera quedarme aquí desde el tres hasta el diez de ☐.

g) Somos dos adultos y tres ☐.

h) Quisiera una habitación con media ☐, por favor.   [8]

2 Match the statements **A, B, C, D, E, F, G** and **H** to the correct destinations **1–8**.

1   **España**

2   **Escocia**

3   **Francia**

4   **Italia**

5   **Estados Unidos**

6   **Alemania**

7   **País de Gales**

8   **Suiza**

A   Tengo muchas ganas de visitar Edimburgo, dicen que es precioso.   ☐

B   Vamos a ir de compras a Nueva York, ¡qué ilusión!   ☐

C   El año pasado fuimos a Berlín y visitamos todos los monumentos.   ☐

D   Vamos a hacer senderismo en las montañas y visitar la capital, Bern.

E   Quiero ver la catedral de Sevilla y comer paella.

F   Fuimos al teatro en Cardiff y también subimos la montaña Snowdon.

G   Me encanta la pizza y la pasta, y los monumentos históricos son preciosos.

H   Quiero visitar la capital, subir la Torre Eiffel e ir de excursión por el río Sena.   [8]

3 Read the following passage about Rosa's holiday. Then answer the questions that follow in English.

> En julio del año pasado pasé un mes con mi familia en la costa en nuestro apartamento. Me encanta estar allí porque puedo ver a mis amigos y paso todos los días en la playa con ellos. Por la mañana solemos bañarnos en el mar y a mí me gusta mucho practicar los deportes acuáticos. El año pasado fui un día con mi familia a un pueblo en la montaña y dimos una vuelta en bici, que me encantó. ¡Fue precioso! Luego saqué muchas fotos y compré unos recuerdos para mis abuelos. Por la noche volvimos a la costa y cenamos en un restaurante cerca del apartamento. ¡Fue un día perfecto!

a) How long did Rosa go on holiday for?

.... [1]

b) Where did she stay?

.... [1]

c) Why does she like going there?

.... [2]

d) What does she usually do in the morning?

.... [1]

e) Where did she go one day last year?

.... [1]

f) What did she do after the bike ride?

.... [2]

g) Where did they have dinner?

.... [1]

Travel and Tourism

4 Lees el pronóstico meteorológico mientras estás de vacaciones.

lunes	Las temperaturas van a mejorarse hoy pero no hará mucho calor todavía.
martes	Cielos despejados. En la mayoría del país hará viento pero también bastante calor.
miércoles	Por la mañana veremos muchas nubes que resultarán en lluvia fuerte por la tarde.
jueves	Un día perfecto de playa con temperaturas altas y cielos claros.
viernes	Un día muy tranquilo. No hará tanto sol pero hará una temperatura agradable.

Escoge el tiempo más adecuado para las siguientes situaciones.

Escribe el día más adecuado.

a) Necesitas un buen día para hacer surf, no muy frío y con aire. _____

b) Quieres pasar el día descansando y tomando el sol. _____

c) Quieres dar una vuelta por la sierra y no quieres que haga demasiado sol, pero tampoco quieres frío. _____ [3]

5 Read the blog about Elena's holidays.

El verano pasado fui de vacaciones a Italia con mi familia y mi mejor amigo. Viajamos en coche y el viaje duró tres días en total. Pasamos por el túnel de la Mancha y luego viajamos por Francia hasta los Alpes. Este año estamos pasándolo bien en España. El hotel tiene una piscina enorme y está muy cerca de la playa que es preciosa.

En Italia nos quedamos en un camping bonito cerca de un lago enorme. Había buenas instalaciones y el paisaje era precioso. Me gustaría volver algún día para subir una montaña con mi padre. El mejor día fue cuando hicimos senderismo por el lago. Fue muy duro pero merecía la pena porque las vistas eran increíbles. Llevamos un picnic para el almuerzo y lo comimos al lado de una cascada.

Cuando sea mayor, me gustaría ir a Australia con mi familia. Tenemos amigos allí y queremos visitarles. No he estado nunca y me parece que sería una buena experiencia conocer a partes diferentes del país.

Which stages do the following situations apply to?

Write **P** for something that happened in the **past**.

Write **N** for something that is happening **now**.

Write **F** for something that is going to happen in the **future**.

Write the correct letter in each box.

a) Holidaying in Spain

b) Staying on a campsite

c) Travelling through France

d) Having a picnic

e) Climbing a mountain

f) Holidaying in Australia [6]

6 Match the descriptions **A, B, C, D, E** and **F** with the images **1–6**.

1

2

3

4

5

6

A   Tengo una reserva para cuatro días.

B   ¿Hay agua potable aquí?

C   ¿Hay sitio para una tienda para una noche?

D   Quisiera reservar una habitación doble, por favor.

E   ¿El desayuno está incluido?

F   ¡No hay agua caliente!

[6]

Studies and Employment

1 Read these opinions about school and say whether each one is **positive** or **negative**.

a) **Normalmente las clases son aburridas.** ....

b) **Para mí, los exámenes son fáciles y no me preocupan.** ....

c) **Recibimos un montón de deberes todos los días.** ....

d) **Siempre aprendo mucho porque los profesores explican bien.** ....

e) **Tengo muchos amigos en mi instituto.** ....

f) **Suelo sacar buenas notas.** ....

g) **Tenemos un uniforme muy bonito.** ....

h) **Estoy deseando dejar el colegio.** ....   [8]

2 Read the accounts below and then say whether the statements that follow are **true** or **false**.

Jesús: De momento estoy estudiando mucho porque quiero ir a la universidad y entonces tengo que sacar buenas notas en mis exámenes. Voy bastante bien en todas mis clases. La única asignatura que encuentro un poco difícil es la historia pero me gusta y el profesor es muy bueno.

Inma: Mi asignatura preferida es la historia porque es fascinante. Lo que no me gusta mucho es la física, es muy complicada y siempre saco malas notas. Quiero trabajar en un banco en el futuro entonces tengo que trabajar muchísimo en la clase de matemáticas. No aguanto el inglés.

a) Jesús wants to go to university. ....

b) Both Jesús and Inma like history. ....

c) Jesús is not doing well at school. ....

d) Inma gets good marks in physics. ....

e) Inma loves English. ....

f) Jesús doesn't think his history teacher is very good. ....   [6]

3 Read about Ramón's school routine.

Which stages do the following situations apply to?

Me levanto sobre las siete y me arreglo para ir al colegio. Desayuno y salgo de casa a las ocho y cuarto. Voy al colegio en autobús con mis amigos o en el verano voy andando. Hace dos días me levanté tarde y no llegué al colegio hasta las nueve.

Paso el recreo en el patio jugando al fútbol con mis amigos. Luego como en el comedor y por la tarde tenemos dos clases. A mí me gusta el miércoles porque tenemos dos clases de dibujo por la tarde y ¡me encanta! Este miércoles, vamos a pintar un cuadro.

Ayer estudié las matemáticas y luego tuve un examen de español que fue bastante difícil. Mañana vamos a ver una obra de teatro durante la clase de inglés que será divertido. Luego por la tarde, después del colegio, voy a practicar el boxeo.

Write **P** for something that happened in the **past**.

Write **N** for something that happens in the present/**now**.

Write **F** for something that is going to happen in the **future**.

Write the correct letter in each box.

a) Getting up at seven o'clock. ☐

b) Arriving at school at nine o'clock ☐

c) Eating in the dining room ☐

d) Painting a picture ☐

e) Doing a Spanish exam ☐

f) Going boxing ☐ [6]

4 Read Inma's thoughts about her future plans and complete the text using words from the list.

Write the correct letter in the boxes.

Cuando sea mayor, creo que quiero ser contable ya que me ☐ las matemáticas. Al terminar mis exámenes, voy a ir al colegio para ☐ con mis estudios. Después, espero ☐ a la universidad para estudiar las matemáticas y mientras ☐, quiero buscar un trabajo a tiempo parcial, preferiblemente en un banco, para ☐ un poco de dinero y experiencia también.

A	iré
B	estudio
C	estudiar
D	encantan
E	ganar
F	continuar
G	dinero
H	ir
I	gastar

[5]

5 Translate the following sentences into Spanish.

a) I like maths. _____ [1]

b) I don't like ICT. _____ [1]

c) I'm interested in science. _____ [1]

d) I don't like homework at all. _____ [1]

e) Science is more difficult than maths. ....

.... [1]

f) Spanish is as easy as French. ....

.... [1]

g) My RE teacher is the best teacher in the school. ....

.... [1]

6 **Lee lo que dicen estos estudiantes sobre el colegio.**

¿Cómo son las opiniones?

Elena	Paco	Miguel

Estudio muchas asignaturas que me interesan como las ciencias y la informática. El año pasado estudiaba la geografía y al final la dejé porque no se me daba muy bien.	Suelo sacar buenas notas en mis clases, sobre todo en la clase de inglés, que me resulta bastante interesante y fácil.	Este año estoy estudiando la tecnología que es práctica y también la informática, que es útil para mí. Lo que pasa es que siempre hay muchos deberes y los odio.

Escribe   **P**   **(Positivo)**

               N   **(Negativo)**

               P+N   **(Positivo + Negativo)**

Escribe la letra en la casilla correcta.

a) Elena

b) Paco

c) Miguel   [3]

7 Read Manolita's email about school pressures.

Choose the four correct statements.

Hola, ¿qué tal? Aquí todo va bien menos en el colegio. Estoy muy estresada de momento a causa de la cantidad de deberes que tengo. Estamos haciendo exámenes de momento y ¡no quiero hacerlos! Hace falta repasar tanto y luego hay mucha presión pensando en lo que quiero hacer en el futuro porque la verdad es que no tengo mucha idea. ¿Y tú – qué quieres hacer? Yo he estado pensando en hacer algo útil como ser enfermera o profesora, pero hay que estudiar mucho y no sé si ir a la universidad o no. Mis padres dicen que es mi decisión si voy o si busco un trabajo. Ellos no fueron a la universidad, entonces no entienden el proceso muy bien. ¡Estoy muy confundida!

A	Manolita is enjoying school.
B	She is going to do exams soon.
C	She needs to revise a lot.
D	Manolita doesn't know what she wants to do in the future.
E	The stress is making her ill.
F	She is wondering whether to become a teacher.
G	Her parents want her to look for a job.
H	Her parents didn't go to university.

Write the correct letters in the boxes.

☐ ☐ ☐ ☐ [4]

Grammar 1

1 Read the list of nouns and say whether each one is **Masculine** or **Feminine** and also **Singular** or **Plural**.

Write **M** or **F** in the first box, followed by **S** or **P** in the second box.

a) bolígrafo ☐ ☐

b) mermelada ☐ ☐

c) árboles ☐ ☐

d) mano ☐ ☐

e) padres ☐ ☐

f) catedrales ☐ ☐

g) regiones ☐ ☐

h) ciudad ☐ ☐

i) problemas ☐ ☐

j) fotos ☐ ☐

[10]

2 Complete the description about Jorge's family choosing the correct adjective from the list below.

Write the correct letter in the boxes.

En mi familia somos seis personas. Mi madre se llama Beatriz y es muy ☐ y amable. Diría que me parezco mucho a mi padre porque él tiene el pelo y los ojos muy ☐ y yo también soy ☐. Mis hermanas son bastante ☐ físicamente y a veces pueden ser ☐.

A	rubio
B	molestas
C	simpático
D	claros
E	ruidosos
F	graciosa
G	parecidas
H	antipáticos
J	grosero

[5]

3 Translate the following sentences into English.

a) **No te dije la verdad.** ....

b) **Dame el dinero.** ....

c) **Nunca nos habla.** ....

d) La vi ayer en el colegio. _____

e) María le dijo 'hola'. _____

f) Dale el helado a ella. _____

g) Pregúntaselo a él. _____ [7]

4 Choose the most appropriate adverb from the list below to complete the sentences.

Write the correct answer in the space provided.

a) Mi madre dice que hablo _____ pero no lo creo. Hablo
    lentamente en mi opinión.

b) Yo he visto esa película _____.

c) ¡Ay! Me duele el estómago. Creo que he comido _____.

d) Sí yo conozco muy _____ a Manuel. Somos buenos amigos.

e) Lo siento _____.

f) ¡Mamá, estoy _____!

generosamente
aquí
muchas veces
allí
bien
poco
deprisa
sinceramente
demasiado

[6]

5 Choose either **por** or **para** to complete these sentences and write in the answer space provided.

a) _____ mí, es muy bonito.

b) Mañana tenemos que pasar _____ casa de tu tía _____ darle
    el regalo.

c) Yo siempre hago mis deberes _____ la tarde al llegar del instituto.

d) No te preocupes, yo lo haré _____ ti esta vez, como no tienes mucho tiempo.

e) El sábado voy al centro _____ comprar unas botas.

f) Tengo que terminar esto _____ mañana.

g) El bocadillo de jamón es _____ tu padre.

h) ¿Cuándo vamos a ir? ¿_____ la noche?　　　　　　[9]

6 Choose the most appropriate interrogative from the list below to complete the sentences.

Write the correct answer in the space provided.

cuántas
adónde
cuándo
cuál
quién
por qué
dónde
cómo

[8]

a) ¿_____ vamos mañana – al pueblo o a la playa?

b) ¿_____ piensas eso?

c) ¿_____ es tu hermana María, es muy alta?

d) ¿_____ es aquel chico al lado de tu hermano?

e) ¿_____ vamos a ir al cine – el jueves?

f) ¿_____ galletas quieres?

g) ¿_____ quieres, el verde o el azul?

h) ¿_____ te gustaría vivir en el futuro?

Grammar 2

1 Choose the correct verb from the options given to complete the sentences.

comparto   madrugar   me ducho   está   lavo   enciendo   limpiar

a) _____ en el cuarto de baño todos los días.

b) _____ los platos para mi madre.

c) _____ la luz para leer el libro de cocina.

d) Voy a _____ el cuarto de baño esta tarde.

e) Yo _____ mi dormitorio con mi hermano.

f) Tengo que _____ los días de colegio.

g) <<¿Dónde _____ el sacacorchos? Tengo una botella de vino.>>   [7]

2 Draw lines between the boxes to match the radical changing verbs with the English meaning.

Me despierto	He/She wakes up
Pensamos	I think
Quieren	It begins
Te diviertes	I want
Pienso	I wake up
Cierras	It closes
Se despierta	We think
Quiero	You amuse / enjoy yourself
Empieza	You close
Cierra	They want

[10]

3 Translate the following sentences into Spanish.

a) They follow the instructions. _____

b) He always laughs a lot. _____

c) We repeat the verbs every day. _____

d) I get dressed at seven o'clock. _____

e) She always asks for the bill in Spanish. _____

f) It sometimes snows in January. _____   [6]

4 Choose the most appropriate negative to complete the following description about Eva's free time. Write the correct letter in the boxes.

Yo ☐ hago deporte en mi tiempo libre porque ☐ me gusta nada. Prefiero ver películas y me encantan las comedias. Sin embargo ☐ veo películas de terror porque me dan miedo y ☐ me gustan las películas románticas. No he visto ☐ .

A	jamás
B	ninguna
C	tampoco
D	nunca
E	nadie
F	no
G	nada

5 Translate the following sentences into Spanish using the present continuous tense.

a) I am reading a book.

....

b) What are you doing?

....

c) Julio is swimming in the pool.

....

d) María and Nico are talking on the telephone.

....

e) Where are you spending your holidays? (**tú**)

....

f) What is he eating?

.... [6]

6 Read the following sentences and complete each one with the correct part of either **ser** or **estar**.

a) Mi madre .... **muy simpática.**

b) Esos chicos .... **mis hermanos.**

c) ¿Dónde .... **el banco, por favor?**

d) Mi tío .... **trabajando en el colegio porque** .... **profesor.**

e) ¡Qué bien! .... **muy contento ahora.** [6]

Grammar 3

1 **a)** Which of the following verbs is in the preterite tense? Tick the correct option.

A Decidí ☐ B Decido ☐ C Decidiré ☐

b) Which of the following verbs is in the imperfect tense? Tick the correct option.

A Esperé ☐ B Espero ☐ C Esperaba ☐

c) Which of the following verbs is in the pluperfect tense? Tick the correct option.

A Empecé ☐ B Empezábamos ☐ C Había empezado ☐

d) Which of the following verbs is in the future tense? Tick the correct option.

A Terminaré ☐ B Termino ☐ C Terminé ☐

e) Which of the following verbs is in the conditional tense? Tick the correct option.

A Preferiré ☐ B Prefería ☐ C Preferiría ☐

f) Which of the following verbs is in the subjunctive mood? Tick the correct option.

A Tengo ☐ B Tendré ☐ C Tenga ☐ [6]

2 Draw lines between the boxes to link the sentence parts and create full sentences in the perfect tense.

Está mañana he…	…descubierto en el Amazonas?
Mi amiga francesa me ha …	…vuelto nunca al restaurante.
No encuentro mi móvil. ¿Mamá has…	…visto mi teléfono?
¿Sabes lo que han…	…hablado con mi madre y está de acuerdo conmigo.
¡Ay, qué lástima! Las nubes han…	…cubierto las montañas y ahora no podemos ver nada.
¿Nosotros? No, no hemos…	… escrito una carta para describirme su pueblo.

[6]

3 Complete the following sentences with the correct form of the verb. Tick the correct option.

a) Guillermo _____ el accidente, entonces habló con la policía.

A vio ☐ B ver ☐ C ve ☐

b) Mi hermano tuvo un accidente con su moto y _____ el tobillo.

A se rompió ☐ B se rompe ☐ C roto ☐

c) El fin de semana que viene _____ al cine con mis amigos.

A iba ☐ B iré ☐ C fui ☐

d) Mis amigos _____ un incendio esta mañana.

A vi ☐ B ven ☐ C vieron ☐

e) El coche iba muy rápido y después _____ con el camión.

A chocar ☐ B chocó ☐ C choca ☐

f) ¿Yo .... usar tu coche mamá? El mío tiene un pinchazo.

A podrías ☐   B podréis ☐   C podría ☐

g) Si pudiera elegir, ... en Estados Unidos en el futuro.

A viviría ☐   B vivo ☐   C viviré ☐   [7]

4 Translate the following sentences into Spanish using the imperfect tense.

a) I used to speak German well. ....

b) My brother used to go to the park at weekends. ....

....

c) My parents always went to France. ....

....

d) I used to go out a lot. ....   [4]

5 a) Which of the following is the correct past participle of **comer**? Tick the correct option.

A comado ☐   B comido ☐   C comer ☐

b) What is the correct form of **haber** for the following sentence? Tick the correct option.

Mis amigas .... leído el libro.

A ha ☐   B he ☐   C han ☐

c) Which of the following is the correct past participle of **romper**? Tick the correct option.

A romper ☐   B rompido ☐   C roto ☐

d) What is the correct form of **haber** for the following sentence? Tick the correct option.

¿Qué....hecho vosotros?

A habéis ☐   B has ☐   C han ☐

e) Which of the following verb forms completes this sentence? Tick the correct option.

Acabo de .... a Raúl en el cine.

A visto ☐   B ver ☐   C vi ☐   [5]

6 Translate the following sentences into Spanish to practise the imperative. Use **usted**.

a) Take the first on the right and go straight on. ....

....

b) Cross the square and go down the street. ....

c) Go up the street and take the third on the right. ....

....

d) Cross the bridge and turn left. ....   [4]

Collins

GCSE
Spanish

H

Higher Tier Paper 1 Listening

Time allowed: 45 minutes
(including 5 minutes' reading time before the test)

Instructions

- Download the audio material to use with this test from **www.collins.co.uk/collinsGCSErevision**
- Use black ink or black ball-point pen.

Instructions

- The marks for questions are shown in brackets.
- The maximum mark for this paper is 50.
- You must **not** use a dictionary.

Advice

For each item, you should do the following:

- Carefully listen to the recording. Read the questions again.
- Listen again to the recording. Then answer the questions.
- You may write at any point during the test.
- In Section A, answer the questions in English. In Section B, answer the questions in Spanish.
- Answer all questions in the spaces provided.
- Write down all the information you are asked to give.
- You have 5 minutes to read through the question paper before the test begins. You may make notes during this time.

Name: ....

Section A Questions and answers in English

Opinions about people's houses

Listen to your Spanish friends, Nico and Laura, talking about their houses.

What is their opinion of the following aspects?

Write **P** for a **positive** opinion.

N for a **negative** opinion.

P+N for a **positive** and **negative** opinion.

0 1 Nico

His house ☐ His bedroom ☐

[2 marks]

0 2 Laura

Bedroom space ☐ The colour ☐

[2 marks]

Shopping in a department store

A	Perfumery
B	Men's Fashion
C	Music
D	Travel
E	Sports Clothes and Equipment
F	Food
G	Children's Section
H	Women's Fashion

You are listening to advertisements in a Spanish department store.

Match the correct advert to each of the departments above.

For each advert, write the correct letter in the box.

0 3 ☐

[1 mark]

0 4 ☐

[1 mark]

0 5 ☐

[1 mark]

0 6 ☐

[1 mark]

0 7 ☐

[1 mark]

0 8 ☐

[1 mark]

Relationships

Your new Spanish friend Juanita tells you about the relationships within her family.

What does Juanita say?

Answer both parts of the question in English.

0 9 · 1 How does Juanita generally get on with her brother?

_____

[1 mark]

0 9 · 2 Why does Juanita say that she gets on well with her sister? Give two details.

_____

_____

[2 marks]

0 9 · 3 Why does Juanita say that she is lucky?

_____

[1 mark]

0 9 · 4 Who does Juanita say is the strictest in her family?

_____

[1 mark]

A public announcement

While in a shopping centre in Spain, you hear the following announcement.

Answer the question in **English.**

1 0 What is going to happen in 30 minutes' time?

_____

[1 mark]

A radio programme about health and fitness in Argentina

On the Internet, you hear a report about health and fitness issues in South America, in particular, in Argentina.

Answer the questions in **English**.

| 1 | 1 | What do 64% of young Argentinians say?

....

[1 mark]

| 1 | 2 | What percentage of young people say that they regularly eat junk food?

....

[1 mark]

| 1 | 3 | What do 75% admit to?

....

[1 mark]

| 1 | 4 | · | 1 | What is happening to the number of young people that smoke?

....

[1 mark]

| 1 | 4 | · | 2 | What does the increasing figure of 58% refer to?

....

[1 mark]

Easter Celebrations

Your friend explains to your Spanish teacher about his Easter celebrations.

1 5 Which two things from the list below refer to your friend?

A	He receives lots of Easter eggs.
B	Last year he went to the Dominican Republic for Easter.
C	He goes to church at Easter.
D	He thought the Easter processions were boring.
E	He loves chocolate.

Write the correct letters in the boxes.

[2 marks]

Charitable work

Your Spanish friend is interviewed about her job in a charity shop.

Answer the questions in **English**.

| 1 | 6 | What does she have to do in the shop? Give two details.

....

....

[2 marks]

| 1 | 7 |·| 1 | Why does she say that she likes her job?

....

[1 mark]

| 1 | 7 |·| 2 | What does she want to do next year?

....

[1 mark]

School Pressures

You hear part of a radio documentary about modern day pressures at school.

Answer the question in **English**.

| 1 | 8 | What does the student say causes the most stress?

....

[1 mark]

Shopping

Your Spanish friend Magdalena tells you her thoughts on going shopping.

Which three things from the list below are true?

A	Magdalena thinks the shops in her town are expensive.
B	She likes to go shopping with her friends.
C	She prefers to go with her family.
D	Magdalena bought a birthday present.
E	Her sister is having a party.
F	Her friend bought a jacket.

1 9 Write the correct letters in the boxes.

[3 marks]

Answer the question in **English.**

2 0 Although she prefers designer clothes, where does Magdalena also buy clothes?

Give two details.

....

....

[2 marks]

The shopping centre…

A	is close to the town.
B	has a lot of shops.
C	has just opened.

2 1 Write the correct letter in the box.

[1 mark]

Poverty

Listen to these two friends discussing a programme that they have seen about poverty.

Answer the questions in **English**.

2 2 · 1 Why did María feel bad after watching the programme?

_____

[1 mark]

2 2 · 2 What does Juan suggest that they can do to help the situation?

_____

[1 mark]

2 2 · 3 Name two things that Juan suggests they could send to help the poor in Africa.

_____

_____

[2 marks]

What does María say that she already does on a weekly basis?

A	Works with a community group selling things for charity
B	Helps to complete useful tasks around her local community
C	Sends money to charity

2 2 · 4 Write the correct letter in the box.

[1 mark]

Practice Exam Paper 1: Listening

Future Plans

You listen to Andrés and Carmen discussing what they are going to do when they leave school.

What does Carmen think about her dream of becoming a vet?

A	It will be too difficult to achieve.
B	She is going to try very hard to achieve it, despite it being difficult.
C	It is too much studying and she will be too tired.

2 3 · 1 Write the correct letter in the box.

[1 mark]

Answer the question in **English.**

2 3 · 2 Apart from the money, why does Andrés want to have his own plumbing business?

....

[1 mark]

Section B Questions and answers in Spanish

Los móviles

Tus amigos Jorge y Olivia hablan de sus móviles.

¿Qué piensan ellos de los móviles y qué piensan sus padres?

2 4 Completa la tabla en español.

Jorge	Sus padres
es necesario es conveniente	

[2 marks]

2 5 Completa la tabla en español.

Sus padres	Olivia
La distrae mucho de los deberes	

[1 mark]

Las vacaciones

Tu amigo Javi está planeando sus vacaciones del año que viene con su novia.

Escuchas su conversación.

¿Qué le gustaría hacer Javi durante las vacaciones? Selecciona las dos respuestas correctas.

A	Deportes de invierno
B	Hacer submarinismo
C	Nadar
D	Salir en barco
E	Practicar el esquí acuático

`2 6` Escribe las dos letras correctas en las casillas. ☐ ☐

[2 marks]

`2 7` · `1` ¿Qué quiere hacer su novia?

....

....

[1 mark]

`2 7` · `2` ¿Qué piensa Javi que deben hacer?

....

....

[1 mark]

Problemas en la capital

Escuchas un informe sobre problemas en la ciudad.

¿Cuál es el mayor problema según el estudio?

A	Delitos menores como escribir en lugares públicos o hacer mucho ruido
B	Crímenes de dinero
C	Problemas medioambientales

2 8 · 1 Escribe la letra correcta en la casilla.

[1 mark]

2 8 · 2 ¿Qué ha pasado para formar esta opinión?

....

....

[1 mark]

END OF QUESTIONS

Collins

GCSE
Spanish
Higher Tier Paper 2 Speaking

H

Candidate's material – Photo card

Candidate's material – Role play

Time allowed: 10-12 minutes

(+ 12 minutes' preparation time)

Instructions

- During the preparation time you must prepare the photo card and role play cards given to you.
- You may make notes during the preparation time.
- You must ask one question during the General Conversation.

Information

- The photo card test will last approximately 3 minutes. The role play test will last approximately 2 minutes. The General Conversation will last between 5 and 7 minutes.
- You must **not** use a dictionary, either in the test or during the preparation time.

Name: _____

Photo card

- Look at the photo.

- Prepare your <u>spoken</u> answers to the questions below.

- Then think of other questions you might be asked on the topic of 'Me, My Family and Friends' and prepare answers to those, too.

- **¿Qué hay en la foto ?**

- **En tu opinión, ¿cómo debe ser un buen amigo / una buena amiga? ¿Por qué ?**

- **¿Qué hiciste con tus amigos la semana pasada?**

Practice Exam Paper 2: Speaking

You will be asked two further questions, on the same topic.

Other questions you might be asked are:

- **Describe a tu mejor amigo / mejor amiga.**

- **¿Os lleváis bien siempre ? ¿Por qué ? ¿Por qué no?**

- **¿Qué os gusta hacer juntos?**

- **¿Qué vas a hacer con tus amigos mañana?**

- **¿Dónde se puede encontrar nuevos amigos?**

- **¿Prefieres pasar tiempo con tu familia o con tus amigos?**

- **¿Por qué son importantes para ti los amigos?**

Prepare your answers to these questions, too.

Role Play

Prepare your spoken answers to this role play.

Instructions to candidates

Your teacher will play the part of your Spanish friend and will speak first.

You should address your friend as 'tú'.

When you see this – ! – you will have to respond to something you have not prepared.

When you see this – ? – you will have to ask a question.

Estás hablando con tu amigo español / tu amiga española sobre las vacaciones.

- Tus vacaciones el año pasado – **(dos detalles)**
- !
- Actividades durante las vacaciones – **(dos detalles)**
- Planes para tus próximas vacaciones
- ? Tipo de vacaciones

Practice Exam Paper 2: Speaking

General Conversation

Sample Questions:

Theme 1: Identity and Culture

1) ¿Con quién te llevas mejor en tu familia y por qué?

2) ¿Te gustaría casarte en el futuro? ¿Por qué (no)?

3) Háblame de una fiesta que sueles celebrar con tu familia / tus amigos.

4) ¿Te gustaría hacer un deporte de riesgo?

5) ¿Para qué sueles usar el Internet?

Theme 2: Local, National, International and Global Areas of Interest

1) ¿Cómo sería tu casa ideal?

2) ¿Qué es lo bueno de tu región?

3) ¿Cuáles son los beneficios de practicar el deporte?

4) ¿Por qué beben algunos jóvenes demasiado alcohol?

5) En tu opinión, ¿cuáles son los problemas más serios en nuestra sociedad?

Theme 3: Current and Future Studies and Employment

1) ¿Opinas que el acoso escolar es un problema muy corriente en tu instituto?

2) ¿Preferirías ir a la universidad o conseguir un trabajo? ¿Por qué?

3) Para ti, ¿qué es lo más importante de un trabajo?

4) ¿Crees que los jóvenes deben trabajar a tiempo parcial mientras estudian?

5) ¿Te gustaría trabajar al extranjero? ¿Por qué (no)?

END OF QUESTIONS

Collins

GCSE
Spanish
Higher Tier Paper 3 Reading

H

Time allowed: 1 hour

Instructions

- Use black ink or black ball-point pen.
- Answer **all** questions.
- You must answer the questions in the spaces provided.
- In **Section A**, answer the questions in **English**. In **Section B**, answer the questions in **Spanish**. In **Section C**, translate the passage into **English**.

Information

- The marks for questions are shown in brackets.
- The maximum mark for this paper is 60.
- You must **not** use a dictionary.

Name: _____

Practice Exam Paper 3: Reading

Section A Questions and answers in English

Holidays

Ramón writes about his holidays in France. Read what he says.

> El año pasado fuimos de vacaciones cerca de las montañas pero lejos de la costa en Francia. Nos quedamos en un camping grande con una piscina muy buena. Había mucho que hacer para los jóvenes como pistas de tenis y de baloncesto, una sala de juegos con una televisión y el camping estaba muy cerca del pueblo donde se podía ir al parque, ir de compras y comer en restaurantes típicos.
>
> Hacía sol y bastante calor y a mi madre le gustaba tomar el sol todos los días, mientras mi hermano y yo jugábamos en la piscina o al tenis.
>
> *Ramón*

Complete the sentences.

Write the correct letter in the box.

$\boxed{0}\boxed{1}\cdot\boxed{1}$ Ramón stayed on a camp-site...

A	on the coast.
B	near the mountains.
C	in a town.

[1 mark]

$\boxed{0}\boxed{1}\cdot\boxed{2}$ For young people...

A	there was only a park.
B	there wasn't much to do.
C	there was lots to do.

[1 mark]

$\boxed{0}\boxed{1}\cdot\boxed{3}$ Ramón's mother...

A	played tennis with Ramón's brother.
B	liked to sunbathe.
C	swam in the pool.

[1 mark]

School Life

Read María's blog about school life:

> Realmente, no me gusta mucho el colegio. No me gustan muchos de los profesores porque son bastante antipáticos y no explican bien. Sin embargo, me cae bien a mi profesora de francés porque aunque es estricta, me ayuda mucho. También, creo que los exámenes causan mucho estrés porque hay que trabajar muchísimo y nunca tengo tiempo libre.
>
> Para mí, lo que menos me gusta de mi cole es un grupo de estudiantes que intenta intimidar a otros estudiantes. Pero supongo que el problema del acoso escolar existe en todos los institutos hasta cierto punto y por lo menos los profesores intentan resolverlo.
>
> Tenemos que llevar uniforme, que es muy feo – pantalones marrones y un jersey marrón con camisa blanca, pero por lo menos todos los estudiantes se visten de la misma manera. A mi parecer, esto es mejor porque es más elegante y así todos parecen iguales.
>
> En cuanto a mis amigos – tengo muchos y normalmente charlo con ellos durante el recreo. Es la única oportunidad de estar con ellos que tengo porque por la noche estoy muy ocupada con el trabajo del cole. ¡Qué aburrido!

0 2 · 1 Now read the sentences below and choose the four sentences that are correct.

Write the letters in the boxes below.

A	María doesn't like any of her teachers.
B	Her French teacher helps her.
C	The teachers don't do anything about the bullying problem.
D	She thinks bullying is a problem in all schools.
E	María thinks it's good to have a uniform.
F	She likes her uniform.
G	She has a job in the evenings.
H	María spends time with her friends at breaktime.

[ ] [ ] [ ] [ ]

[4 marks]

Alcohol

Read the interview about alcohol and write the correct name in the space provided.

Emilio: Mis amigos y yo nos emborrachamos por la calle porque los bares son caros. Me encanta estar con mis amigos y pasarlo bien y el alcohol nos ayuda a hacerlo. No molestamos a nadie.

Rosa: Nosotros salimos de copas una vez a la semana pero como las bebidas en los bares son muy caras, no solemos beber mucho. Sin embargo, me encanta el ambiente en los bares.

Carolina: Yo no bebo alcohol y a veces cuando salgo con mis amigas y ellas se emborrachan, me siento un poco aislada. Me molesta un poco pero no voy a empezar a beber porque no me gusta el sabor.

Jesús: Yo sé que el alcohol puede ser muy perjudicial para la salud y por eso no bebo con mis amigos. Si celebramos un cumpleaños en casa, pues a veces tomo una copa de vino pero nada más.

0 3 · 1 Who feels a little uncomfortable when friends are drinking alcohol?

_____

[1 mark]

0 3 · 2 Who prefers going out to the bars?

_____

[1 mark]

0 3 · 3 Who feels that alcohol helps them to have a good time?

_____

[1 mark]

0 3 · 4 Who sometimes has a glass of wine?

_____

[1 mark]

Local Area

0 4 · 1 Read the blog about Sergio's town and complete the text using words from the list.

Write the correct letter in the boxes.

> **Hola. Vivo en un barrio tranquilo en las afueras de una ciudad. Para mí lo ☐ es que no estoy muy lejos del centro de la ciudad y por eso, los sábados suelo ir de compras con mis amigos o vamos al cine o a la bolera. En el pasado no ☐ mucho que hacer para los jóvenes pero ahora se puede ☐ muchas cosas divertidas. En cuanto a los turistas, lo interesante es el castillo histórico al lado del río. Diría que la catedral también ☐ la pena visitar porque es preciosa.**

A	suele
B	había
C	visitar
D	era
E	mejor
F	merece
G	peor
H	hacer
J	valer

[4 marks]

Practice Exam Paper 3: Reading

Social Issues

You read this newspaper article about social issues.

Answer the questions in **English**.

En una investigación realizada en las calles de la capital, preguntamos al público sobre los asuntos sociales que más le preocupan. Un enorme 32% dijo que el desempleo es la cosa más preocupante de nuestra sociedad con un 19% preocupándose por la inmigración. Unos dijeron que ésta también afecta al paro.

Una sorpresa es que el 15% del público cree que hay que hacer más para mejorar el problema de la delincuencia que existe en nuestras comunidades, 5% más que el año pasado.

También, 9% de los madrileños piensa que el sexismo en el trabajo es todavía un problema, <<¡los jefes son siempre hombres!>> dijo una señora, mientras un 12% se inquieta por asuntos medioambientales. Y finalmente, 8% de personas cree que el terrorismo es algo que tenemos que vencer.

0 5 · 1 What is the most worrying issue for the people of Madrid?

....

[1 mark]

0 5 · 2 How has the percentage changed, regarding the problem of delinquency, since last year?

....

[1 mark]

0 5 · 3 What percentage of people is worried about the environment?

....

[1 mark]

0 5 · 4 What do people worry about least in Madrid?

....

[1 mark]

Social Media

You do some research about social media and read this interview with a student in the school magazine.

Hola, soy Paco. Uso la informática cada vez más en el colegio en mis clases y para hacer los deberes, etc. Sin embargo, lo que más me gusta es usar las redes sociales para una gama de cosas, tales como comunicarme con amigos, estar al día con lo que pasa en mi pueblo y en el mundo, buscar trabajo, colgar fotos y mucho más.

Mis padres no entienden por qué paso tanto tiempo usando sitios de web como Facebook y Twitter. Supongo que es porque, cuando eran jóvenes, mis padres nunca usaban los ordenadores para hacer las cosas que hago yo. En el cole escribían todo en los cuadernos y nadie tenía ordenadores en casa. Dicen que les preocupa mucho porque muchos jóvenes no salen nunca de su casa para quedarse con sus amigos, porque se comunican por el ordenador. Piensan que esto va a causar problemas sociales dentro de los próximos años.

Which stages do the following situations apply to?

Write **P** for something that happened in the **past**.
Write **N** for something that is happening **now**.
Write **F** for something that is going to happen in the **future**.

Write the correct letter in each box.

| 0 6 · 1 | Being up-to-date | | |

[1 mark]

| 0 6 · 2 | Using exercise books | | |

[1 mark]

| 0 6 · 3 | Staying at home | | |

[1 mark]

| 0 6 · 4 | Social problems | | |

[1 mark]

Lifestyle

Read the account of a singer's daily life and answer the questions.

Me llamo Virginia y soy cantante desde hace tres años. Ahora soy muy famosa y mi vida es muy diferente que antes.

Por la mañana suelo levantarme bastante temprano, sobre las seis y media, y paseo al perro por la playa. Antes de ser cantante profesional, podía despertarme a la hora que quería. ¡Cómo han cambiado las cosas! Después de desayunar, tengo que ensayar con mi grupo y por la tarde tenemos que hacer entrevistas y practicar más. Por la noche, hago una clase de aerobic.

El fin de semana me gusta charlar con mis padres un rato. Diría que me han influido mucho durante mi vida porque siempre me han escuchado y siempre he podido hablarles de cualquier cosa. Creo que es muy importante tener a alguien con quien puedes hablar de tus esperanzas y tus preocupaciones.

Answer the questions in **English**.

0 7 · 1 For how long has Virginia been a singer?

....

[1 mark]

0 7 · 2 Before becoming a famous singer, what time did Virginia used to get up?

....

[1 mark]

0 7 · 3 How many times a day does she practise her music?

....

[1 mark]

0 7 · 4 In which two ways have her parents helped influence her in the past?

....

....

[2 marks]

0 7 · 5 Which two things does Virginia think it is important to talk to someone about?

....

....

[2 marks]

Relationships

Read the article about relationships within the family.

¿Problemas familiares?

¿Te llevas mal con tus padres? ¿Estáis siempre peleando? Pues, según una encuesta reciente, eso es lo normal para los jóvenes de 15 años para arriba. Muchos jóvenes se quejan de que sus padres no les entienden y dicen que les exigen demasiado en el colegio y que hay siempre muchas peleas sobre los deberes. "No hablo mucho con mis padres" dicen.

Para intentar evitar estas peleas, hay que charlar más con tus padres y explicarles cómo te sientes, si te molesta algo o si estás estresado por algo. Tus padres quieren ayudarte y no quieren pasar todo el tiempo discutiendo. Puede que tengan sugerencias que te ayudarán, ellos antes eran jóvenes también.

Una buena idea es establecer unas reglas básicas entre vosotros mismos y así sabrás lo que te van a permitir hacer y por qué, y eso puede ayudar a mantener la paz un poco. Son tus padres no son extraterrestres – ¡Háblales!

08 · 1 According to the article, which four statements are true?

Write the correct letters in the boxes.

A	Many young people aged 15 and above don't get on with their parents.
B	Many parents want their children to leave school and get a job.
C	There are lots of arguments about homework.
D	Young people should avoid arguments by not talking to their parents so much.
E	Parents don't want to hear about stress from their children.
F	Parents may be able to make some helpful suggestions.
G	Establishing ground rules can help to keep the peace.
H	Sometimes parents are like aliens!

[4 marks]

Section B Questions and answers in Spanish

Planes para el futuro

Lee lo que dicen Beatriz y Paco sobre sus planes para el futuro.

Beatriz: En septiembre iré al colegio para estudiar las ciencias. Sueño con ser médica y voy a intentar hacer unas prácticas en un hospital en el verano.

Paco: Hice mis prácticas laborales en un garaje trabajando como mecánico y me gustó mucho. Pienso dejar el instituto después de los exámenes y buscar un trabajo. No tengo ganas de trabajar en una oficina porque me parece monótono.

Contesta las preguntas **en español**.

0 9 · 1 ¿Qué trabajo quiere hacer Beatriz en el futuro?

....

[1 mark]

0 9 · 2 ¿Qué planes tiene Beatriz para el verano?

....

[1 mark]

0 9 · 3 ¿Qué piensa hacer Paco al terminar el instituto?

....

[1 mark]

0 9 · 4 ¿Qué es lo que no quiere hacer Paco?

....

[1 mark]

El turismo

Vas a una agencia de viajes para elegir tus próximas vacaciones. Lees este folleto.

Los Andes Si lo suyo es escaparse a la tranquilidad para respirar el aire libre y hacer senderismo, venga a las montañas más famosas de América Latina.

México Si busca usted una gran fiesta, venga a México para celebrar el Carnaval con nosotros. Si quiere disfrutar de las procesiones y bailes tradicionales, o quiere ver los combates de flores, éste es el sitio ideal para usted.

Perú Si le impresionan los Incas y sus magníficas creaciones arquitectónicas, venga a visitar Perú, donde encontrará unos sitios de interés internacional. Está aquí esperándole.

Argentina Si goza usted de la cocina, venga a nuestra rica tierra para saborear unos de los mejores platos del mundo.

Colombia Si quiere disfrutar de unas costas poco conocidas y relajarse en la arena dorada, y luego, descubrir la fascinante vida marina de nuestras aguas cristalinas, este país sería su destino ideal.

Contesta las preguntas **en español**.

Ejemplo ¿Dónde irías para probar comida deliciosa?

Argentina

1 0 · 1 ¿Dónde irías para pasar los días caminando y estar en paz?

[1 mark]

1 0 · 2 ¿Dónde pasarías las vacaciones si querías relajarte o pasar el día nadando?

[1 mark]

1 0 · 3 ¿Dónde irías para aprender sobre una civilización anciana y ver los edificios antiguos?

[1 mark]

1 0 · 4 ¿Dónde irías para festejar una celebración típica del país?

[1 mark]

El medio ambiente

Lee el blog sobre los problemas medioambientales.

> El tema del medio ambiente me preocupa mucho porque no creo que hagamos lo suficiente para mejorar la situación. En el futuro, me gustaría ver más centros de reciclaje en todas las ciudades. A la vez, los gobiernos locales deben invertir más dinero en otros métodos de producir energía como la energía eólica. Es imprescindible que todos hagamos lo más posible para mejorar la situación.
>
> En el pasado no había mucho tráfico pero ahora todo el mundo viaja en coche y muchas familias tienen dos coches. Como resultado hay mucha contaminación del aire, que me parece muy serio.
>
> Los problemas del medio ambiente afectan al mundo entero. Tenemos que trabajar juntos para buscar alternativas a los combustibles fósiles porque se están agotando. No es suficiente decir que un problema en otro país no nos afecta aquí en nuestro país, como por ejemplo, la deforestación. ¡Hay que salvar el planeta!
>
> Paco Hernández

Contesta las preguntas **en español.**

Ejemplo ¿Por qué piensa Paco que el medio ambiente es un problema serio?

Porque no hacemos lo necesario para mejorarlo.

1 1 · 1 Según Paco, ¿qué deben hacer los políticos?

[1 mark]

1 1 · 2 ¿Qué está causando la contaminación atmosférica, según Paco?

[1 mark]

1 1 · 3 ¿Qué cree Paco que no debemos usar más?

[1 mark]

1 1 · 4 ¿A quiénes les afecta la deforestación?

[1 mark]

Escritores famosos

Lee los textos.

A	*Federico García Lorca*	Quiero beber agua y no hay vaso ni agua; quiero subir al monte y no tengo pies, quiero bordar mis enaguas y no encuentro los hilos.
B	*Laura Esquivel*	Con un día de anticipación se tenían que empezar a pelar ajos, limpiar chiles y a moler especias.
C	*Fernando Fernán Gómez*	Esto podría ser un buen campo de batalla. En aquel bosquecillo está emboscada la infantería. Por la explanada avancen los tanques.
D	*Carmen Martín Gaite*	Yo también compré sandía, que la vendían por rajas gordas, y… me goteaba el zumo por la barbilla.
E	*Gustavo Adolfo Bécquer*	…me gustan tanto los ojos de ese color; son tan expresivos, tan melancólicos…y sus cabellos, negros, muy negros, y largos para que floten…

Escribe la letra correcta en cada casilla.

1 2 · 1 ¿Quién habla de una guerra imaginaria?

[1 mark]

1 2 · 2 ¿Quién está describiendo a alguien?

[1 mark]

1 2 · 3 ¿Quién habla de la frustración y la futilidad?

[1 mark]

1 2 · 4 ¿Quién está preparando la comida?

[1 mark]

1 2 · 5 ¿Quién describe comer una fruta?

[1 mark]

Practice Exam Paper 3: Reading

Section C Translation into English

1 3 · 1 Your friend is trying to get fit and asks you to translate part of an article that they have read in a Spanish magazine, on the topic of health and fitness. Translate into English.

> Estoy intentando comer sanamente y entonces, suelo comer una dieta equilibrada. Ayer preparé lentejas y me gustaron mucho. También, quiero hacer más ejercicio y sé que si hago deporte cuatro veces por semana, me sentiré mejor. Si pudiera, lo haría todos los días pero no tengo tiempo. ¡Venga, hazlo conmigo!

[9 marks]

END OF QUESTIONS

Collins

GCSE
Spanish

H

Higher Tier Paper 4 Writing

Time allowed: 1 hour 15 minutes

Instructions

- Use black ink or black ball-point pen.
- You must answer **three** questions.
- You must answer **either** Question 1.1 **or** Question 1.2. You must **not** answer **both** of these questions.
- You must answer **either** Question 2.1 **or** Question 2.2. You must **not** answer **both** of these questions.
- You must answer Question 3.
- Answer all questions in **Spanish**.
- Answer the questions in the spaces provided.

Instructions

- The marks for questions are shown in brackets.
- The maximum mark for this paper is 60.
- You must **not** use a dictionary.
- To score the highest marks for Question 1.1/Question 2.1, you must write something about each bullet point. Use a variety of vocabulary and structures and include your opinions.
- To score the highest marks for Question 1.2/Question 2.2, you must write something about each bullet point. Use a variety of vocabulary and structures and include your opinions and reasons.

Name: ....

Practice Exam Paper 4: Writing

Answer **either** Question 1.1 **or** Question 1.2.

You must **not** answer **both** of these questions.

EITHER Question 1.1

0 1 · 1 Acabas de ir de compras al nuevo centro comercial y decides escribir a tu amigo español para contarle todo.

Escríbele un correo electrónico.

Menciona:

- dónde prefieres ir de compras normalmente y por qué

- qué compraste y para quién

- tus opiniones sobre el centro comercial

- dónde vas a ir de compras en el futuro

Escribe aproximadamente **90** palabras en **español**. Responde a todos los aspectos de la pregunta.

[16 marks]

OR Question 1.2

0 1 · 2 Escribes un correo electrónico a tu amigo español sobre tu fin de semana y tu tiempo libre.

Escríbele un correo electrónico.

Menciona:

- qué hiciste el fin de semana pasado en tu tiempo libre

- qué te gusta hacer con tus amigos

- tus planes para el próximo fin de semana

- tus opiniones sobre el tiempo libre

Escribe aproximadamente **90** palabras en **español**. Responde a todos los aspectos de la pregunta.

[16 marks]

Practice Exam Paper 4: Writing

Answer **either** Question 2.1 **or** Question 2.2.

You must **not** answer **both** of these questions.

EITHER Question 2.1

0 2 . 1 Lees un blog sobre los problemas medioambientales y mandas un mensaje a tu amigo español.

Escríbele un mensaje.

Menciona:

- los problemas medioambientales que existen en tu región

- las posibles soluciones y tus opiniones

Escribe aproximadamente **150** palabras en **español**. Responde a los dos aspectos de la pregunta.

[32 marks]

OR Question 2.2

0 2 . 2   Lees un artículo en una revista española sobre los jóvenes y la paga. La revista quiere información sobre jóvenes de países diferentes. Decides responder.

Escribe un artículo.

Menciona:

- cómo ganas dinero y tus opiniones

- qué vas a hacer con tu dinero en el futuro

Escribe aproximadamente **150** palabras en **español**. Responde a los dos aspectos de la pregunta.

[32 marks]

0 3 . 1 Translate the following passage into **Spanish**.

> Last year I went on holiday to Spain. I didn't go by plane. We usually go to Italy which is very beautiful. This year we have to visit England because my parents want to go to the countryside. I think it is going to be boring. Beaches are much more fun.

[12 marks]

END OF QUESTIONS

Answers

Pages 148–152

Me, My Family and Friends

1. a) i)–ii) **Any two from**: He's Italian; He's a doctor; He's funny; He's kind. [2]
    b) i)–iii) She's good-looking/beautiful; She's intelligent; She's hard-working. [3]
    c) He's a cook. [1]
    d) She's unfriendly. [1]
    e) She's quiet/shy. [1]
    f) A teacher. [1]

2. Creo que mi hermano es muy inteligente…–…porque aprobó todos sus exámenes. [1]
    Mi madre tiene el pelo largo…–…y rizado con los ojos verdes. [1]
    En mi opinión mi padre es muy…–…estricto, pero también puede ser muy gracioso. [1]
    Mi abuela es muy simpática y…–…cariñosa y siempre me ayuda con todo. [1]
    Tengo dos hermanas que pueden ser…–…impacientes y a veces me molestan. [1]
    Mi tía Paula es muy activa y…–…practica deporte cinco veces a la semana. [1]

3. a) B [1]
    b) B [1]
    c) B [1]

4. a) Yes – she checks it every 10 minutes, (including during lessons) [1]
    b) To keep in contact with family / friends / To send messages [1]
    c) Yes – she would ask her parents to bring it to school for her if she forgot it / she couldn't go for a day without it [1]
    d) If you use it safely/carefully, it's fine/not a problem [1]

5. B, C, F, G (in any order) [4]

6. C, G, F, A, D (must be in this order) [5]

Pages 153–156

Free-time Activities

1. a) las canciones [1]
    b) la cocina [1]
    c) los deportes de invierno [1]
    d) el rugby [1]
    e) los videojuegos [1]
    f) la vela [1]

2. D, F, I, A, H (must be in this order) [5]

3. a) Ángel [1]
    b) Jaime [1]
    c) Rosi [1]
    d) Ángel [1]
    e) Jaime [1]
    f) Rosi [1]
    g) Jaime [1]
    h) Ángel [1]
    i) Jaime [1]
    j) Jaime [1]

Qu		Key idea	Accept	Reject	Mark
4.	Me gusta mucho escuchar música y…	I really like listening to music and…	I like listening to music a lot and…		1
	…lo que más me gusta es la música rock.	…what I like the most is rock music.	…what I most like is rock music.	…what more I like is…	1
	Suelo escucharla en mi móvil…	I usually listen to it on my (mobile) phone…			1
	…cuando voy en autobús al colegio…	…when I go to school on the bus…		…when I go by bus to school…	1
	…y también durante los recreos….	…and also during breaks…			1
	…y por la noche en casa.	…and in the evening / at night at home.			1
	La semana pasada fui a un concierto…	Last week I went to a concert…			1
	…de mi grupo preferido.	…of my favourite group.			1
	¡Fue estupendo!	It was wonderful! / brilliant!	great, etc.		1

5. a) Practicar deporte; ir al cine; leer (novelas) [3]
    b) Es una manera de mantenerse en forma. / Se mantiene en forma / Para mantenerse en forma. [1]
    c) (A) (los /sus) abuelos [1]
    d) (Con) (los / sus) amigos [1]
    e) (Con) cuatro compañeros / amigos (del colegio) [1]

6. ¿Cuánto cuestan las manzanas? – 2 [1]
    Sí, deme un kilo de peras, por favor. – 6 [1]
    No, nada más, gracias. ¿Cuánto es? – 8 [1]
    ¿Qué desea? – 1 [1]
    Dos euros el kilo. – 3 [1]
    Aquí tiene, gracias, adiós. – 10 [1]
    Aquí tiene. ¿Algo más? – 5 [1]
    ¿Quiere algo más? – 7 [1]
    Pues, un kilo de manzanas, por favor. – 4 [1]
    Son tres euros cincuenta. – 9 [1]

7. a) D [1]
    b) F [1]
    c) A [1]
    d) C [1]
    e) B [1]
    f) E [1]

8. ¿Perdone, dónde están los aseos? – Excuse me, where are the toilets? [1]
    ¿Qué sabores hay? – What flavours are there? [1]
    Perdone, falta un tenedor aquí. – Excuse me, there's a fork missing here. [1]
    Hoy, vamos a almorzar temprano. – Today, we're going to have lunch early. [1]
    ¿Pedimos la cuenta? – Shall we ask for the bill? [1]
    ¿Cuánto le debo? – How much do I owe you? [1]
    La comida aquí es muy rica. – The food here is really delicious. [1]

Pages 157–161

Environment and Social Issues

1. C, D, F, H (in any order) [4]

Qu		Accept	Mark
2.	I live in a small town...	Vivo en un (pequeño) pueblo pequeño...	1
	...in the country.	...en el campo.	1
	I like it a lot because...	Me gusta mucho porque...	1
	...it is pretty.	...es bonito.	1
	We have a church and some shops.	Tenemos una iglesia y unas tiendas.	1
	Also, there is a park where...	También hay un parque donde...	1
	...I like to play football with my friends.	..me gusta jugar al fútbol con mis amigos.	1
	In the future I would like...	En el futuro, me gustaría/querría...	1
	...to live in the mountains.	...vivir en las montañas.	1

3. A 5 [1]
    B 3 [1]
    C 6 [1]
    D 1 [1]
    E 2 [1]
    F 4 [1]

4. a) Tiredness, depression and stress. [3]
    b) A bit of everything (except fish). [1]
    c) Swimming. [1]
    d) There are a lot of health risks. [1]
    e) She thinks it makes them feel more grown up. [1]

5. 1 B [1]
    2 C [1]
    3 E [1]

6. a) N [1]
    b) P [1]
    c) P [1]
    d) N [1]
    e) P [1]

    f) N [1]
    g) N [1]
    h) P [1]

7. A 4 [1]
    B 6 [1]
    C 1 [1]
    D 7 [1]
    E 2 [1]
    F 5 [1]
    G 3 [1]

8. A 5 [1]
    B 2 [1]
    C 6 [1]
    D 1 [1]
    E 4 [1]
    F 3 [1]

9. a) i) Perdone (usted), ¿dónde está Correos, por favor? [1]
       ii) Siga todo recto y está enfrente del mercado. [1]
    b) i) ¿Por dónde se va al museo, por favor? [1]
       ii) Tome la primera a la derecha y siga todo recto. [1]
    c) i) Perdone, ¿puede decirme dónde está la plaza mayor, por favor? [1]
       ii) Sí, cruce el puente y siga todo recto. Está a la izquierda. [1]
    d) i) ¿Está lejos la comisaría? [1]
       ii) No, está a cinco minutos a pie; baje la calle y está al final, al lado del cine. [1]
    e) i) ¿Puede ayudarme por favor? No encuentro el mercado. [1]
       ii) Cruce el río y siga todo recto. Está en la plaza mayor. [1]

Pages 162–165

Travel and Tourism

1. a) F [1]
    b) C [1]
    c) E [1]
    d) A [1]
    e) H [1]
    f) D [1]
    g) B [1]
    h) G [1]

2. A 2 [1]
    B 5 [1]
    C 6 [1]
    D 8 [1]
    E 1 [1]
    F 7 [1]
    G 4 [1]
    H 3 [1]

3. a) 1 month. [1]
    b) In her family's apartment. [1]
    c) See her friends; spend all day at the beach. [2]
    d) Swim / practise water sports. [1]
    e) A village in the mountains. [1]
    f) Took photos; bought souvenirs for grandparents. [2]
    g) In a restaurant near their apartment. [1]

4. a) martes [1]
    b) jueves [1]
    c) viernes [1]

5. a) N [1]
   b) P [1]
   c) P [1]
   d) P [1]
   e) F [1]
   f) F [1]

6. A 2 [1]
   B 5 [1]
   C 1 [1]
   D 4 [1]
   E 3 [1]
   F 6 [1]

Pages 166–169

Studies and Employment

1. a) Negative [1]
   b) Positive [1]
   c) Negative [1]
   d) Positive [1]
   e) Positive [1]
   f) Positive [1]
   g) Positive [1]
   h) Negative [1]

2. a) True [1]
   b) True [1]
   c) False [1]
   d) False [1]
   e) False [1]
   f) False [1]

3. a) N [1]
   b) P [1]
   c) N [1]
   d) F [1]
   e) P [1]
   f) F [1]

4. D, F, H, B, E (must be in this order) [5]

5. a) Me gustan las matemáticas. [1]
   b) No me gusta la informática. [1]
   c) Me interesan las ciencias. [1]
   d) No me gustan nada los deberes. [1]
   e) Las ciencias son más difíciles que las
      matemáticas. [1]
   f) El español es tan fácil como el francés. [1]
   g) Mi profesor de religión es el mejor profesor en el
      colegio. [1]

6. a) Elena P+N [1]
   b) Paco P [1]
   c) Miguel P+N [1]

7. C, D, F, H (in any order) [4]

Pages 170–172

Grammar 1

1. a) M, S [1]
   b) F, S [1]
   c) M, P [1]
   d) F, S [1]
   e) M, P [1]
   f) F, P [1]
   g) F, P [1]

   h) F, S [1]
   i) M, P [1]
   j) F, P [1]

2. F, D, A, G, B (must be in this order) [5]

3. a) I didn't tell you the truth. [1]
   b) Give me the money. [1]
   c) She/He never speaks to us. [1]
   d) I saw her yesterday at school. [1]
   e) María said 'hello' to him/her. [1]
   f) Give her the ice-cream. [1]
   g) Ask him. [1]

4. a) deprisa [1]
   b) muchas veces [1]
   c) demasiado [1]
   d) bien [1]
   e) sinceramente [1]
   f) aquí [1]

5. a) para [1]
   b) por; para (in that order) [2]
   c) por [1]
   d) por [1]
   e) para [1]
   f) para [1]
   g) para [1]
   h) por [1]

6. a) adónde [1]
   b) por qué [1]
   c) cómo [1]
   d) quién [1]
   e) cuándo [1]
   f) cuántas [1]
   g) cuál [1]
   h) dónde [1]

Pages 173–174

Grammar 2

1. a) me ducho [1]
   b) lavo [1]
   c) enciendo [1]
   d) limpiar [1]
   e) comparto [1]
   f) madrugar [1]
   g) está [1]

2. Me despierto – I wake up [1]
   Pensamos – We think [1]
   Quieren – They want [1]
   Te diviertes – You amuse / enjoy yourself [1]
   Pienso – I think [1]
   Cierras – You close [1]
   Se despierta – He/She wakes up [1]
   Quiero – I want [1]
   Empieza – It begins [1]
   Cierra – It closes [1]

3. a) Siguen las instrucciones. [1]
   b) Siempre ríe mucho. [1]
   c) Repetimos los verbos todos los días. [1]
   d) Me visto a las siete. [1]
   e) Siempre pide la cuenta en español. [1]
   f) A veces nieva en enero. [1]

4. A/D (nunca/jamás); F (no); D/A (jamás/nunca); C
   (tampoco); B (ninguna) (in that order) [5]

5. a) Estoy leyendo un libro. [1]
b) ¿Qué estás haciendo? [1]
c) Julio está nadando en la piscina. [1]
d) María y Nico están hablando por teléfono. [1]
e) ¿Dónde estás pasando las vacaciones? [1]
f) ¿Qué está comiendo? [1]

6. a) es [1]
b) son [1]
c) está [1]
d) está, es (in that order) [2]
e) estoy [1]

Pages 175–176

Grammar 3

1. a) A [1]
b) C [1]
c) C [1]
d) A [1]
e) C [1]
f) C [1]

2. Está mañana he…–…hablado con mi madre y está de acuerdo conmigo. [1]
Mi amiga francesa me ha …–… escrito una carta para describirme su pueblo. [1]
No encuentro mi móvil. ¿Mamá has…–…visto mi teléfono? [1]
¿Sabes lo que han…–…descubierto en el Amazonas? [1]
¡Ay, qué lástima! Las nubes han…–…cubierto las montañas y ahora no podemos ver nada. [1]
¿Nosotros? No, no hemos…–…vuelto nunca al restaurante. [1]

3. a) A [1]
b) A [1]
c) B [1]
d) C [1]
e) B [1]
f) C [1]
g) A [1]

4. a) (Yo) hablaba bien el alemán. [1]
b) Mi hermano iba al parque los fines de semana. [1]
c) Mis padres siempre iban a Francia. [1]
d) (Yo) salía mucho. [1]

5. a) B [1]
b) C [1]
c) C [1]
d) A [1]
e) B [1]

6. a) Tome la primera a la derecha y siga todo recto. [1]
b) Cruce la plaza y baje la calle. [1]
c) Suba la calle y tome la tercera a la derecha. [1]
d) Cruce el puente y gire a la izquierda. [1]

Pages 177–189

Higher Tier Paper 1 Listening – Mark Scheme

Section A Questions and answers in English

Qu	Accept	Mark
1	His house **P** = 1; His bedroom **P + N** = 1 (must be in this order)	2

Qu	Accept	Mark
2	Bedroom space **P** = 1 The colour **N** = 1 (must be in this order)	2

Qu	Accept	Mark
3	E	1

Qu	Accept	Mark
4	B	1

Qu	Accept	Mark
5	F	1

Qu	Accept	Mark
6	A	1

Qu	Accept	Mark
7	H	1

Qu	Accept	Mark
8	C	1

Qu	Key idea	Accept	Reject	Mark
9.1	Quite well	They get on quite well most of time	He can be a pain	1
9.2	She is understanding AND she can talk to her about anything			2
9.3	Her stepfather / Ángel is nice / she gets on well with her stepfather			1
9.4	Her mum			1

Qu	Key idea	Mark
10	The shopping centre is going to close	1

Qu	Key idea	Reject	Mark
11	They don't do <u>enough</u> exercise / they have weight problems	They don't do exercise	1
12	68%		1
13	They don't know how to cook / prepare <u>healthy</u> food	They don't know how to cook	1

Qu				Mark
14.1	It is decreasing / going down (a little)			1
14.2	(the number of) young people that get drunk (at weekends)	The number of boys that get drunk		1

Qu	Accept	Mark
15	C, E (in any order)	2

Qu	Key idea	Mark
16	Organise the clothes AND attend to / deal with / serve the customers	2
17.1	She finds it fun / there is a variety of people (that come to the shop) / she (sometimes) chats to the customers	1
17.2	Do charitable / charity work in South America	1

Qu	Key idea	Accept	Reject	Mark
18	Trying to get good marks (all of the time)	Having to study so much / having to do homework every night		1

Qu	Accept	Mark
19	B, D, F (in any order)	3

Qu	Key idea	Mark
20	In the supermarket On the Internet	2

Qu	Accept	Mark
21	C	1

Qu	Key idea	Accept	Reject	Mark
22.1	Because she can't do anything (about the situation)	It was hard to see what is happening to people (in Africa)		1
22.2	Pressurise the government to intervene in the problem	Pressurise the government to act / into action		1
22.3	ANY TWO OF: clothes, food, medication, anything else that they need			2
22.4	C			1

Qu	Accept	Mark
23.1	B	1

Qu	Key idea	Mark
23.2	He won't have to work when he doesn't want to	1

Section B Questions and answers in Spanish

Qu	Accept	Reject	Mark
24	Son (demasiado) caros Prefieren que (lo) tenga uno / un móvil / Prefieren que pueda ponerse en contacto		2
25	Es útil para el trabajo escolar / buscar información para hacer los deberes	Buscar información	1

Qu	Accept	Mark
26	B and D	2

Qu	Accept	Reject	Mark
27.1	Ir a sitios (nuevos) para conocer (los) / entender la cultura de un lugar		1
27.2	Ir de vacaciones apartes / separados		1

Qu	Accept	Mark
28.1	C	1

Qu	Key idea	Mark
28.2	Un aumento en las enfermedades <u>respiratorias</u>	1

Pages 190–194

Higher Tier Paper 2 Speaking – Mark Scheme

Photo card – Example answers:

1st question
En la foto hay un grupo de siete jóvenes jugando al voleibol en la playa. Me parece que lo están pasando bien porque todos están sonriendo. Creo que es durante el verano porque hace buen tiempo y todos llevan ropa de verano como pantalones cortos con camiseta. También van descalzos. Creo que es un grupo de amigos y en mi opinión se están divirtiendo mucho.

> **Tip**
> When asked to describe the photo, try to give as much detail as possible and include an opinion. Useful words to know to describe this photo: pasarlo bien (to have a good time), sonreír (to smile – a stem-changing verb), divertirse (to enjoy oneself – stem-changing and reflexive).

2nd question
Para mi un buen amigo debe ser leal y honesto porque creo que es importante poder tener confianza en mis amigos. También me gusta pasarlo bien con mis amigos, así que creo que un buen amigo tiene que tener un

buen sentido de humor. Mis amigos suelen tener gustos parecidos a los míos en cuanto a música y cine o deportes y eso puede ser algo importante también, porque así nos gusta hacer cosas similares.

Tip
Always aim to develop your answer, by going beyond what the question asks you. Note how, in the example above, the answer moves on from what makes a good friend to why this is important.

3rd question

La semana pasada fui al gimnasio con mi mejor amigo para hacer ejercicio y luego el sábado, fui de compras en el centro con otros amigos. ¡Lo pasamos fenomenal! Creo que es importante pasar tiempo con tus amigos porque puedes hablar de muchas cosas con ellos, incluso los problemas. Este fin de semana voy a quedar con unos amigos de mi colegio para ir al cine.

Tip
There will always be a question which requires you to answer in a tense other than the present tense. In this case, the question is in the preterite tense. However, make sure you show that you can combine several different tenses in your answer. Note how the answer above uses the preterite tense, the present tense and then the near future tense. Note how the answer above also has a change of person of the verb, which always impresses the examiner!

Role Play – Example answers and information:

Your teacher will start the role play by saying an introductory text such as:

Introduction: Estás hablando con tu amigo español sobre las vacaciones. Yo soy tu amigo.

1. **Teacher:** ¿Adónde fuiste de vacaciones el año pasado?
   Where did you go on holiday last year?

   Student: El año pasado fui de vacaciones a España con mi familia.
   Last year I went on holiday to Spain with my family.

Tip
Make sure you include two elements as required in the question.

2. Unprepared question
   Teacher: ¿Cómo prefieres viajar cuando vas de vacaciones?
   How do you prefer to travel when you go on holiday?

   Student: Suggested answers- any of- Normalmente prefiero viajar/ir en avión / en barco / en tren / en coche.
   Usually I prefer to travel/go by plane / boat / train / car.

Tip
Make sure you listen carefully to the question word and the tense in the question. Any method of transport expressed in the present tense is acceptable.

3. **Teacher:** ¿Qué hiciste durante tus vacaciones?
   What did you do on your holiday?

   Student: Visité muchos pueblos bonitos y también nadé en la piscina.
   I visited lots of pretty towns and I also swam in the pool.

Tip
The question requires two elements in the past tense.

4. **Teacher:** ¿Adónde vas de vacaciones este año?
   Where are you going to go on holiday this year?

   Student: Voy a ir a Italia en el verano.
   I am going to go to Italy in the summer.

Tip
The question is in the future tense and the student has added an extra element to the answer.

5. Asking a question
   Student: ¿Qué tipo de vacaciones prefieres?
   What type of holiday do you prefer?

   Teacher: Pues, prefiero hacer turismo cuando estoy de vacaciones.
   Well, I prefer to go sightseeing when I am on holiday.

Tip
There will always be a question to ask, so ensure that you revise how to ask a question.

Tip
When you are preparing for your role-play consider:

- How many elements you need to include in each of your answers.

- Whether you need to use 'tú' or 'usted'.

- The tense that is expected – the tense will be inferred. For example in this role-play we have the past implied by el año pasado (last year).

- For the question you need to ask, examine the tense of the question and whether you are going to say 'tú' or 'usted'.

General Conversation – Example answers:

Theme 1: Identity and Culture

1. Diría que me llevo mejor con mi hermana mayor porque es muy simpática y podemos hablar de cualquier cosa. También es más madura que mi hermano y solemos pasar mucho tiempo juntas.

2. Pues sí, a mí me gustaría casarme pero solo quiero una boda pequeña porque creo que es más íntima. Y las bodas pueden ser muy caras también, que me parece una pérdida de dinero.

3. Mi familia entera siempre se junta para celebrar el día de Navidad. Comemos mucha comida rica y siempre lo pasamos muy bien. ¡El año pasado eramos diecinueve personas!

4. Creo que me gustaría hacer el paracaidismo porque me parece muy emocionante. Sería una experiencia inolvidable aunque bastante cara.

5. Lo uso para muchas cosas, por ejemplo, suelo descargar música y películas y también puedo buscar información para completar mis deberes. Y por supuesto me encanta acceder a las redes sociales y comunicarme con mis amigos.

Theme 2: Local, National, International and Global Areas of Interest

1. Mi casa ideal sería muy grande y tendría un gimnasio y una piscina porque me encantan los deportes. Lo ideal sería estar situada cerca del centro de la ciudad.

2. Lo que más me gusta de mi región es que hay mucho que hacer. Se puede ir a la playa o dar una vuelta por el campo y luego, si te apetece, hay un montón de bares y restaurantes en el centro.

3. Practicar deporte es una buena manera de mantenerte en forma y te hace relajarte y evitar el estrés. La semana pasada, jugué dos veces al fútbol y también fui a la piscina y al gimnasio.

4. En mi opinión, algunos jóvenes piensan que es muy guay emborracharse y creen que tienen que beber mucho para pasarlo bien. Yo no estoy de acuerdo.

5. Lo que más me preocupa es el medio ambiente. Creo que tenemos que hacer más porque estamos destruyendo el planeta a un ritmo alarmante. Voy a hacerme socio de una organización benéfica porque creo que es imprescindible que actuemos ahora.

Theme 3: Current and Future Study and Employment

1. Pues, no creo que sea tan serio en mi instituto. Los profesores son muy buenos si hay un problema entre alumnos y siempre intentan ayudarnos a resolverlo. Pero creo que en algunos sitios, sí, es un problema.

2. Personalmente, quiero ir a la universidad porque quiero ser veterinario. Estudiaré las ciencias, que sería bastante difícil, pero es mi sueño.

3. Para mí, lo más importante es que te guste el trabajo y que estés contento. No quiero hacer un trabajo simplemente porque paga bien si el trabajo es muy monótono.

4. A mí me gustaría tener un trabajo para poder ganar un poco de dinero, pero me resultaría muy difícil porque siempre tengo un montón de deberes para hacer. Quizás el año que viene pueda buscar algo.

5. Pues, sí, me encantaría trabajar en España o Francia para poder usar mis idiomas y también sería una experiencia muy útil para el futuro.

Pages 195–208

Higher Tier Paper 3 Reading – Mark Scheme

Section A Questions and answers in English

Qu	Accept	Mark
1.1	B	1
1.2	C	1
1.3	B	1

Qu	Accept	Mark
2.1	B	1
	D	1
	E	1
	H (in any order)	1

Qu	Accept	Mark
3.1	Carolina	1
3.2	Rosa	1
3.3	Emilio	1
3.4	Jesús	1

Qu	Accept	Mark
4.1	E B H F (in this order)	4

Qu	Key idea	Accept	Mark
5.1	Unemployment	Being out of work	1
5.2	It's increased/gone up by 5%		1
5.3	12%		1
5.4	Terrorism		1

Qu	Accept	Mark
6.1	N	1
6.2	P	1
6.3	N	1
6.4	F	1

Qu	Key idea	Reject	Mark
7.1	3 years	Since she was 3 years old	1
7.2	Whenever (she wanted)	Any specific time	1
7.3	Twice		1
7.4	(they) have (always) listened (to her) (She has) always been able to talk to them (about anything)		2
7.5	Your hopes and worries		2

Qu	Accept	Mark
8.1	A	1
	C	1
	F	1
	G (in any order)	1

Section B Questions and answers in Spanish

Qu	Key idea	Accept	Reject	Mark
9.1	(Quiere ser) médica	doctora		1
9.2	(intentar) hacer prácticas (en un hospital)		Ir a un hospital	1
9.3	Buscar un trabajo	Encontrar un trabajo		1
9.4	Trabajar en una oficina			1

Qu	Accept	Mark
10.1	Los Andes	1
10.2	Colombia	1
10.3	Perú	1
10.4	México	1

Qu	Key idea	Accept	Reject	Mark
11.1	Invertir/ gastar más dinero en otros métodos de (producir) energía	Dar más dinero a otros métodos de (producir) energía		1
11.2	El tráfico / los coches	Todo el mundo viaja en coche / muchas familias tienen dos coches		1
11.3	Los combustibles fósiles			1
11.4	(a) todos / todo el mundo		(a) Nosotros / nuestro país	1

Qu	Accept	Mark
12.1	C	1
12.2	E	1
12.3	A	1
12.4	B	1
12.5	D	1

Section C Translation into English

Qu		Key Idea	Accept	Reject	Mark
13.1	Estoy intentando comer sanamente y entonces…	I am trying to eat healthily and so/therefore…			1
	…suelo comer una dieta equilibrada.	I usually eat a balanced diet.	I am accustomed to eating a balanced diet.		1
	Ayer preparé lentejas y me gustaron mucho.	Yesterday I cooked /prepared lentils and I really liked them.	… and I liked them a lot.	Wrong tense	1
	También, quiero hacer más ejercicio…	Also, I want to do more exercise…	…exercise more…		1
	…y sé que si hago deporte cuatro veces por semana…	…and I know that if I do sport 4 times a week…	…four times per week…		1
	…me sentiré mejor.	…I will feel better.		It will make me feel better.	1
	Si pudiera, lo haría todos los días…	If I could, I would do it every day…		Wrong tense	1
	…pero no tengo tiempo.	…but I don't have time.		Wrong tense	1
	¡Venga, hazlo conmigo!	Come on, do it with me!			1

Pages 209–218

Higher Tier Paper 4 Writing – Mark Scheme

Question 1

For this question (1.1 or 1.2) there are 4 compulsory bullet points, which must all be attempted, although there does not need to be an equal amount written for each point. The marks are awarded for Content (10 marks) and Quality of Language (6 marks). The number of words is 90 and the maximum mark is 16.

Content

Level	Marks	Response
5	9–10	Very good response covering all bullet points. Communication mainly clear and opinions given.
4	7–8	Good response covering all bullet points. Communication is mostly clear with only a few ambiguities. Quite a lot of information given with opinions.
3	5–6	Reasonable response covering most of the bullet points. Communication mostly clear but with some ambiguities. Some information and an opinion given.
2	3–4	Basic response covering some bullet points. Communication sometimes clear but messages sometimes break down. Little information. Opinion given.
1	1–2	Limited response covering some bullet points. Communication may not be clear and messages break down. Very little information. Opinion may be given.
0	0	Content does not meet the standard for Level 1.

Quality of Language

Level	Marks	Response
3	5–6	A variety of vocabulary used. Attempts at complex structures evident. Three time frames attempted, largely successfully. Mainly minor errors. Some errors may occur in more complex sentences, but meaning usually clear. Appropriate style and register.
2	3–4	Some variety of vocabulary used. Some attempts at complex structures evident. Two time frames attempted, largely successfully. Some major errors and more frequent minor errors. Some errors may occur in more complex sentences, but meaning usually clear. More accurate then inaccurate. Style and register may not always be correct.
1	1–2	Not a wide range of vocabulary used and may be repetitive. Sentences often not constructed correctly and usually short and simple. Frequent errors. Incorrect style and register.
0	0	The language does not meet the standard for Level 1.

- A major error seriously affects communication.
- If a mark of 0 is given for Content, a mark of 0 must also be given for Quality of Language.

Sample Answer Question 1.1

Hola Miguel. Me encanta ir de compras y normalmente voy al pueblo con mis amigos porque es muy divertido. Siempre pasamos un día entero allí.
El sábado pasado fui al nuevo centro comercial y lo pasé muy bien. Compré un regalo para el cumpleaños de mi madre. Le compré un jersey de su tienda preferida. ¡Es muy bonito! Me gustó el centro comercial porque hay una buena variedad de tiendas distintas. ¡Es muy guay!

En el futuro me encantaría ir de compras a Nueva York porque creo que sería muy emocionante.

[16 marks]

Sample Answer Question 1.2

El fin de semana pasado visité a mis abuelos y luego, mis amigos y yo jugamos al críquet en el parque. Me encanta el fin de semana porque suelo ir al cine con mi amiga María. Nos gusta mucho ver películas de acción. Pero el fin de semana que viene, voy a ir al teatro con mi familia y estoy muy emocionada. ¡Será estupendo!
En mi opinión, es muy importante hacer algo relajante en tu tiempo libre, como practicar deporte o salir con amigos, para aliviar el estrés del instituto.

[16 marks]

Question 2

For this question (2.1 or 2.2) there are 2 compulsory bullet points, which must both be attempted, although there does not need to be an equal amount written for each point. The marks are awarded for Content (15 marks) Range of Language (12 marks) and Accuracy (5 marks). The number of words is 150 and the maximum mark is 32.

Content

Level	Marks	Response
5	13–15	Fully relevant with lots of detail and information. Communication mainly clear and opinions and reasons given.
4	10–12	Almost always relevant with a lot of information. Communication mostly clear with only a few ambiguities. Opinions and reasons given.
3	7–9	Generally relevant with quite a lot of information. Communication usually clear but with some ambiguities. Opinions and some reasons given.
2	4–6	Some relevant information. Communication sometimes clear but messages sometimes break down. Opinion given.
1	1–3	Limited relevant information. Communication may not be clear and messages break down. Opinion may be given.
0	0	Content does not meet the standard for Level 1.

Range of Language

Level	Marks	Response
4	10–12	Very good variety of vocabulary and structures. Some complex sentences used. A fluent piece of writing. Appropriate style and register.
3	7–9	Good variety of vocabulary and structures. Some complex sentences attempted and mainly successful. Largely fluent piece of writing with occasional lapses. Appropriate style and register.
2	4–6	Some variety of vocabulary and structures. Some longer sentences used with linking words, often correctly. Style and register may not always be correct.

Level	Marks	Response
1	1–3	Not a wide range of vocabulary used. Sentences usually short and simple. Incorrect style and register.
0	0	The range of language produced does not meet the standard for Level 1.

Accuracy

Level	Marks	Response
5	5	Accurate. Could be a few errors, particularly in complex sentences. Secure verbs and tenses.
4	4	Generally accurate. May be some minor errors. Occasional major errors, often when attempting complex sentences. Verbs and tenses almost always correct.
3	3	Fairly accurate. Some minor and some major errors. Verbs and tenses are usually correct.
2	2	More accurate than inaccurate. Meaning usually fairly clear. Some verbs and tenses incorrect.
1	1	A lot of major and minor errors. Meaning not clear most of the time. Largely incorrect verbs and tenses.
0	0	Accuracy does not meet the standard for Level 1.

- A major error seriously affects communication.
- If a mark of 0 is given for Content, a mark of 0 must also be given for Quality of Language.

Sample Answer Question 2.1

En mi región, hay unos cuantos problemas medioambientales. Para mí, lo peor es la contaminación atmosférica, a causa del tráfico que circula por la ciudad. Lo que pasa es que la red de transporte público es muy mala en esta región y como consecuencia, la gente usa su propio coche. Pero, ¿por qué no cogen la bici o por qué no van a pie? No sería tan difícil ya que la ciudad es bastante compacta. Además, hay mucha basura en las calles y todo parece muy feo.
Soy de la opinión de que deberían construir más carriles bici, para que la gente decida dejar el coche en casa. Si pudiéramos convertir el centro del pueblo en una zona peatonal con espacio para bicis también, mejoraría el problema de la contaminación del aire y a la vez, todo el mundo estaría más en forma. También el ayuntamiento debe instalar más cubos de basura. ¡Así me gustaría mi región!

[32 marks]

Sample Answer Question 2.2

Para ganar dinero tengo un trabajo a tiempo parcial. Trabajo todos los sábados en una tienda de ropa y la verdad es que me gusta mucho. Diría que es muy divertido porque no sólo puedo ayudar a los clientes, sino también hablar con mis colegas todo el día. La semana pasada trabajé más horas y entonces gané más dinero. ¡Qué bien! Lo único es que al final de la semana estaba muy cansada y era difícil completar todos mis deberes para el colegio.

Cuando tenga suficiente dinero, voy a comprarme un nuevo portátil porque el mío no funciona bien y va muy lento. Voy a ir con mis padres a buscar uno dentro de poco. Si trabajo muchas horas, podré comprar el portátil dentro de unos meses. También estoy pensando en intentar ahorrar un poco de dinero para mis vacaciones del año que viene. Vamos a ir a Estados Unidos y necesitaré mucho dinero para gastar allí.

[32 marks]

Question 3

The translation is awarded marks for Conveying Key Messages (6 marks) and Application of Grammatical Knowledge of Language and Structures (6 marks). The maximum mark is 12 and the sense of the whole passage must be taken into account when awarding marks.

Conveying Key Messages

Level	Marks	Response
6	6	All key messages communicated.
5	5	Nearly all key messages communicated.
4	4	Most key messages communicated.
3	3	Some key messages communicated.
2	2	Few key messages communicated.
1	1	Very few key messages communicated.
0	0	Content does not meet the standard for Level 1.

Application of Grammatical Knowledge of Language and Structures

Level	Marks	Response
6	6	Excellent knowledge of vocabulary and structures; almost faultless.
5	5	Very good knowledge of vocabulary and structures; highly accurate.
4	4	Good knowledge of vocabulary and structures; mostly accurate.
3	3	Reasonable knowledge of vocabulary and structures; more accurate than inaccurate.
2	2	Limited knowledge of vocabulary and structures; mostly inaccurate.
1	1	Very limited knowledge of vocabulary and structures; highly inaccurate.
0	0	Language produced does not meet the standard for Level 1.

- If a mark of 0 is awarded for Conveying Key Messages, a mark of 0 is automatically awarded for Application of Grammatical Knowledge of Language and Structures.

Sample Answer (Indicative Content)

The following indicative content is an example of an answer that would achieve full marks.
El año pasado fui de vacaciones a España. No fui / viajé en avión. Solemos ir / normalmente vamos a Italia que es muy bonita / preciosa. Este año tenemos que visitar Inglaterra porque mis padres quieren ir a / visitar el campo. Creo / Pienso que va a ser muy aburrido / pesado. Las playas son mucho más divertidas.

Notes

Notes